12-9-08

American Constitutional Law: Powers and Liberties

2004 Supplement

2004 Supplement

American Constitutional Law: Powers and Liberties

Calvin Massey
Professor of Law
University of California
Hastings College of the Law

ASPEN
PUBLISHERS

1185 Avenue of the Americas, New York, NY 10036
www.aspenpublishers.com

A Wolters Kluwer Company
www.aspenpublishers.com

Printed in the United States of America.

ISBN 0-7355-4053-5

1 2 3 4 5 6 7 8 9 0

Library of Congress Cataloging-in-Publication Data

Massey, Calvin R.
American constitutional law: powers and liberties / Calvin Massey.
p. cm.
Includes bibliographical references and index.
ISBN 0-7355-2032-1 (casebook)
ISBN 0-7355-4053-5 (supplement)
1. Constitutional law — United States — Cases. I. Title.

KF4549.M318 2001
342.73—dc21 00-067539

About Aspen Publishers

Aspen Publishers, headquartered in New York City, is a leading information provider for attorneys, business professionals, and law students. Written by preeminent authorities, our products consist of analytical and practical information covering both U.S. and international topics. We publish in the full range of formats, including updated manuals, books, periodicals, CDs, and online products.

Our proprietary content is complemented by 2,500 legal databases, containing over 11 million documents, available through our Loislaw division. Aspen Publishers also offers a wide range of topical legal and business databases linked to Loislaw's primary material. Our mission is to provide accurate, timely, and authoritative content in easily accessible formats, supported by unmatched customer care.

To order any Aspen Publishers title, go to *www.aspenpublishers.com* or call 1-800-638-8437.

To reinstate your manual update service, call 1-800-638-8437.

For more information on Loislaw products, go to *www.loislaw.com* or call 1-800-364-2512.

For Customer Care issues, e-mail *CustomerCare@aspenpublishers.com*; call 1-800-234-1660; or fax 1-800-901-9075.

Aspen Publishers
A Wolters Kluwer Company

Contents

Chapter 1

Judicial Review and Constitutional Structure

C. The Adequate and Independent State Grounds Doctrine

Page 38: Insert the following immediately before section D:

BUSH v. GORE
531 U.S. 98 (2000)

CHIEF JUSTICE REHNQUIST, joined by JUSTICES SCALIA and THOMAS, concurring.

We join the *per curiam* opinion [in which the Court voided the Florida Supreme Court's ordered manual recount of all ballots cast in the Florida 2000 presidential election that had failed to register a choice for President in the machine tally (so-called "undervotes"), as an equal protection violation]. We write separately because we believe there are additional grounds that require us to reverse the Florida Supreme Court's decision.

I. We deal here not with an ordinary election, but with an election for the President of the United States. In Burroughs v. United States, 290 U.S. 534 (1934), we said:

"While presidential electors are not officers or agents of the federal government, they exercise federal functions under, and discharge duties in virtue of authority conferred by, the Constitution of the United States. The President is vested with the executive power of the nation. The importance of his election and the vital character of its relationship to and effect upon the welfare and safety of the whole people cannot be too strongly stated."

Likewise, in Anderson v. Celebrezze, 460 U.S. 780, 794-795 (1983), we said: "In the context of a Presidential election, state-imposed restrictions implicate a uniquely important national interest. For the President and the Vice President of the United States are the only elected officials who represent all the voters in the Nation."

In most cases, comity and respect for federalism compel us to defer to the decisions of state courts on issues of state law. That practice reflects our understanding that the decisions of state courts are definitive pronouncements of the will of the States as sovereigns. Of course, in ordinary cases, the distribution of powers among the branches of a State's government raises no questions of federal constitutional law, subject to the requirement that the government be republican in character. But there are a few exceptional cases in which the Constitution imposes a duty or confers a power on a particular branch of a State's government. This is one of them. Article II, §1, cl. 2, provides that "each State shall appoint, in such Manner as the *Legislature* thereof may direct," electors for President and Vice President. (Emphasis added.) Thus, the text of the election law itself, and not just its interpretation by the courts of the States, takes on independent significance.

In McPherson v. Blacker, 146 U.S. 1 (1892), we explained that Art. II, §1, cl. 2, . . . "leaves it to the legislature exclusively to define the method" of appointment. A significant departure from the legislative scheme for appointing Presidential electors presents a federal constitutional question. . . .

In Florida, the legislature has chosen to hold statewide elections to appoint the State's 25 electors. Importantly, the legislature has delegated the authority to run the elections and to oversee election disputes to the Secretary of State (Secretary) and to state circuit courts. Isolated sections of the code may well admit of more than one interpretation, but the general coherence of the legislative scheme may not be altered by judicial interpretation so as to wholly change the statutorily provided apportionment of responsibility among these various bodies. In any election but a Presidential election, the Florida Supreme Court can give as little or as much deference to Florida's executives as it chooses, so far as Article II is concerned, and this Court will have no cause to question the court's actions. But, with respect to a Presidential election, the court must be both mindful of the legislature's role under Article II in choosing the manner of appointing electors and deferential to those bodies expressly empowered by the legislature to carry out its constitutional mandate.

In order to determine whether a state court has infringed upon the legislature's authority, we necessarily must examine the law of the State as it existed prior to the action of the court. Though we generally defer to state courts on the interpretation of state law there are of course areas in which the Constitution requires this Court to undertake an independent, if still deferential, analysis of state law. For example, in NAACP v. Alabama ex rel. Patterson, 357 U.S. 449 (1958), it was argued that we were without jurisdiction because the petitioner had not pursued the correct appellate remedy in Alabama's state courts. Petitioners had sought a state-law writ of certiorari in the Alabama Supreme Court when a writ of mandamus, according to that court, was proper. We found this state-law ground inadequate to defeat our jurisdiction because we were "unable to reconcile the procedural holding of the Alabama Supreme Court" with prior Alabama precedent. The purported state-law ground was so novel, in our independent estimation, that "petitioner could not fairly be deemed to have been apprised of its existence." Six years later we decided Bouie v. City of Columbia, 378 U.S. 347 (1964), in which the state court had held, contrary to precedent, that the state trespass law applied to black sit-in demonstrators who had consent to enter private property but were then asked to leave. Relying upon *NAACP*, we concluded that the South Carolina Supreme Court's interpretation of a state penal statute had impermissibly broadened the scope of that statute beyond what a fair reading provided, in violation of due process. What we would do in the present case is precisely parallel: Hold that the Florida Supreme Court's interpretation of the Florida election laws impermissibly distorted them beyond what a fair reading required, in violation of Article II.[1] This inquiry does not imply a disrespect for state *courts* but rather a respect for the constitutionally prescribed role of state *legislatures*. To attach definitive weight to the pronouncement of a state court, when the very question at issue is whether the court has actually departed from the statutory meaning, would be to abdicate our responsibility to enforce the explicit requirements of Article II.

II. Acting pursuant to its constitutional grant of authority, the Florida Legislature has created a detailed, if not perfectly crafted, statutory scheme that provides for appointment of Presidential electors by direct election. Under the statute, "votes cast for the actual candidates for President and Vice President shall be counted as votes cast for the presidential electors supporting such candidates." The legislature has designated the Secretary of State as the "chief election officer," with the responsibility to "obtain and maintain uniformity in the application, operation, and interpretation of the election laws." The state legislature has delegated to county canvassing boards the duties of administering elections. Those boards are responsible for providing results to the state Elections Canvassing Commission, comprising the Governor, the Secretary of State, and the Director of the Division of Elections. After the election has taken place, the canvassing boards receive returns from precincts, count the votes, and in the event that a candidate was defeated by .5% or less, conduct a mandatory recount. The county canvassing boards must file certified election returns with the Department of State by 5 p.m. on the seventh day following the election. The Elections Canvassing Commission must then certify the results of the election.

The state legislature has also provided mechanisms both for protesting election returns and for contesting certified election results. [Any] protest must be filed prior to the certification of election results by the county canvassing board. Once a protest has been filed, "the county canvassing board may authorize a manual recount." . . . Contests to the certification of an election, [based on] "receipt of a number of illegal votes or rejection of a number of legal votes sufficient to change or place in doubt the result of the election," must be filed in the appropriate Florida circuit court, and [in] Presidential elections, the contest period necessarily terminates on

1. Similarly, our jurisprudence requires us to analyze the "background principles" of state property law to determine whether there has been a taking of property in violation of the Takings Clause. That constitutional guarantee would, of course, afford no protection against state power if our inquiry could be concluded by a state supreme court holding that state property law accorded the plaintiff no rights. See Lucas v. South Carolina Coastal Council, [p. 614]. In one of our oldest cases, we similarly made an independent evaluation of state law in order to protect federal treaty guarantees. In Fairfax's Devisee v. Hunter's Lessee, 11 U.S. [7 Cranch] 603 (1813), we disagreed with the Supreme Court of Appeals of Virginia that a 1782 state law had extinguished the property interests of one Denny Fairfax, so that a 1789 ejectment order against Fairfax supported by a 1785 state law did not constitute a future confiscation under the 1783 peace treaty with Great Britain.

the date set by 3 U.S.C. §5 for concluding the State's "final determination" of election controversies.

In its first decision, Palm Beach Canvassing Bd. v. Harris, (*Harris I*), the Florida Supreme Court extended the 7-day statutory certification deadline established by the legislature. This modification of the code, by lengthening the protest period, necessarily shortened the contest period for Presidential elections. Underlying the extension of the certification deadline and the shortchanging of the contest period was, presumably, the clear implication that certification was a matter of significance: The certified winner would enjoy presumptive validity, making a contest proceeding by the losing candidate an uphill battle. In its latest opinion, however, the court empties certification of virtually all legal consequence during the contest, and in doing so departs from the provisions enacted by the Florida Legislature.

The court determined that canvassing boards' decisions regarding whether to recount ballots past the certification deadline (even the certification deadline established by *Harris I*) are to be reviewed *de novo*, although the election code clearly vests discretion whether to recount in the boards, and sets strict deadlines subject to the Secretary's rejection of late tallies and monetary fines for tardiness. Moreover, the Florida court held that all late vote tallies arriving during the contest period should be automatically included in the certification regardless of the certification deadline (even the certification deadline established by *Harris I*), thus virtually eliminating both the deadline and the Secretary's discretion to disregard recounts that violate it.

Moreover, the court's interpretation of "legal vote," and hence its decision to order a contest-period recount, plainly departed from the legislative scheme. Florida statutory law cannot reasonably be thought to *require* the counting of improperly marked ballots. Each Florida precinct before election day provides instructions on how properly to cast a vote; each polling place on election day contains a working model of the voting machine it uses and each voting booth contains a sample ballot. . . . No reasonable person would call it "an error in the vote tabulation," or a "rejection of legal votes," when electronic or electromechanical equipment performs precisely in the manner designed, and fails to count those ballots that are not marked in the manner that these voting instructions explicitly and prominently specify. The scheme that the Florida Supreme Court's opinion attributes to the legislature is one in which machines are *required* to be "capable of correctly counting votes," but which nonetheless regularly produces elections in which legal votes are predictably *not* tabulated, so that in close elections manual recounts are regularly required. This is of course absurd. The Secretary of State, who is authorized by law to issue binding interpretations of the election code, rejected this peculiar reading of the statutes. The Florida Supreme Court, although it must defer to the Secretary's interpretations, rejected her reasonable interpretation and embraced the peculiar one. See Palm Beach County Canvassing Board v. Harris (*Harris III*).

But as we indicated in our remand of the earlier case, in a Presidential election the clearly expressed intent of the legislature must prevail. And there is no basis for reading the Florida statutes as requiring the counting of improperly marked ballots. . . . The State's Attorney General (who was supporting the Gore challenge) confirmed in oral argument here that never before the present election had a manual recount been conducted on the basis of the contention that "undervotes" should have been examined to determine voter intent. For the court to step away from this established practice, prescribed by the Secretary of State, the state official charged by the legislature with "responsibility to . . . obtain and maintain uniformity in the application, operation, and interpretation of the election laws," was to depart from the legislative scheme. . . .

For these reasons, in addition to those given in the *per curiam*, we would reverse.

JUSTICE STEVENS, joined by JUSTICE GINSBURG and JUSTICE BREYER, dissenting.

The Constitution assigns to the States the primary responsibility for determining the manner of selecting the Presidential electors. See Art. II, §1, cl. 2. When questions arise about the meaning of state laws, including election laws, it is our settled practice to accept the opinions of the highest courts of the States as providing the final answers. On rare occasions, however, either federal statutes or the Federal Constitution may require federal judicial intervention in state elections. This is not such an occasion. . . .

Article II [does] not create state legislatures out of whole cloth, but rather takes them as they come — as creatures born of, and constrained by, their state constitutions. Lest there be any doubt, we stated over 100 years ago in *McPherson* that "what is forbidden or required to be done by a State" in the Article II context "is forbidden or required of the legislative power under state constitutions as they exist." [The] legislative power in Florida is subject to judicial review pursuant to Article V of the Florida Constitution, and nothing in Article II of the Federal Constitution frees the state legislature from the constraints in the state constitution that created it. Moreover, the Florida Legislature's own decision to employ a unitary code for all elections indicates that it intended the Florida Supreme Court to play the same role in Presidential elections that it has historically played in resolving electoral disputes. The Florida Supreme Court's exercise of appellate jurisdiction therefore was wholly consistent with, and indeed contemplated by, the grant of authority in Article II. . . .

Article II does not grant federal judges any special authority to substitute their views for those of the state judiciary on matters of state law.

JUSTICE GINSBURG, joined by JUSTICES STEVENS, SOUTER, AND BREYER, dissenting.

. . . Rarely has this Court rejected outright an interpretation of state law by a state high court. [This] case involves nothing close to the kind of recalcitrance by a state high court that warrants extraordinary action by this Court. The Florida Supreme Court concluded that counting every legal vote was the overriding concern of the Florida Legislature when it enacted the State's Election Code.

[Chief Justice Rehnquist] says that Article II, by providing that state legislatures shall direct the manner of appointing electors, authorizes federal superintendence over the relationship between state courts and state legislatures, and licenses a departure from the usual deference we give to state court interpretations of state law.

The Framers of our Constitution, however, understood that in a republican government, the judiciary would construe the legislature's enactments. . . . By holding that Article II requires our revision of a state court's construction of state laws in order to protect one organ of the State from another, [Chief Justice Rehnquist] contradicts the basic principle that a State may organize itself as it sees fit. Article II does not call for the scrutiny undertaken by this Court.

The extraordinary setting of this case has obscured the ordinary principle that dictates its proper resolution: Federal courts defer to state high courts' interpretations of their state's own law. This principle reflects the core of federalism, on which all agree. [Were] the other members of this Court as mindful as they generally are of our system of dual sovereignty, they would affirm the judgment of the Florida Supreme Court.

NOTES

1. *The Independent State Interest in Presidential Elections.* Does Article II establish a federal interest in a state's election law when it governs the state's presidential election? Or does Justice Stevens have the better argument when he argues that Article II contemplates that a state's legislature must always act in accordance with a state's constitution? But suppose that a state's constitution assigned to the state's supreme court the exclusive power to determine how the state's presidential electors are to be selected. Surely such a provision would be offensive to Article II. Would the United States Supreme Court have power to say so? Is it merely a difference in degree if a state supreme court interprets the state election law in a fashion that is at odds with the legislative intent? If so, does the U.S. Supreme Court have power to decide this issue? The concurring justices surely think so.

The justices disagreed about whether the Court should have reviewed the Florida Supreme Court's reading of Florida election law and also about whether that reading constituted a plain departure from the preexisting election law, sufficient to constitute a change in the law. Can the two issues be separated? If not, does the justices' answer to the first question depend on their view as to the proper answer to the second question?

Are presidential elections special? Perhaps the nation as a whole has an extraordinary interest in the impartial administration of each state's election law, especially when the dispute arises in the unique context of a disputed state election, the outcome of which will determine the entire presidential vote. In that context, is there a heightened federal interest in ensuring that a state supreme court's interpretation of its election law is free of expedient urges to influence the outcome of the national election? Partisan Democrats assailed the Court's decision; partisan Republicans assailed the Florida Supreme Court's decisions. Putting partisanship aside (if you can), whose interest in the proper interpretation of Florida election law in the context of the 2000 presidential election was greater — the nation's or Florida's?

2. *The Independent State Interest in Congressional Elections.* Article I, §4 empowers "the Legislature" of each state to prescribe the "Times, Places, and Manner

of holding Elections for Senators and Representatives," a provision that mimics Article II, §1's provision with respect to presidential elections. Is the argument of the concurring justices equally applicable to state election laws governing congressional elections? Note that a basic premise of U.S. Term Limits v. Thornton, p. 147, was that a state's congressional delegation "owe[s] primary allegiance not to the people of a State, but to the people of the Nation." By contrast, a central premise of Garcia v. San Antonio Metropolitan Transit Authority, p. 210, was that federalism limits on congressional power can safely be entrusted to Congress because the members of Congress represent state rather than national interests.

D. The Eleventh Amendment

1. *Hans v. Louisiana* and the Current Doctrine

Page 122: Insert the following at the end of section 1, immediately before section 2:

The premise underlying *Hans* was that the Eleventh Amendment was adopted not so much to do what it literally says, but to express in the Constitution a preconstitutional understanding that after constitutional union the states continued to possess plenary sovereign immunity except to the extent explicitly surrendered in the Constitution. A principal attribute of that sovereign immunity was thought to be immunity from private suit in federal court. In Alden v. Maine, 527 U.S. 706 (1999), the Court relied on that premise to conclude that Congress may not use its Article I powers to authorize private suits against states in their own courts without regard to a state's consent to such suit. In Federal Maritime Commission v. South Carolina State Ports Authority, 535 U.S. 743 (2002), the Court relied on the same principle to hold that a federal administrative agency is barred from adjudicating a private party's complaint against a nonconsenting state.

Because the only recognized source of congressional power to abrogate Eleventh Amendment immunity is section five of the Fourteenth Amendment, the scope of Congress's section five power is critically important to determining the extent of Eleventh Amendment immunity. In a series of cases, beginning with City of Boerne v. Flores, p. 1231, and continuing with *Garrett*, 2004 Supplement, chapter 11, the Supreme Court has circumscribed the extent of the section five power and imposed on Congress a requirement that it make particularized findings of unconstitutional state behavior as a predicate for invocation of the section five power. But in *Hibbs* and Tennessee v. Lane, 2004 Supplement, chapter 11, the Court has deferred to Congress when the underlying constitutional right Congress has sought to protect receives heightened judicial scrutiny. These cases essentially work to broaden Eleventh Amendment immunity by narrowing congressional ability to abrogate that immunity.

Eleventh Amendment immunity applies to *in personam* jurisdiction asserted against a state. The Eleventh Amendment does not prevent federal courts from asserting *in rem* jurisdiction to adjudicate a state's interest in a *res* that is not possessed by the state. In California v. Deep Sea Research, Inc., 523 U.S. 491 (1998), the Court applied this principle to permit a federal court to determine California's interest in an historic shipwreck located by a private party in California's territorial waters. In Tennessee Student Assistance Corp. v. Hood, 124 S. Ct. 1905 (2004), the Court applied the same principle to uphold the ability of a federal bankruptcy court to hear and decide an adversary proceeding against a state, in which the remedy sought was discharge of a student loan obligation owed to an arm of the state. In a footnote the Court noted that a bankruptcy court's *in rem* jurisdiction does not override sovereign immunity; rather, the exercise of such jurisdiction "is not an affront to the sovereignty of the State." The Court cautioned that it did *not* "hold that every exercise of a bankruptcy court's *in rem* jurisdiction will not offend the sovereignty of the State."

Chapter 2

Doctrines Limiting the Scope of Judicial Review

C. Justiciability: The Proper Role of Federal Courts

4. Political Questions

Page 117: Insert immediately before subsection C.5:

BUSH v. GORE
531 U.S. 98 (2000)

[In a *per curiam* decision the Court voided as a violation of equal protection the Florida Supreme Court's ordered manual recount of all ballots that failed to register a vote for President in the machine count of Florida's balloting in the 2000 presidential election.]

JUSTICE BREYER, joined by JUSTICES STEVENS, SOUTER, and GINSBURG, dissenting.

Despite the reminder that this case involves "an election for the President of the United States," no preeminent legal concern, or practical concern related to legal questions, required this Court to hear this case. . . . With one exception, petitioners' claims do not ask us to vindicate a constitutional provision designed to protect a basic human right. Petitioners invoke fundamental fairness, namely, the need for procedural fairness, including finality. But with the one "equal protection" exception, they rely upon law that focuses . . . upon the constitutional allocation of power. Respondents invoke a competing fundamental consideration — the need to determine the voter's true intent. But they look to state law, not to federal constitutional law, to protect that interest. Neither side claims electoral fraud, dishonesty, or the like. . . . Of course, the selection of the President is of fundamental national importance. But that importance is political, not legal. And this Court should resist the temptation unnecessarily to resolve tangential legal disputes.

The Constitution and federal statutes themselves make clear that restraint is appropriate. They set forth a road map of how to resolve disputes about electors, even after an election as close as this one. . . . But it nowhere provides for involvement by the United States Supreme Court. To the contrary, the Twelfth Amendment commits to Congress the authority and responsibility to count electoral votes. A federal statute, the Electoral Count Act, enacted after the close 1876 Hayes-Tilden Presidential election, specifies that, after States have tried to resolve disputes (through "judicial" or other means), Congress is the body primarily authorized to resolve remaining disputes. See Electoral Count Act of 1887, 24 Stat. 373, 3 U.S.C. §§5, 6, and 15.

The legislative history of the Act makes clear its intent to commit the power to resolve such disputes to Congress, rather than the courts:

"The two Houses are, by the Constitution, authorized to make the count of electoral votes. They can only count legal votes, and in doing so must determine, from the best evidence to be had, what are legal votes. . . . The power to determine rests with the two Houses, and there is no other constitutional tribunal." H. Rep. No. 1638, 49th Cong., 1st Sess., 2 (1886) (report submitted by Rep. Caldwell, Select Committee on the Election of President and Vice-President). . . .

The Act goes on to set out rules for the congressional determination of disputes about those votes. [3 U.S.C. §15]. Given this detailed, comprehensive scheme for counting electoral votes, there is no reason to believe that federal law either foresees or requires resolution of such a political issue by this Court. . . .

The decision by both the Constitution's Framers and the 1886 Congress to minimize this Court's role in resolving close federal presidential elections is as wise as it is clear. However awkward or difficult it may be for Congress to resolve difficult electoral disputes, Congress, being a political body, expresses the people's will far more accurately than does an unelected Court. And the people's will is what elections are about.

Moreover, Congress was fully aware of the danger that would arise should it ask judges, unarmed with appropriate legal standards, to resolve a hotly contested Presidential election contest. Just after the 1876 Presidential election, Florida, South Carolina, and Louisiana each sent two slates of electors to Washington. Without these States, Tilden, the Democrat, had 184 electoral votes, one short of the number required to win the Presidency. With those States, Hayes, his Republican opponent, would have had 185. In order to choose between the two slates of electors, Congress decided to appoint an electoral commission composed of five Senators, five Representatives, and five Supreme Court Justices. Initially the Commission was to be evenly divided between Republicans and Democrats, with Justice David Davis, an Independent, to possess the decisive vote. However, when at the last minute the Illinois Legislature elected Justice Davis to the United States Senate, the final position on the Commission was filled by Supreme Court Justice Joseph P. Bradley.

The Commission divided along partisan lines, and the responsibility to cast the deciding vote fell to Justice Bradley. He decided to accept the votes by the Republican electors, and thereby awarded the Presidency to Hayes. Justice Bradley immediately became the subject of vociferous attacks. Bradley was accused of accepting bribes, of being captured by railroad interests, and of an eleventh-hour change in position after a night in which his house "was surrounded by the carriages" of Republican partisans and railroad officials. C. Woodward, Reunion and Reaction 159-160 (1966). Many years later, Professor Bickel concluded that Bradley was honest and impartial. He thought that " 'the great question' for Bradley was, in fact, whether Congress was entitled to go behind election returns or had to accept them as certified by state authorities," an "issue of principle." The Least Dangerous Branch 185 (1962).... For present purposes, the relevance of this history lies in the fact that the participation in the work of the electoral commission by five Justices, including Justice Bradley, did not lend that process legitimacy. Nor did it assure the public that the process had worked fairly, guided by the law. Rather, it simply embroiled Members of the Court in partisan conflict, thereby undermining respect for the judicial process. And the Congress that later enacted the Electoral Count Act knew it....

Those who caution judicial restraint in resolving political disputes have described the quintessential case for that restraint as a case marked, among other things, by the "strangeness of the issue," its "intractability to principled resolution," its "sheer momentousness, . . . which tends to unbalance judicial judgment," and "the inner vulnerability, the self-doubt of an institution which is electorally irresponsible and has no earth to draw strength from." Bickel, supra, at 184. Those characteristics mark this case....

I fear that in order to bring this agonizingly long election process to a definitive conclusion, we have not adequately attended to that necessary "check upon our own exercise of power," "our own sense of self-restraint." Justice Brandeis once said of the Court, "The most important thing we do is not doing." What it does today, the Court should have left undone.

NOTE

A Nonjusticiable Political Question? Which strand or strands of the political question doctrine does Justice Breyer invoke? Is there a constitutionally "textually demonstrable commitment" of resolution of the issue to Congress? If so, is it the Twelfth Amendment? What part of the Twelfth Amendment? Was there a "lack of judicially discoverable and manageable standards" for decision? The justices certainly were not at a loss for arguments as to the merits of the case.

Perhaps the principal emphasis of Justice Breyer's opinion is upon the prudential reasons for the political question doctrine. Did Justice Breyer emphasize a judicially inappropriate policy decision upon which decision necessarily rested? Was there such a policy decision? Partisan cynics bitterly charge that the antecedent policy decision was the decision of which candidate to prefer. But is there good evidence in the opinion for that rather scurrilous charge? Alternatively, did the decision evidence a lack of respect to the other coordinate branches of the federal government? Note that the political question cases have not deferred to states. Consider, in this regard, Baker v. Carr. There was no unusual need to defer to a political fait accompli; the final outcome of the Florida election was much in doubt and it was the Court's decision that seemed to seal its outcome. Nor was there any risk of national embarrassment resulting from multiple inconsistent resolutions.

Was this a case in which a new strand in the political question doctrine might have been appropriately created? If so, how would you state such a principle?

Chapter 3

The Limits of Federal Legislative Power

A. Implementing Enumerated Powers and "Default" Rules

1. Implementing Enumerated Powers: The "Necessary and Proper Clause"

Page 142: Insert the following at the end of note 2, immediately before note 3:

In Sabri v. United States, 124 S. Ct. 1941 (2004), the Court characterized *McCulloch* as "establishing review for means-ends rationality under the Necessary and Proper Clause." Justice Thomas concurred in the judgment, but noted that *McCulloch* described the scope of the implementing power under the Necessary and Proper Clause as consisting of all lawful "means which are appropriate [and] which are plainly adapted" to the accomplishment of constitutionally legitimate ends. To Justice Thomas this was "hardly synonymous with 'means-ends rationality.' " He thought that "plainly adapted" means "obvious" or "clear." Thus, a "statute can have a 'rational' connection to an enumerated power without being obviously or clearly tied to that enumerated power. To show that a statute is 'plainly adapted' to a legitimate end . . . it would seem necessary to show some obvious, simple, and direct relation between the statute and the enumerated power." Is this a distinction without a difference? If not, what sort of judicial review would this entail?

2. Implying "Default" Rules for Federal and State Power

Page 158: Insert the following as an additional note following U.S. Term Limits v. Thornton *and immediately before subsection B:*

Postscript: "Scarlet Letter" Designations. After the *Thornton* decision, some states enacted laws instructing their federal congressional delegations to seek a constitutional amendment to establish state power to set term limits and requiring a ballot designation next to incumbents who failed to do so, noting that fact. Typical of these laws was Missouri's Article VIII to its constitution, which required that the ballot bear the designation, "DISREGARDED VOTERS' INSTRUCTION ON TERM LIMITS," next to the names of incumbent members of Congress who failed to take action to support a constitutional amendment, and which required that the designation, "DECLINED TO PLEDGE TO SUPPORT TERM LIMITS," be printed next to the names of nonincumbent candidates for Congress who refused to sign such a pledge. In Cook v. Gralike, 531 U.S. 510 (2001), the Court voided this "scarlet letter" provision on much the same theory as *Thornton*. States have power to control the conduct of federal elections only to the extent that they are given such power under the elections clause of Article I, §4, which grants to the states the power to prescribe the time, place, and manner of such elections, subject to congressional control. Missouri's Article VIII was not a regulation bearing on the manner of the election because its clear intent and probable effect was to handicap candidates holding a specific policy view and thus influence the outcome of the election. Moreover, while citizens may "instruct their representatives" they may punish them for disregarding those instructions by their vote, not by a public announcement on the ballot to that effect.

B. Commerce

1. The General Scope of the Commerce Power

Page 183: Insert the following as an additional note after Lopez *and immediately before subsection B.2:*

7. Interpreting Statutes to Avoid Constitutional Issues. Recall that in Ashwander v. T.V.A., p. 21, Justice Brandeis summarized "a series of rules" the Court uses to avoid the necessity of constitutional decisions. One of those rules was that "if a case can be decided on either of two grounds, one involving a constitutional question, the other a question of statutory construction or general law, the Court will decide only the latter." More recently the Court has stated that "where a statute is susceptible of two constructions, by one of which grave and doubtful constitutional questions arise and by the other of which such questions are avoided, our duty is to adopt the latter." Jones v. United States, 529 U.S. 848, 857 (2000). This principle has been vigorously applied of late to avoid deciding difficult issues posed by the scope of the commerce power.

In *Jones* the Court applied this canon to overturn a conviction under the federal arson statute, 18 U.S.C. §844 (i), as applied to the arson of an owner-occupied private residence. The statute made criminal arson of "any building . . . used in interstate or foreign commerce or *in any activity affecting interstate or foreign commerce*." Because the Court was of the view that a reading of the arson statute that included within its coverage any arson that merely "affected interstate commerce" would raise a significant question of the validity of the statute, it interpreted the statutory language to include only arson of buildings actually used in a commercial manner. A related version of this canon is the requirement, associated with United States v. Bass, 404 U.S. 336, 349 (1971), that "unless Congress conveys its purpose clearly, it will not be deemed to have significantly changed the federal-state balance in the prosecution of crimes."

The two approaches were fused in Solid Waste Agency of Northern Cook County v. United States Army Corps of Engineers, 531 U.S. 159 (2001). Section 404(a) of the federal Clean Water Act grants authority to the Corps to issue permits "for the discharge of dredged or fill material into the navigable waters." Pursuant to that authority the Corps issued regulations that defined navigable waters as including "intrastate . . . mudflats, sandflats, wetlands, sloughs, prairie potholes, [or] wet meadows, . . . the use, degradation or destruction of which could affect interstate commerce," including intrastate waters "which are or would be used" as habitat for migratory birds or endangered species. The Corps refused to issue a permit to Solid Waste Agency, a consortium of suburban Chicago municipalities, to deposit their solid waste into an abandoned gravel pit that now collected rainwater into permanent and seasonal ponds. The Supreme Court ruled that the regulations exceeded the statutory authority given to the Corps. In so doing the Court noted that

> Where an administrative interpretation of a statute invokes the outer limits of Congress's power, we expect a clear indication that Congress intended that result. This requirement stems from our prudential desire not to needlessly reach constitutional issues and our assumption that Congress does not casually authorize administrative agencies to interpret a statute to push the limit of congressional authority. This concern is heightened where the administrative interpretation alters the federal-state framework by permitting federal encroachment upon a traditional state power. [United States v. Bass]. Thus, "where an otherwise acceptable construction of a statute would raise serious constitutional problems, the Court will construe the statute to avoid such problems unless such construction is plainly contrary to the intent of Congress." . . .
>
> Respondents argue that the "Migratory Bird Rule" falls within Congress's power to regulate intrastate activities that "substantially affect" interstate commerce. They note that the protection of migratory birds is a "national interest of very nearly the first magnitude," [Missouri v. Holland, p. 260] and that . . . millions of people spend over a billion dollars annually on recreational pursuits relating to migratory birds. These arguments raise significant constitutional questions. For example, we would have to evaluate the precise object or activity that, in the aggregate, substantially affects interstate commerce. This is not clear, for although the Corps has claimed jurisdiction over petitioner's land because it contains water areas used as habitat by migratory birds, respondents now . . . focus upon the fact that the regulated activity is petitioner's municipal landfill, which is "plainly of a commercial nature." But this is a far cry, indeed, from the "navigable waters" and "waters of the United States" to which the statute by its terms extends.
>
> These are significant constitutional questions . . . and yet we find nothing approaching a clear statement from Congress that it intended §404(a) to reach an abandoned sand and gravel pit such as we have here. Permitting respondents to claim federal ju-

> risdiction over ponds and mudflats falling within the "Migratory Bird Rule" would result in a significant impingement of the States' traditional and primary power over land and water use. Rather than expressing a desire to readjust the federal-state balance in this manner, Congress chose to "recognize, preserve, and protect the primary responsibilities and rights of States . . . to plan the development and use . . . of land and water resources. . . ." We thus read the statute as written to avoid the significant constitutional and federalism questions raised by respondents' interpretation, and therefore reject the request for administrative deference. We hold that [the regulations], as clarified and applied to petitioner's [disposal] site pursuant to the "Migratory Bird Rule" exceeds the authority granted to respondents under §404(a) of the [Clean Water Act].

Suppose that you were asked by a member of Congress to draft an amendment to the Clean Water Act that would give the Army Corps of Engineers authority to regulate dumping in the waters described by the "Migratory Bird Rule." After *Solid Waste Agency*, how would you draft such statute to ensure that the Corps had maximum regulatory authority consistent with the scope of Congress's commerce power?

2. The Historical Development of Commerce Clause Doctrine

Page 207: Insert the following new subsection immediately before section 3:

iv. Reconciling *Lopez*, *Morrison*, and *Wickard*

In a trio of recent cases, the United States Court of Appeals for the Ninth Circuit has applied the commerce power principles of *Lopez* and *Morrison* to invalidate, as applied, federal criminal laws prohibiting possession of child pornography, cultivation or use of marijuana for personal medically-approved purposes, and possession of a homemade machine gun. In each of the three cases the Court of Appeals explores the tension between the *Lopez-Morrison* principles and *Wickard*'s aggregation principle, which the Court did not overturn in either *Lopez* or *Morrison*. Do these cases adequately reconcile the competing doctrine? Do they misapply *Wickard*? Do these cases treat *Wickard*'s aggregation principle as being overruled *sub silentio* by *Lopez* and *Morrison*? What is the modern role for the *Wickard* aggregation principle? Finally, do these cases suggest that *Lopez* and *Morrison* are untenable? If so, why?

UNITED STATES v. McCOY

323 F.3d 1114 (9th Cir. 2003)

REINHARDT, Circuit Judge. Rhonda McCoy entered a conditional plea of guilty to possession of child pornography after photo shop employees discovered a picture of her and her daughter with their genital areas exposed. . . . [She contended that 18 U.S.C. §2252(a)(4)(B),[1] which] prohibits the possession of child pornography made with materials that have traveled in interstate commerce, [is] an unconstitutional exercise of Congress's power under the Commerce Clause. We hold that 18 U.S.C. §2252(a)(4)(B) is unconstitutional as applied to simple intrastate possession of a visual depiction (or depictions) that has not been mailed, shipped, or transported interstate and is not intended for interstate distribution, or for any economic or commercial use, including the exchange of the prohibited material for other prohibited material.

[In April 2000, Rhonda McCoy spent an evening at home with her ten-year-old daughter and naval petty officer husband,] painting Easter eggs and taking family photographs. Rhonda, who, according to the presentence report, has a substance abuse problem as well as mental health problems, had substantial amounts of alcohol that night. At some point during the evening, Rhonda and [her daughter], partially unclothed, posed side by side for the camera, with their genital areas exposed. This pose was captured in one photograph [which was later developed by a photo shop operated by the U.S. Navy base on which the McCoys lived. A manager of the photo shop contacted law enforcement officials, informing them] of the existence of photographs that appeared to present a child in sexually suggestive poses. [A] search of the McCoy home pursuant to a federal search warrant [resulted in the seizure of] numerous photographs, as well as the family still camera, video camera, and computer. . . .

The government does not allege that the photograph of Rhonda and her child was mailed, shipped, or transported in interstate or foreign commerce, nor that [McCoy] intended to sell or distribute the photograph in interstate commerce. Rather, federal jurisdiction was premised upon the place of manufacture of the camera and film used to take the pictures. Both were ordinary commercial products. . . . Neither the type of film nor the model of camera is produced anywhere in California.

. . . At issue here is whether a statute enacted pursuant to the Commerce Clause may constitutionally reach non-commercial, non-economic individual conduct that is purely intrastate in nature, when there is no reasonable basis for concluding that the conduct had or was intended to have any significant interstate connection or any substantive effect on interstate commerce. . . .

---

1. The statute imposes criminal penalties upon any "person who — (4) . . . (B) knowingly possesses 1 or more books, magazines, periodicals, films, video tapes, or other matter which contain any visual depiction that has been mailed, or has been shipped or transported in interstate or foreign commerce, or which was produced using materials which have been mailed or so shipped or transported, by any means including by computer, if — (i) the producing of such visual depiction involves the use of a minor engaging in sexually explicit conduct; and (ii) such visual depiction is of such conduct. . . ." [Ed.]

We apply the four *Morrison* factors in order to decide whether §2252(a)(4)(B) as applied is a constitutional exercise by Congress of its Commerce Clause power. . . . First, we discuss whether simple intrastate possession of child pornography, without more, is a commercial or economic activity, and then whether the connection between such possession and interstate commerce is attenuated. We begin with these two factors not only because they are related and require a similar analytic approach, but because they are the most important ones. An activity that is utterly lacking in commercial or economic character would likely have too attenuated a relationship to interstate commerce and would, accordingly, not be subject to regulation under the Commerce Clause. Finally, we consider the remaining two factors: the express jurisdictional element of the statute, and whether it poses discrete limitations, and the statute's findings and legislative history. These latter factors aid our analysis but are ordinarily not, in themselves, dispositive.

B.1. Regulation of Commerce or Economic Activity

While not denying the existence of a vast interstate commercial child pornography market, McCoy argues that the simple intrastate possession of a home-produced sexually explicit picture of a child, with no intent to distribute interstate or by commercial means, is not properly characterized as commercial or economic activity. The government, relying on Wickard v. Filburn, argues that "the possession of such matter is the reason interstate trafficking in such obscenity exists," [and] contends that all such pictures are a part of interstate commerce, even if the possessor is a parent who possesses a picture of his own child solely for his own personal use and the picture was locally created . . . . *Wickard*'s "aggregation principle" does not determine the question here. . . . In *Lopez* [and *Morrison*], the Court approved of *Wickard*'s rationale only in relation to activity the *economic* nature of which was obvious. . . . Here, McCoy's photograph is much farther removed from interstate activity than Filburn's wheat. Filburn's "[h]ome-grown wheat . . . compete[d] with wheat in commerce," and reduced the *demand* for the wheat grown for commercial sales, in direct contravention of the purposes of the Agricultural Adjustment Act — to reduce the *supply* and, accordingly, to bolster the price. McCoy's venture, in contrast, was purely non-economic and non-commercial, and had no connection with or effect on any national or international commercial child pornography market, substantial or otherwise. The picture . . . which McCoy possessed for her own personal use did not "compete" with other depictions exchanged, bought, or sold in the illicit market for child pornography and did not affect their availability or price. Nor are pictures of the type McCoy possessed connected in any respect with commercial or economic enterprises. Section 2252(a)(4)(B) is, thus, not "an essential part of a larger regulation of economic activity, in which the regulatory scheme could be undercut unless the intrastate activity were regulated." *Lopez*, 514 U.S. at 561. . . . [We] conclude that simple intrastate possession of home-grown child pornography not intended for distribution or exchange is "not, in any sense of the phrase, economic activity." . . .

2. Attenuated Effect

McCoy argues that the connection between the simple intrastate possession of child pornography and interstate commerce is too attenuated to warrant a valid exercise of Commerce Clause power. In response, the government . . . argues that Congress can reach purely intrastate conduct if it rationally determines that doing so is necessary to effectively regulate the national market. . . . Reasoning similar to the government's has been rejected by the Supreme Court twice recently, in both [*Lopez* and *Morrison*.] It is particularly important that in the field of criminal law enforcement, where state power is preeminent, national authority be limited to those areas in which interstate commerce is truly affected. . . . [Application of] §2252(a)(4)(B) to McCoy in the circumstances present here (or to others in similar circumstances) does not regulate economic or commercial activity; nor does it show a relationship, attenuated or otherwise, between the regulated activity and interstate commerce — and certainly not the type of direct or substantial relationship necessary to justify the invocation by Congress of its Commerce power in order to regulate intrastate criminal activity. . . .

3. Express Jurisdictional Element

Unlike the statutes at issue in *Lopez* and in *Morrison*, §2252(a)(4)(B) contains an express jurisdictional element that is intended to satisfy Commerce Clause concerns. [Such] statutory attempts to comply with the Commerce Clause [are so-called] "jurisdictional hooks": a [statutory requirement that the government] "establish specific facts justifying the exercise of federal jurisdiction in connection with any individual application of the statute." The purpose of a jurisdictional hook is to limit the reach of a particular statute to a discrete set of cases that substantially affect interstate commerce. [*Morrison, Lopez*.] The language of the jurisdictional hook in question here fails totally to achieve that purpose. It not only fails to limit the reach of the statute to any category or categories of cases that have a particular effect on interstate commerce, but, to the contrary, it encompasses virtually *every* case imaginable, so long as any modern-day photographic equipment or material has been used. . . . In McCoy's case, the "jurisdictional hook" is the use of a camera and film, made somewhere outside of California. [But this] "limiting" jurisdictional provision . . . completely fails to "guarantee[ ] that the final product regulated substantially affects interstate commerce."

4. Legislative History

While neither necessary nor conclusive, congressional findings addressing the national impact of the regulated activity in question can assist in determining whether that activity substantially affects interstate commerce. *Lopez*. As the Supreme Court noted in *Morrison*, however, it is not the mere *existence* of legislative findings that is determinative. Rather, "[w]hether particular operations affect interstate commerce sufficiently to come under the constitutional power of Congress to regulate them is ultimately a judicial rather than a legislative question." [*Morrison*, quoting *Lopez*.]

[Our reading of the legislative history is] that §2252(a)(4)(B), as applied to McCoy and others similarly situated, would be unconstitutional. First, it is true that Congress declared *commercial* child pornography to be a national problem. These determinations, however, speak only to the general phenomenon of commercial child pornography; they do not speak to the relationship between *intrastate non-commercial* conduct like McCoy's and the interstate commercial child pornography market. . . . At most, the legislative history here tells us that Congress intended to eliminate the interstate commercial child pornography market, and nothing more. . . . Second, doubt existed from the outset regarding Congress's authority to regulate intrastate activity. When [§2252 was first proposed in 1978 the Department of Justice] recommended that the bill cover only conduct in which the prohibited pictures themselves had been moved in interstate or foreign commerce . . . . The jurisdictional problem recognized by the Department of Justice some twenty-five years ago is only exacerbated by the Supreme Court's recent adoption of an even more restrictive view of the scope of Congress's Commerce Clause power, in *Lopez* and *Morrison*. . . .

5. Summary

[We] conclude that [when] the first, and ordinarily the most important, [*Morrison*] factor [is] applied in the circumstances before us, §2252(a)(4)(B) does not regulate activity that is economic or commercial in nature. The remaining *Morrison* factors also support our conclusion that simple intrastate possession of child pornography does not fall within *Lopez*'s third category of permissible *Commerce Clause* regulation: activity that "substantially affects" interstate commerce. The relationship between purely intrastate non-commercial possession of prohibited home-grown depictions and the highly commercial interstate activity engaged in by the "multi-million dollar industries" involved is highly attenuated at best. . . .

We hold that §2252(a)(4)(B)'s application to the simple intrastate possession of a visual depiction (or depictions) that has not been mailed, shipped, or transported interstate and is not intended for interstate distribution or for economic or commercial use, including the exchange of the prohibited material for other prohibited material, cannot be justified under the Commerce Clause. If punishment for the conduct in which McCoy engaged is desirable and lawful, it is the state that must seek to attain that result, not the federal government. The statute is unconstitutional as applied. . . .

UNITED STATES v. STEWART

348 F.3d 1132 (9th Cir. 2003)

KOZINSKI, Circuit Judge. We decide whether Congress can, under its Commerce Clause power, prohibit the mere possession of homemade machineguns. . . . Stewart was charged and convicted of . . . five counts of unlawful possession of a machinegun in violation of 18 U.S.C. §922(o).[1] . . . Stewart did not acquire his machineguns from someone else: He fabricated them himself. The government has never contested Stewart's claim that the machineguns were entirely homemade, and the evidence supports his claim. . . . The district court ruled against Stewart's Commerce Clause argument, reasoning that "the parts, at least, moved in interstate commerce." Indeed, some of the machinegun parts did move in interstate commerce. At some level, of course, everything we own is composed of something that once traveled in commerce. This cannot mean that *everything* is subject to federal regulation under the Commerce Clause, else that constitutional limitation would be entirely meaningless. As *Lopez* reminds us, Congress's power has limits, and we must be mindful of those limits so as not to " 'obliterate the distinction between what is national and what is local and create a completely centralized government.' " [*Lopez*, quoting *NLRB v. Jones & Laughlin Steel Corp.*] Some components of Stewart's machineguns had crossed state lines, but these components did not add up to a gun. Not even close. . . . This is quite different than if Stewart had ordered a disassembled gun and simply put the parts together, the way one might assemble a chair from IKEA. These machineguns were a "unique type of firearm," with legal parts mixed and matched from various origins; they required more than a simple turn of a screwdriver or a hit of a hammer to become machineguns. We therefore cannot say that the machineguns themselves — in any recognizable form — traveled in interstate commerce. Because these firearms were genuinely homemade, we find that Stewart did not obtain his machineguns by "using the channels of interstate commerce." . . .

Even if Stewart did not *use* the channels of interstate commerce, his possession of machineguns may still have substantially *affected* interstate commerce. Several courts of appeals have held section 922(o) constitutional on this ground [but we] cannot agree that simple possession of machineguns — particularly possession of homemade machineguns — has a substantial effect on interstate commerce. . . . Possession of a machinegun is not, without more, economic in nature. . . . Whatever its intended use, without some evidence that it will be sold or transferred — and there is none here — its relationship to interstate commerce is highly attenuated. Moreover, the regulation itself does not have an economic purpose: whereas the statute in *Wickard* was enacted primarily to control the market price of wheat, there is no evidence that section 922(o) was enacted to regulate commercial aspects of the machinegun business. More likely, section 922(o) was intended to keep machineguns out of the hands of criminals — an admirable goal, but not a commercial one. . . .

Lopez already rejected the reasoning that, because the cost of violent crimes is spread through insurance, regulations intended to prevent violent crimes significantly affect the national economy. Nor did *Lopez* buy the argument that violent crime substantially affects commerce by reducing people's willingness to travel to unsafe areas of the country. Though prohibition of all machinegun possession may have a greater chance of reducing violent crime than a prohibition that extends only

1. 18 U.S.C. §922(o) makes it unlawful to "transfer or possess a machinegun." [Ed.]

to school zones, this does not change what the Court said in *Lopez*: that under these expansive theories, "it is difficult to perceive any limitation on federal power, even in areas such as criminal law enforcement . . . where States historically have been sovereign." . . .

Moreover, nothing in the legislative history . . . speaks to the relationship between mere possession of firearms and interstate commerce. Instead, the legislative findings focus primarily on the need for federal enforcement where firearms cross state and international borders, and are thus difficult for individual states to regulate on their own. . . . Nothing in the legislative history suggests that Congress ever considered the impact of purely intrastate possession of homemade machineguns on interstate commerce, and there is no reason to assume that prohibiting local possession of machineguns would have the same national and commercial consequences as prohibiting the interstate and foreign traffic in firearms. . . .

We therefore conclude that section 922(o) is unconstitutional as applied to Stewart. . . .

RAICH v. ASHCROFT

352 F.3d 1222 (9th Cir. 2003)

PREGERSON, Circuit Judge. [Appellants Raich and Monson] are seriously ill Californians who use marijuana for medical purposes on the recommendation of their doctors. Such use is legal under [California law.] The remaining two appellants . . . assist Raich in growing her marijuana. [Appellants seek] injunctive and declaratory relief based on the alleged unconstitutionality of the federal Controlled Substances Act, [the "CSA," 21 U.S.C. §801 *et seq.*, under which marijuana is a prohibited controlled substance.][1] . . . [The] district court denied the appellants' motion for a preliminary injunction. . . . We have jurisdiction to hear this interlocutory appeal pursuant to 28 U.S.C. §1292 (a)(1). . . . The grant or denial of a preliminary injunction will be reversed only where the district court abused its discretion or based its decision on an erroneous legal standard or on clearly erroneous findings of fact. [A significant and relevant factor in deciding whether a preliminary injunction is warranted is the probability or] likelihood of success on the merits . . . . We find that the appellants have demonstrated a strong likelihood of success on their claim that, as applied to them, the CSA is an unconstitutional exercise of Congress' Commerce Clause authority. . . .

[Appellees] correctly note that " 'where a *general regulatory statute bears a substantial relation to commerce*, the *de minimis* character of individual instances arising under that statute is of no consequence.' " [*Lopez*, quoting Maryland v. Wirtz, 392 U.S. 183, 197 n.27 (1968), (first emphasis added in *Lopez*).[2]] But here the ap-

---

1. 21 U.S.C. §841(a)(1) makes it unlawful to knowingly or intentionally "manufacture, distribute, or dispense, or possess with intent to manufacture, distribute, or dispense, a controlled substance," and §844(a) makes possession of a controlled substance unlawful. [ED.]

2. The Supreme Court has restated this principle: "Where the *class of activities* is regulated and that *class* is within the reach of federal power, the courts have 'no power to excise, as trivial, indi-

pellants . . . contend that, whereas . . . earlier cases [upholding the CSA] concerned drug *trafficking*, [their] conduct constitutes a *separate and distinct class of activities*: the intrastate, noncommercial cultivation and possession of cannabis for personal medical purposes as recommended by a patient's physician pursuant to valid California state law.

Clearly, the way in which the activity or class of activities is defined is critical. We find that the appellants' class of activities — the intrastate, noncommercial cultivation, possession and use of marijuana for personal medical purposes on the advice of a physician — is, in fact, different in kind from drug trafficking. [Concern] regarding users' health and safety is significantly different in the medicinal marijuana context, where the use is pursuant to a physician's recommendation. Further, the limited medicinal use of marijuana as recommended by a physician arguably does not raise the same policy concerns regarding the spread of drug abuse. Moreover, this limited use is clearly distinct from the broader illicit drug market — as well as any broader commercial market for medicinal marijuana — insofar as the medicinal marijuana at issue in this case is not intended for, nor does it enter, the stream of commerce. . . .

We must now answer the question whether this class of activities has an effect on interstate commerce sufficient to make it subject to federal regulation under the Commerce Clause. [The question is whether this case involves] "activities that substantially affect interstate commerce." . . .

As applied to the limited class of activities presented by this case, the CSA does not regulate commerce or any sort of economic enterprise. The cultivation, possession, and use of marijuana for medicinal purposes and not for exchange or distribution is not properly characterized as commercial or economic activity. Lacking sale, exchange or distribution, the activity does not possess the essential elements of commerce. . . . As the regulated activity in this case is not commercial, *Wickard*'s aggregation analysis is not applicable. [*Morrison*, 529 U.S. at 611 n.4.] . . .

Congress['s] findings in the CSA regarding the effects of intrastate activity on interstate commerce . . . are primarily concerned with the trafficking or distribution of controlled substances. Nevertheless, they provide some evidence that intrastate possession of controlled substances may [have an impact upon] interstate commerce. [But] there is no indication that Congress was considering anything like the class of activities at issue here when it made its findings. The findings are not specific to marijuana, much less intrastate medicinal use of marijuana that is not bought or sold and the use of which is based on the recommendation of a physician. Common sense indicates that the findings related to this specific class of activities would be significantly different from the findings relating to the effect of drug trafficking, generally, on interstate commerce. [In any case,] *Morrison* counsels courts to take congressional findings with a grain of salt. . . .

---

vidual instances' of the class." Perez v. United States, 402 U.S. 146, 154 (1971), quoting Maryland v. Wirtz, 392 U.S. 183, 193 (1968) (emphasis in original). [ED.]

[The] link between the regulated activity and a substantial effect on interstate commerce is "attenuated." [While] the intrastate cultivation, possession and use of medical marijuana on the recommendation of a physician could, at the margins, have an effect on interstate commerce by reducing the demand for marijuana that is trafficked interstate[, it] is far from clear that such an effect would be substantial. . . . On the basis of our consideration of the [*Morrison*] factors, we find that the CSA, as applied to the appellants, is likely unconstitutional. . . .

BEAM, Circuit Judge, dissenting. It is simply impossible to distinguish the relevant conduct surrounding the cultivation and use of the marijuana crop at issue in this case from the cultivation and use of the wheat crop that affected interstate commerce in Wickard v. Filburn, 317 U.S. 111 (1942). . . . Except for why the marijuana at issue in this case is consumed, i.e., for medicinal rather than nutritional purposes, plaintiffs' conduct is entirely indistinguishable from that of Mr. Filburn's. . . . .

Plaintiffs argue that *Wickard* is distinguishable because Filburn was engaged in the commercial activity of farming, while their activities are purely non-economic. . . . The argument ignores the fungible, economic nature of the substance at issue — marijuana plants — for which there is a well-established and variable interstate market, albeit an illegal one under federal law. . . . "In any event, the cultivation of marijuana for personal consumption most likely *does* substantially affect interstate commerce . . . because 'it supplies a need of the man who grew it which would otherwise be reflected by purchases in the open market.'" [Proyect v. United States, 101 F.3d 11, 14 n.1 (2d Cir. 1996), quoting *Wickard.*] . . .

If Congress cannot reach individual narcotic growers, possessors, and users, its overall statutory scheme will be totally undermined. [The] conduct in this case is indistinguishable from the conduct at issue in *Wickard*. . . . Accordingly, I dissent.

3. Limits Imposed by Principles of State Autonomy

b. Procedural Immunity

Page 239: Insert as a new note following Printz, *immediately before section C:*

Sovereign Immunity as a Procedural Immunity: Alden v. Maine

In Seminole Tribe of Florida v. Florida, 517 U.S. 44 (1996), the Court held that Congress lacked authority under its Article I powers to abrogate a state's Eleventh Amendment immunity from private damages suits in federal court. Thereafter, employees of the state of Maine filed suit in a Maine court seeking damages for Maine's alleged violation of the federal Fair Labor Standards Act, but the claim was dismissed due to Maine's sovereign immunity. In Alden v. Maine, 527 U.S. 706 (1999), the Supreme Court relied on a structural principle of state sovereign immunity (except as explicitly surrendered in the Constitution) to hold that Congress lacked authority to compel states to entertain in their own courts private damages suits based on federal law. The Court noted that because "the Supremacy Clause enshrines as 'the supreme Law of the Land' only those federal Acts that accord with the constitutional design, [this] merely raises the question of whether a law is a valid exercise of the national power." The Court struck down the law because the principle of state immunity from suit without its consent was a preconstitutional attribute of sovereignty that was not waived by the states in the Constitution, either explicitly or by any implication from the grant to the federal government of its enumerated powers. This conclusion was based on several important structural principles of federalism, foremost of which was the interference with a state's autonomy — its "decisionmaking ability" — presented by a congressional edict that states must entertain unconsented suits for damages:

> A power to press a State's own courts into federal service to coerce the other branches of the State . . . is the power first to turn the State against itself and ultimately to commandeer the entire political machinery of the State against its will and at the behest of individuals. . . . Private suits against nonconsenting States — especially suits for money damages — may threaten the financial integrity of the States. . . . A general federal power to authorize private suits would place unwarranted strain on the States' ability to govern in accordance with the will of their citizens. [The] allocation of scarce resources among competing needs and interests lies at the heart of the political process. . . . If the principle of representative government is to be preserved to the States, the balance between competing interests must be reached after deliberation by the political process established by the citizens of the State, not by judicial decree mandated by the Federal Government and invoked by the private citizen.
>
> [A contrary ruling would] strike[ ] at the heart of the political accountability so essential to our liberty and republican form of government [because it would] blur not only the distinct responsibilities of the State and National Governments but also the separate duties of the judicial and political branches of the state government. . . . A State is entitled to order the processes of its own governance, assigning to the political branches, rather than the courts, the responsibility for directing the payment of debts.

As in *New York* and *Printz*, the "structural postulate at work in *Alden* was the procedural immunity principle. Congress remained free to impose liability on the states for violations of the FLSA and to enforce the states' resulting duty by suit brought by the United States; what Congress could not do was to impose an enforcement mechanism that interfered with the internal governance processes of the states." Massey, Federalism and the Rehnquist Court, 53 Hastings L.J. 431, 469 (2002).

G. Foreign Affairs

Page 267: Insert at the end of the section, immediately before section H:

Note: The Renewed Vigor of Zschernig v. Miller

In American Insurance Ass'n v. Garamendi, 539 U.S. 396 (2003), the Supreme Court invalidated a California law, the Holocaust Victim Insurance Relief Act of 1999 (HVIRA), which required any insurer doing business in California to disclose information about all policies sold in Europe between 1920 and 1945 by the company or any "related" entity upon penalty of loss of its state business license.

During the Nazi era the government of Germany seized the proceeds of insurance policies owned by Jews; after the end of World War II many insurers refused to pay on life insurance policies because of the absence of a death certificate or other proof of death. After German reunification, a spate of lawsuits was filed in American courts against insurers and other companies doing business with the Nazis, seeking restitution of various kinds. Acting in response to concerns raised by foreign governments and businesses, the United States entered into an executive agreement with Germany, known as the German Foundation Agreement, by which Germany established a foundation funded with 10 billion Deutsch marks contributed by the German Government and German companies to compensate Nazi era victims. The United States, for its part, agreed to attempt to cause state and local governments to recognize the foundation as the sole body for resolving such claims, and pledged to assert in any American court in which a German company was sued on a Nazi era claim a statement that it would be in the national interest of the United States to have the claim adjudicated exclusively in the foundation. Similar such executive agreements were reached between the United States and Austria, and the United States and France. The agreements dealt specifically with insurance claims by requiring the foundation to coordinate its activities with the International Commission on Holocaust Era Insurance Claims (ICHEIC), a non-governmental organization conceived to attempt to obtain from European insurers information about and settlement of outstanding insurance policies.

Even before the California HVIRA was challenged in federal court as an impermissible intrusion on the foreign affairs power, federal officials warned California that the HVIRA "has the unfortunate effect of damaging the one effective means now at hand to process quickly and completely unpaid insurance claims from the Holocaust period, the [ICHEIC]," that "actions by California, pursuant to this law, have already threatened to damage the cooperative spirit which the [ICHEIC] requires to resolve [this] issue," and stressed that HVIRA would possibly derail the German Foundation Agreement. California remained obdurate and proceeded with vigorous enforcement of the HVIRA, prompting the litigation ending in the Court's decision in *Garamendi* that the HVIRA was preempted by the federal foreign affairs power. Justice Souter wrote for the Court:

> The principal argument for preemption . . . is that HVIRA interferes with foreign policy of the Executive Branch, as expressed principally in the executive agreements with Germany, Austria, and France. The major premises of the argument, at least, are beyond dispute. There is, of course, no question that at some point an exercise of state power that touches on foreign relations must yield to the National Government's pol-

> icy, given the "concern for uniformity in this country's dealings with foreign nations" that animated the Constitution's allocation of the foreign relations power to the National Government in the first place. . . . Nor is there any question generally that there is executive authority to decide what that policy should be. . . . While Congress holds express authority to regulate public and private dealings with other nations in its war and foreign commerce powers, in foreign affairs the President has a degree of independent authority to act. . . . At a more specific level, our cases have recognized that the President has authority to make "executive agreements" with other countries, requiring no ratification by the Senate or approval by Congress, this power having been exercised since the early years of the Republic. . . . Making executive agreements to settle claims of American nationals against foreign governments is a particularly longstanding practice. [Valid] executive agreements are fit to preempt state law, just as treaties are, and if the agreements here had expressly preempted laws like HVIRA, the issue would be straightforward. [But because] the agreements include no preemption clause . . . their claim of preemption [rests] on asserted interference with the foreign policy those agreements embody.

In Zschernig v. Miller, p. 266, the Court applied a field preemption theory to invalidate the Oregon law at issue. Justices Harlan and White would have applied conflict preemption, leaving the states with freedom to act on matters that might incidentally affect foreign policy, so long as their actions do not "impair the effective exercise of the Nation's foreign policy." Justice Souter, for the Court, thought that

> [it] is a fair question whether respect for the executive foreign relations power requires a categorical choice between the contrasting theories of field and conflict preemption evident in the *Zschernig* opinions, but the question requires no answer here. For even on Justice Harlan's view, the likelihood that state legislation will produce something more than incidental effect in conflict with express foreign policy of the National Government would require preemption of the state law. And since on his view it is legislation within "areas of . . . traditional competence" that gives a State any claim to prevail, it would be reasonable to consider the strength of the state interest, judged by standards of traditional practice, when deciding how serious a conflict must be shown before declaring the state law preempted. . . . Judged by these standards, we think petitioners and the Government have demonstrated a sufficiently clear conflict to require finding preemption here.
>
> [Resolving] Holocaust-era insurance claims that may be held by residents of this country is a matter well within the Executive's responsibility for foreign affairs. [There] is a "longstanding practice" of the national Executive to settle them in discharging its responsibility to maintain the Nation's relationships with other countries. [*Dames & Moore*]. The issue of restitution for Nazi crimes has in fact been addressed in Executive Branch diplomacy and formalized in treaties and executive agreements over the last half century, and . . . resolution of private claims . . . is an express object of diplomacy today. . . . Vindicating victims injured by acts and omissions of enemy corporations in wartime is thus within the traditional subject matter of foreign policy in which national, not state, interests are overriding, and which the National Government has addressed. [Exercise of] federal executive authority means that state law must give way where, as here, there is evidence of clear conflict between the policies adopted by

the two. The . . . consistent Presidential foreign policy has been to encourage European governments and companies to volunteer settlement funds in preference to litigation or coercive sanctions.

California has taken a different tack of providing regulatory sanctions to compel disclosure and payment, supplemented by a new cause of action for Holocaust survivors if the other sanctions should fail. . . . Whereas the President's authority to provide for settling claims in winding up international hostilities requires flexibility in wielding "the coercive power of the national economy" as a tool of diplomacy, HVIRA denies this, by making exclusion from a large sector of the American insurance market the automatic sanction for noncompliance with the State's own policies on disclosure. . . . HVIRA threatens to frustrate the operation of the particular mechanism the President has chosen. . . . In addition to thwarting the Government's policy of repose for companies that pay through the ICHEIC, California's indiscriminate disclosure provisions place a handicap on the ICHEIC's effectiveness (and raise a further irritant to the European allies) by undercutting European privacy protections. . . .

The express federal policy and the clear conflict raised by the state statute are alone enough to require state law to yield. If any doubt about the clarity of the conflict remained, however, it would have to be resolved in the National Government's favor, given the weakness of the State's interest, against the backdrop of traditional state legislative subject matter, in regulating disclosure of European Holocaust-era insurance policies in the manner of HVIRA.

[There] is no serious doubt that the state interest actually underlying HVIRA is concern for the several thousand Holocaust survivors said to be living in the State. [Should] the State's interest [be] recognized as a powerful one, by virtue of the fact that California seeks to vindicate the claims of Holocaust survivors? The answer lies in recalling that the very same objective dignifies the interest of the National Government in devising its chosen mechanism for voluntary settlements, there being about 100,000 survivors in the country, only a small fraction of them in California.

The basic fact is that California seeks to use an iron fist where the President has consistently chosen kid gloves. We have heard powerful arguments that the iron fist would work better, [but the] question relevant to preemption in this case is conflict, and the evidence here is "more than sufficient to demonstrate that the state Act stands in the way of [the President's] diplomatic objectives."

In dissent, Justice Ginsburg, joined by Justices Stevens, Scalia, and Thomas, noted that

[w]e have not relied on *Zschernig* since it was decided, and I would not resurrect that decision here. The notion of "dormant foreign affairs preemption" with which *Zschernig* is associated resonates most audibly when a state action "reflects a state policy critical of foreign governments and involves 'sitting in judgment' on them." L. Henkin, Foreign Affairs and the United States Constitution 164 (2d ed. 1996). The HVIRA entails no such state action or policy. It takes no position on any contemporary foreign government and requires no assessment of any existing foreign regime. It is directed solely at private insurers doing business in California, and it requires them solely to disclose information in their or their affiliates' possession or control. I would not extend *Zschernig* into this dissimilar domain. . . . Neither would I stretch *Belmont*, *Pink* [see pp. 404-405], or *Dames & Moore* [see pp. 392-397] to support implied preemp-

tion by executive agreement. In each of those cases, the Court gave effect to the express terms of an executive agreement. . . . If it is uncertain whether insurance *litigation* may continue given the executive agreements on which the Court relies, it should be abundantly clear that those agreements leave *disclosure* laws like the HVIRA untouched. . . . To fill the agreements' silences, the Court points to statements by individual members of the Executive Branch. But we have never premised foreign affairs preemption on statements of that order. We should not do so here lest we place the considerable power of foreign affairs preemption in the hands of individual sub-Cabinet members of the Executive Branch. . . . The displacement of state law by preemption properly requires a considerably more formal and binding federal instrument. [By] declining to invalidate the HVIRA in this case, we would reserve foreign affairs preemption for circumstances where the President, acting under statutory or constitutional authority, has spoken clearly to the issue at hand.

Chapter 4

Limiting the Scope of State Power Over Interstate Commerce

A. The Dormant Commerce Clause

4. Facially Neutral Regulations with Discriminatory Effects on Commerce

Page 321: Insert new note 3 immediately before subsection A.5:

3. Interstate Commerce *or Interstate* Competition*?* In Pharmaceutical Research and Manufacturers of America v. Walsh, 538 U.S. 644 (2003), the Court held that Maine's "Maine Rx" program did not violate the dormant commerce clause. Maine Rx is designed to reduce prescription drug prices for state residents. Under the program, a drug manufacturer must either reduce its drug prices by granting rebates to Maine pharmacists which are passed through to drug consumers or have its Medicaid drug sales in Maine subjected to a "prior authorization" procedure that requires state agency approval to qualify a prescription drug for reimbursement. In a series of divided opinions, the Court agreed that, at least at the preliminary injunction stage of the litigation, there was an insufficient showing that Maine Rx's prior authorization procedure was preempted by federal law governing Medicaid. However, the Court was unanimous that Maine Rx did not violate the commerce clause.

The pharmaceutical industry alleged "that the rebate requirement constitutes impermissible extraterritorial regulation, and . . . that it discriminates against interstate commerce in order to subsidize in-state retail sales," but the Court rejected both contentions. Maine Rx did not produce extraterritorial price regulation, as in Baldwin v. G. A. F. Seelig, Inc., 294 U.S. 511 (1935), p. 313, and Healy v. Beer Institute, 491 U.S. 324 (1989).[1] Quoting the lower court, the Supreme Court noted

1. In *Healy*, the Court voided a Massachusetts regulation that required beer wholesalers to affirm monthly that the price at which they would sell beer in Massachusetts for the coming month was no higher than the price at which they sold beer in neighboring states. The effect of the regu-

that " 'the Maine Act does not regulate the price of any out-of-state transaction, either by its express terms or by its inevitable effect. Maine does not insist that manufacturers sell their drugs to a wholesaler for a certain price. Similarly, Maine is not tying the price of its in-state products to out-of-state prices.' " The pharmaceutical industry also contended that Maine Rx was similar to the facially neutral but actually discriminatory tax-and-subsidy scheme struck down in *West Lynn Creamery*, p. 316, "because it would be created entirely from rebates paid by out-of-state manufacturers and would be used to subsidize sales by local pharmacists to local consumers. Unlike the situation in *West Lynn*, however, the Maine Rx Program will not impose a disparate burden on any competitors. A manufacturer could not avoid its rebate obligation by opening production facilities in Maine and would receive no benefit from the rebates even if it did so; the payments to the local pharmacists provide no special benefit to competitors of rebate-paying manufacturers."

In Exxon v. Maryland, p. 309, the Court noted that the commerce clause "protects the interstate market, not particular interstate firms, from prohibitive or burdensome regulations." In *Walsh*, the Court relied on the absence of "a disparate burden on any competitors" to find the dormant commerce clause inapplicable. Evidence submitted to the trial court in *Walsh* indicated that use of prior authorization in other states had caused a sharp drop in the market share of non-generic pharmaceutical drugs. Does *Walsh* rest on the unstated proposition that there is one interstate market for pharmaceutical drugs, a market that includes generic and non-generic drugs? Or does *Walsh* rest on the proposition that in the absence of a disparate impact on interstate firms, the dormant commerce clause is not offended? If the latter proposition is correct, is *Exxon* still good law? If the former proposition is correct, should there have been some examination into the nature of the market for pharmaceutical drugs? An economist, for example, might want to know the degree to which generic and non-generic drugs are actual substitutes for each other. A physician might wish to assess the medical efficacy of such substitution. Are those inquires relevant to a determination of the interstate market in pharmaceutical drugs for purposes of the commerce clause?

C. Preemption and Consent: Congress Has the Final Word

1. Preemption

Page 353: Insert the following at the end of the note, immediately before subsection C.2:

---

lation was to require beer wholesalers to sell beer in other states at a price no higher than the affirmed price in effect for Massachusetts.

The Presumption Against Preemption: Observed in the Breach? The Court continues to recite that there is a presumption against preemption when Congress regulates an activity that has "traditionally" been a subject of state regulation. But observe what it has done in recent years.

In Geier v. American Honda Motor Co., 529 U.S. 861 (2000), the Court held that ordinary state tort law was such an obstacle to Congress's intent to formulate auto safety standards that it was in actual conflict with a Department of Transportation regulation mandating air bags on some but not all vehicles and was thus impliedly preempted by the regulation. Geier, a Honda driver injured in an auto accident, sued Honda on the theory that it was negligent in manufacturing an auto without an air bag. Honda claimed that its compliance with an interim Department of Transportation regulation that required it to equip some of its models (but not Geier's) with air bags insulated it from liability by reason of the regulation's preemption of state tort law.

Even though the presumption against preemption imposes on the party seeking to establish preemption the burden of proving a clear and manifest intent of Congress to preempt contrary state law the Court concluded that the checkered history of the safety standard (an on-again off-again attempt to compel automakers to equip their cars with devices that would overcome the public's resistance to seat belt use) indicated that the Department of Transportation had as its objective a gradual phasing in of air bags, an objective that would be frustrated by a state's imposition of tort liability on an auto manufacturer who complied with the standard by manufacturing a vehicle without an air bag.

Does this result cast doubt on the continuing vitality of Commonwealth Edison v. Montana, 453 U.S. 609 (1981)? In *Commonwealth Edison* the Court opined that conflict preemption is not normally to be found where the conflict is between state law and a general, broad, or abstract federal objective and went on to hold that there was no conflict between Montana's substantial severance tax on coal, which admittedly made coal more expensive to the electrical generation utilities that use it, and a variety of federal laws that specifically have as their objective the production and consumption of coal.

Should it make any difference that the federal objective identified by the Court in *Geier* was an agency objective, not a congressional objective? Should an unequivocally clear statement of agency intent to preempt be required? Justice Stevens so argued in his dissent in *Geier*, noting that "[u]nlike Congress, administrative agencies are clearly not designed to represent the interests of States, yet with relative ease they can promulgate comprehensive and detailed regulations that have broad preemption ramifications for state law." Should preemption implied from an agency regulation be especially disfavored on the theory that agency administrators are politically unaccountable and concerned primarily about their narrow bailiwick, but members of Congress are politically accountable?

Finally, is there reason to wonder whether the entire category of "implied obstacle conflict preemption" is really warranted? See Nelson, "Preemption," 86 Va. L. Rev. 225, 231-232 (2000): "[The Supremacy Clause supports preemption] if and only if state law contradicts a valid rule established by federal law, and the mere fact that the federal law serves certain purposes does not automatically mean that it contradicts everything that might get in the way of those purposes."

In United States v. Locke, 529 U.S. 89 (2000), the Court unanimously held that Washington State's regulations of oil tankers plying its waters were impliedly preempted by a series of federal laws regulating similar but not identical aspects of tanker traffic in American waters. Washington had adopted rules governing tanker navigation procedures, crew training and procedures, and reporting of casualty incidents. The Court held that federal law had impliedly preempted the entire field of design, construction, equipping, and operation of oil tankers, and that conflict preemption applied to the narrow area of state regulation of matters peculiar to local waters, such as depth or narrowness of marine passages. The Court firmly rejected any suggestion that the presumption against preemption should apply at all when "the State regulates in an area where there has been a history of significant federal presence."

Was this rejection of the presumption against preemption wise? In a field preemption case the entire inquiry is to decide whether what Congress has done is sufficiently pervasive to constitute an implicit declaration that no other regulation of the area is to be allowed. An important part of this inquiry is to identify the boundaries of the field. Should the presumption against preemption be retained as a device to hem in the field boundaries and prevent judges from deciding that the field is so vast as to be virtually limitless? Or is it appropriate to discard the presumption as soon as Congress embarks upon significant valid regulation on the theory that Congress is occupying the field and the degree of that occupation should be resolved in favor of federal power? Note that field preemption can produce a regulatory vacuum when the federal scheme (which totally displaces state power to regulate in the field) fails to address some particular point that may be of concern to a state. Of course, Congress can correct that oversight, but it may de disinclined to do so if the vacuum is of consequence only to a tiny minority of states.

In Lorillard Tobacco v. Reilly, 533 U.S. 525 (2001), the Court ruled that Massachusetts regulations banning cigarette advertising within 1,000 feet of a school or playground were preempted by the Federal Cigarette Labeling and Advertising Act, 15 U.S.C. §1334(b), which provides that "no requirement or prohibition based on smoking and health shall be imposed under state law with respect to the advertising or promotion of any cigarettes" that bear the warning labels prescribed by federal law. The Court denied any distinction between regulations addressing the content of such advertising and those directed to the location of cigarette advertisements.

> We believe that Congress wished to ensure that "a State could not do through negative mandate (e.g., banning all cigarette advertising) that which it already was forbidden to do through positive mandate (e.g., mandating particular cautionary statements)." [We] hold only that the FCLAA pre-empts state regulations targeting cigarette advertising. States remain free to enact generally applicable zoning regulations, and to regulate conduct with respect to cigarette use and sales.

In its ruling on appeal, the First Circuit had applied the presumption against preemption on the theory that the subject of the Massachusetts regulations was zoning, a traditional state-regulated activity. The Court said the regulations involved only cigarette advertising and that the presumption against preemption did not apply because that activity is not a traditionally state-regulated activity. Should the presumption against preemption have applied? How can you determine which activities are traditionally regulated by states and which are not? Suppose that Massachusetts had regulated yard signs or hand-lettered community bulletin board advertisements of cigarettes; would that produce a different outcome?

Chapter 5

Separation of Powers

B. Executive Action

2. In Foreign Affairs

b. War

Page 403: Insert the following new note 4 immediately before subsection B.2.c:

4. The War Against Terrorism after September 11, 2001. On September 11, 2001, four commercial airliners were hijacked and three were used as missiles to destroy New York's World Trade Center and damage the Pentagon with the loss of some 3,000 lives. (The fourth airliner, apparently headed for Congress or the White House, crashed in Pennsylvania as a result of passenger resistance.) Three days later, Congress enacted a joint resolution authorizing the President to use military force. The Joint Resolution recited that the "acts of treacherous violence . . . committed against the United States and its citizens . . . render it both necessary and appropriate that the United States exercise its rights to self-defense and to protect United States citizens both at home and abroad," declared that "such acts . . . pose an unusual and extraordinary threat to the national security and foreign policy of the United States," asserted that "the President has authority under the Constitution to take action to deter and prevent acts of international terrorism against the United States," and resolved that

> the President is authorized to use all necessary and appropriate force against those nations, organizations, or persons he determines planned, authorized, committed, or aided the terrorist attacks that occurred on September 11, 2001, or harbored such organizations or persons, in order to prevent any further acts of international terrorism against the United States by such nations, organizations or persons.

The Joint Resolution also stated that "[c]onsistent with section 8(a)(1) of the War Powers Resolution, the Congress declares that this [resolution] is intended to constitute specific statutory authorization within the meaning of section 5(b) of the

War Powers Resolution" and further declared that "[n]othing in this resolution supercedes any requirement of the War Powers Resolution." H.J.R. 64, S.J.R. 23, Sept. 14, 2001.

Queries: Is this a declaration of war? If so, against what state? International law holds that war is between states. If this is not a declaration of war, is the Joint Resolution constitutionally sufficient to permit the President to wage war in accordance with its terms? Is the Joint Resolution an impermissible delegation to the President of the power to declare war? Consider United States v. Curtiss-Wright Export Corporation, 299 U.S. 304 (1936), and *The Prize Cases*, 67 U.S. (2 Black) 635 (1863).

Consider these same queries in connection with the October 2002 congressional resolution that authorized the President to use American armed forces "as he determines to be necessary and appropriate in order to (1) defend the national security of the United States against the continuing threat posed by Iraq; and (2) enforce all relevant United Nations Security Council resolutions regarding Iraq," so long as the President determined these two objectives could not be attained by "further diplomatic or peaceful means" and that military action is "consistent" with the American response to the terrorist attacks of September 11, 2001. Was the Iraq War of 2003 unconstitutional? If so, why? What remedy is available if you conclude that the Iraq War was unconstitutional?

5. Bulletins from the War on Terror: Hamdi *and* Rasul (Guantanamo Detainees Case). After the September 11 attacks the United States and its allies invaded Afghanistan and overturned its fundamentalist Islamic Taliban government. In the process it captured a number of enemy combatants, some 600 of which were removed to and imprisoned in an American naval base at Guantanamo, Cuba. Among those detained was an American citizen, Yaser Hamdi, who was later transferred to a naval brig in Charleston, S.C. Through his father Hamdi brought a habeas corpus petition to challenge the validity of his imprisonment. The District Court ordered production of various documents and witnesses under the control of the U.S. government in order to facilitate determination of the validity of Hamdi's detention. On certified appeal, the Fourth Circuit reversed, concluding that because it was "undisputed that Hamdi was captured in a zone of active combat in a foreign theater of conflict," he was not entitled to any "factual inquiry or evidentiary hearing" in which Hamdi might plead his case and rebut the government's claims.

In Hamdi v. Rumsfeld, 124 S. Ct. 2633 (2004), the Supreme Court reversed. A four-justice plurality consisting of Justice O'Connor, joined by Chief Justice Rehnquist and Justices Kennedy and Breyer, first addressed the "threshold question [of] whether the Executive has the authority to detain citizens who qualify as 'enemy combatants,' [a term that] for purposes of this case [refers to] individual[s alleged to be] 'part of or supporting forces hostile to the United States or coalition partners' in Afghanistan and who 'engaged in an armed conflict against the United States' there. We . . . answer only the narrow question before us: whether the detention of citizens falling within that definition is authorized." The plurality concluded that a federal statute, 18 U.S.C. §4001(a), which provides that "no citizen shall be imprisoned or otherwise detained by the United States except pursuant to an Act of

Congress," was inapplicable because Congress had authorized such detention in its Joint Resolution of September 14, 2001. "The capture and detention of lawful combatants and the capture, detention, and trial of unlawful combatants, by 'universal agreement and practice,' are 'important incidents of war.' Ex parte Quirin, [317 U.S. 1, 28 (1942)]. The purpose of detention is to prevent captured individuals from returning to the field of battle and taking up arms once again. . . . There is no bar to this Nation's holding one of its own citizens as an enemy combatant. [*Quirin.*]. . . . A citizen, no less than an alien, can be 'part of or supporting forces hostile to the United States or coalition partners' and 'engaged in an armed conflict against the United States'; such a citizen, if released, would pose the same threat of returning to the front during the ongoing conflict." While under "the law of war . . . detention may last no longer than active hostilities," the plurality also recognized that " 'given its unconventional nature, the current conflict is unlikely to end with a formal cease-fire agreement,' [and that if] the Government does not consider this unconventional war won for two generations, and if it maintains during that time that Hamdi might, if released, rejoin forces fighting against the United States, then . . . Hamdi's detention could last for the rest of his life."

Ex parte Milligan, 71 U.S. (4 Wall.) 2 (1866), in which the Court held that a Civil War military tribunal could not try and punish a citizen sympathetic to the Confederacy while the civil courts were available, did not apply because "*Milligan* turned in large part on the fact that Milligan was not a prisoner of war, but a resident of Indiana arrested while at home there. . . . Had Milligan been captured while he was assisting Confederate soldiers by carrying a rifle against Union troops on a Confederate battlefield, the holding of the Court might well have been different."

However, "there remains the question of what process is constitutionally due to a citizen who disputes his enemy-combatant status." Because "the writ of habeas corpus remains available to every individual detained within the United States" unless Congress has validly suspended it (which everyone agreed had not occurred) the plurality proceeded to analyze, under the Mathews v. Eldridge test [p.479], the process to which Hamdi was entitled to evaluate whether he was an enemy combatant.

> Hamdi's "private interest . . . affected by the official action" is the most elemental of liberty interests — the interest in being free from physical detention by one's own government. . . . On the other side of the scale are the weighty and sensitive governmental interests in ensuring that those who have in fact fought with the enemy during a war do not return to battle against the United States. . . . Without doubt, our Constitution recognizes that core strategic matters of warmaking belong in the hands of those who are best positioned and most politically accountable for making them. . . .
>
> The Government [argues] that its interests in reducing the process available to alleged enemy combatants are heightened by the practical difficulties that would accompany a system of trial-like process. In its view, military officers who are engaged in the serious work of waging battle would be unnecessarily and dangerously distracted by litigation half a world away, and discovery into military operations would both intrude on the sensitive secrets of national defense and result in a futile search for evidence buried under the rubble of war. To the extent that these burdens are triggered by

heightened procedures, they are properly taken into account in our due process analysis.

Striking the proper constitutional balance here is of great importance to the Nation during this period of ongoing combat. But it is equally vital that our calculus not give short shrift to the values that this country holds dear or to the privilege that is American citizenship. It is during our most challenging and uncertain moments that our Nation's commitment to due process is most severely tested; and it is in those times that we must preserve our commitment at home to the principles for which we fight abroad. We therefore hold that a citizen-detainee seeking to challenge his classification as an enemy combatant must receive notice of the factual basis for his classification, and a fair opportunity to rebut the Government's factual assertions before a neutral decisionmaker. . . . At the same time, the exigencies of the circumstances may demand that, aside from these core elements, enemy combatant proceedings may be tailored to alleviate their uncommon potential to burden the Executive at a time of ongoing military conflict. Hearsay, for example, may need to be accepted as the most reliable available evidence from the Government in such a proceeding. Likewise, the Constitution would not be offended by a presumption in favor of the Government's evidence, so long as that presumption remained a rebuttable one and fair opportunity for rebuttal were provided. . . .

In so holding, we necessarily reject the Government's assertion that separation of powers principles mandate a heavily circumscribed role for the courts in such circumstances. Indeed, the position that the courts must forgo any examination of the individual case and focus exclusively on the legality of the broader detention scheme cannot be mandated by any reasonable view of separation of powers, as this approach serves only to *condense* power into a single branch of government. We have long since made clear that a state of war is not a blank check for the President when it comes to the rights of the Nation's citizens. Youngstown Sheet & Tube, [p.364]. Whatever power the United States Constitution envisions for the Executive in its exchanges with other nations or with enemy organizations in times of conflict, it most assuredly envisions a role for all three branches when individual liberties are at stake.

Justice Souter, joined by Justice Ginsburg, concurred in the judgment on the ground that the Joint Resolution of September 14, 2001 did not constitute sufficient authorization to the President to detain American citizens as enemy combatants, and that 18 U.S.C. §4001(a) thus applied. Accordingly, Justice Souter "would not reach any questions of what process [Hamdi] may be due . . . [It] suffices that the Government has failed to justify holding him in the absence of a further Act of Congress, criminal charges, a showing that the detention conforms to the laws of war, or a demonstration that [18 U.S.C.] §4001(a) is unconstitutional. . . . Since this disposition does not command a majority of the Court, however, the need to give practical effect to the conclusions of eight members of the Court rejecting the Government's position calls for me to join with the plurality in ordering remand on terms closest to those I would impose. . . . [The] plurality's remand will allow Hamdi to offer evidence that he is not an enemy combatant, and he should at the least have the benefit of that opportunity."

Justices Scalia and Stevens dissented. They reasoned that because Congress had not suspended habeas corpus Hamdi (and other "citizens accused of being enemy combatants who are detained within the territorial jurisdiction of a federal court") could not be detained indefinitely as a enemy combatant but could only be prosecuted under the federal criminal code in federal court. Justice Thomas also dissented, contending that the President's "*constitutional* authority to protect the national security" coupled with the September 14, 2001 Joint Resolution vested in the President "broad discretion" to determine whether or not Hamdi was in fact an enemy combatant. "[A]lthough it is appropriate for the Court to determine the judicial question whether the President has the asserted authority, we lack the information and expertise to question whether Hamdi is actually an enemy combatant, a question the resolution of which is committed to other branches."

In Rasul v. Bush (Guantanamo Detainees Case), 124 S. Ct. 2686 (2004), the Court faced "the narrow but important question whether United States courts lack jurisdiction to consider challenges to the legality of the detention of foreign nationals captured abroad in connection with hostilities and incarcerated" by the United States "in a territory [such as Guantanamo] over which the United States exercises plenary and exclusive jurisdiction, but not 'ultimate sovereignty.' " Guantanamo occupies this unusual status because Cuba has leased it to the United States. The federal habeas corpus statute, 28 U.S.C. §2241, enables federal courts to hear challenges to the validity of imprisonment brought by persons within the jurisdiction of the federal courts. A prior decision, Johnson v. Eisentrager, 339 U.S. 763 (1950), held that "aliens detained outside the sovereign territory of the United States [may not] invoke a petition for a writ of habeas corpus." However, because under "the express terms of its agreements with Cuba, the United States exercises 'complete jurisdiction and control' over the Guantanamo Bay Naval Base, and may continue to exercise such control permanently if it so chooses," the Court thought that the habeas corpus statute included within its coverage all those detained at Guantanamo: "Aliens held at the base, no less than American citizens, are entitled to invoke the federal courts' authority under §2241." But the Court also noted: "Whether and what further proceedings may become necessary after respondents make their response to the merits of petitioners' claims are matters that we need not address now. What is presently at stake is only whether the federal courts have jurisdiction to determine the legality of the Executive's potentially indefinite detention of individuals who claim to be wholly innocent of wrongdoing."

Justice Scalia, joined by Chief Justice Rehnquist and Justice Thomas, dissented, arguing that the text, history, and prior interpretation of the habeas corpus statute indicated that the statute applied only to persons within the territorial jurisdiction of the federal district court in which relief is sought. Because Guantanamo is not within the jurisdiction of any federal district court the dissenters thought the statute did not apply to the Guantanamo detainees. The dissenters charged that the Court "extends the habeas statute, for the first time, to aliens held beyond the sovereign territory of the United States and beyond the territorial jurisdiction of its courts; [indeed,] to the four corners of the earth. . . . The consequence of this holding, as applied to aliens outside the country, is breathtaking. . . . Today's carefree Court disregards, without a word of acknowledgment, the dire warning of a more circumspect Court in *Eisentrager:*

> To grant the writ to these prisoners might mean that our army must transport them across the seas for hearing. This would require allocation for shipping space, guarding personnel, billeting and rations. It might also require transportation for whatever witnesses the prisoners desired to call as well as transportation for those necessary to defend legality of the sentence. The writ, since it is held to be a matter of right, would be equally available to enemies during active hostilities as in the present twilight between war and peace. Such trials would hamper the war effort and bring aid and comfort to the enemy. They would diminish the prestige of our commanders, not only with enemies but with wavering neutrals. It would be difficult to devise more effective fettering of a field commander than to allow the very enemies he is ordered to reduce to submission to call him to account in his own civil courts and divert his efforts and attention from the military offensive abroad to the legal defensive at home. Nor is it unlikely that the result of such enemy litigiousness would be conflict between judicial and military opinion highly comforting to enemies of the United States."

Justice Scalia charged that the Court's treatment of the habeas corpus statute was "a wrenching departure from precedent" that

> ought to be unthinkable when the departure has a potentially harmful effect upon the Nation's conduct of a war. The Commander in Chief and his subordinates had every reason to expect that the internment of combatants at Guantanamo Bay would not have the consequence of bringing the cumbersome machinery of our domestic courts into military affairs. Congress is in session. If it wished to change federal judges' habeas jurisdiction from what this Court had previously held that to be, it could have done so. And it could have done so by intelligent revision of the statute, instead of by today's clumsy, countertextual reinterpretation that confers upon wartime prisoners greater habeas rights than domestic detainees. The latter must challenge their present physical confinement in the district of their confinement, whereas under today's strange holding Guantanamo Bay detainees can petition in any of the 94 federal judicial districts. The fact that extraterritorially located detainees lack the district of detention that the statute requires has been converted from a factor that precludes their ability to bring a petition at all into a factor that frees them to petition wherever they wish — and, as a result, to forum shop. For this Court to create such a monstrous scheme in time of war, and in frustration of our military commanders' reliance upon clearly stated prior law, is judicial adventurism of the worst sort.

C. Legislative Action and the Administrative State

2. Specific Limits

a. Nondelegation

Page 430: Insert the following at the very bottom of the page, immediately before subsection C.2.b:

In Whitman v. EPA, 531 U.S. 457 (2000), the Court reviewed a rare case in which a Court of Appeals had ruled that Congress had impermissibly delegated its legislative power by authorizing the Environmental Protection Agency to interpret the Clean Air Act in an indeterminate manner. The Court reversed, but explained the workings of the nondelegation doctrine and its relation to agency discretion. Justice Scalia wrote for the Court, joined by Chief Justice Rehnquist and Justices O'Connor, Kennedy, Thomas, Ginsburg, and Breyer.

In a delegation challenge, the constitutional question is whether the statute has delegated legislative power to the agency. Article I, §1 of the Constitution vests "all legislative Powers herein granted . . . in a Congress of the United States." This text permits no delegation of those powers, and so we repeatedly have said that when Congress confers decisionmaking authority upon agencies *Congress* must "lay down by legislative act an intelligible principle to which the person or body authorized to [act] is directed to conform." We have never suggested that an agency can cure an unlawful delegation of legislative power by adopting in its discretion a limiting construction of the statute. [The] idea that an agency can cure an unconstitutionally standardless delegation of power by declining to exercise some of that power seems to us internally contradictory. The very choice of which portion of the power to exercise — that is to say, the prescription of the standard that Congress had omitted — would *itself* be an exercise of the forbidden legislative authority. Whether the statute delegates legislative power is a question for the courts, and an agency's voluntary self-denial has no bearing upon the answer.

We agree that the text of §109(b)(1) of the [Clean Air Act] at a minimum requires that the EPA must establish uniform national standards at a level that is requisite to protect public health from the adverse effects of the pollutant in the ambient air." Requisite, in turn, "means sufficient, but not more than necessary." These limits on the EPA's discretion are strikingly similar to the ones we approved in Touby v. United States, 500 U.S. 160 (1991), which permitted the Attorney General to designate a drug as a controlled substance for purposes of criminal drug enforcement if doing so was "necessary to avoid an imminent hazard to the public safety." They also resemble the Occupational Safety and Health Act provision requiring the agency to "set the standard which most adequately assures, to the extent feasible, on the basis of the best available evidence, that no employee will suffer any impairment of health" — which the Court upheld in Industrial Union Dept., AFL-CIO v. American Petroleum Institute, 448 U.S. 607 (1980).

. . . In the history of the Court we have found the requisite "intelligible principle" lacking in only two statutes, one of which provided literally no guidance for the exercise of discretion, and the other of which conferred authority to regulate the entire economy on the basis of no more precise a standard than stimulating the economy by assuring "fair competition." See Panama Refining Co. v. Ryan; A. L. A. Schechter Poultry Corp. v. United States.

It is true enough that the degree of agency discretion that is acceptable varies according to the scope of the power congressionally conferred. [Congress] must provide substantial guidance on setting air standards that affect the entire national economy. But even in sweeping regulatory schemes we have never demanded [that] statutes provide a "determinate criterion" for saying "how much [of the regulated harm] is too much." . . . Section 109(b)(1) of the [Clean Air Act], which to repeat we interpret as requiring the EPA to set air quality standards at the level that is "requisite" — that is, not lower or higher than is necessary — to protect the public health with an adequate margin of safety, fits comfortably within the scope of discretion permitted by our precedent.

D. Immunities and Privileges

2. Executive Immunities

Page 452: Insert the following immediately prior to Clinton v. Jones:

Under the doctrine of qualified immunity, executive officials may not be held liable for their actions that were objectively reasonable under clearly established law at the time of the actions in question. When executive officials, such as police officers, use force that is alleged to be excessive in carrying out their duties, the question of reasonableness becomes bifurcated. The immunity inquiry focuses on whether the official's judgment about the lawful scope of force is reasonable. In Saucier v. Katz, 533 U.S. 194 (2001), the Court stated that "the immunity inquiry [acknowledges] that reasonable mistakes can be made as to the legal constraints on particular police conduct. . . . If the officer's mistake as to what the law requires is reasonable the officer is entitled to [immunity]." The Court conceded that this analytical framework is likely to immunize some police conduct that is objectively unreasonable, so long as the police officer's mistake about the permitted boundaries of force is itself reasonable. In Saucier v. Katz, military police officers dragged Katz, a 60-year-old man with one leg in a brace due to a fractured foot, away from a public appearance of Vice President Gore after Katz unfurled a protest banner. Katz was tossed into a police van where he fell but was otherwise uninjured. On the merits, the Court concluded that, considering the heightened security needs associated with an appearance by the Vice President, this "was within the bounds of appropriate police responses."

What sort of police conduct is objectively unreasonable but entitled to immunity because the executive official is reasonably mistaken as to the lawful limits upon his authority to use force? Consider the following possibilities, and assess whether in any case the police conduct is objectively unreasonable but still entitled to immunity:

(a) A motorist stopped by police for driving at 100 m.p.h. through a residential neighborhood with posted speed limits of 40 m.p.h. charges out of his car brandishing a tire iron. The police react by using electric stun weapons to immobilize him and then beat him with their batons while he is lying on the ground.

(b) A motorist is stopped by police for erratic driving late at night. The apprehending officer smells marijuana in the car, observes a few stray dried marijuana leaves on the front of the female driver's blouse, and thus orders her out of the car and subjects her to a roadside strip search, the fruits of which consist of a plastic bag filled with 10 grams of marijuana.

(c) Same facts as (b) except that the search is fruitless.

Chapter Six

Due Process

A. Procedural Due Process

2. Defining the Process That Is Due

Page 484: Insert as new note 3, immediately before Section B:

3. *"Megan's Laws": Registration and Public Disclosure of the Whereabouts of Sex Offenders.* In Connecticut Department of Public Safety v. Doe, 538 U.S. 1 (2003), the Court upheld a Connecticut law that required convicted sex offenders to register and disclose publicly their whereabouts after release from custody. The Second Circuit had ruled that the law deprived convicted sex offenders of a liberty interest by reason of stigmatizing sex offenders as currently dangerous and imposing "extensive and onerous" registration obligations. The Court reversed the Second Circuit but did not decide whether a liberty interest was implicated. Instead, the Court reasoned that even if Connecticut had deprived convicted sex offenders of a liberty interest, due process did not require a hearing prior to registration and disclosure because those obligations were imposed as a result of conviction, and the criminal trial resulting in conviction afforded ample due process protection. The Court expressed no opinion on whether the registration and disclosure requirements unconstitutionally infringe a fundamental liberty interest protected by substantive due process. Justices Souter and Ginsburg concurred in an opinion suggesting that a feature of the Connecticut law that permits some but not all convicted sex offenders to seek judicial exemption from registration and disclosure might be susceptible to a challenge on equal protection grounds.

Query. For purposes of procedural due process, is a liberty interest implicated by the imposition of a registration and disclosure requirement on a convicted sex offender who has served his sentence and been released into the community?

B. Substantive Due Process

3. The Modern Revival: "Privacy" Rights

c. Consensual Sexual Choices

Page 578: Insert at the end of the subsection, immediately before subsection d:

LAWRENCE v. TEXAS
539 U.S. 558 (2003)

JUSTICE KENNEDY delivered the opinion of the Court.

Liberty protects the person from unwarranted government intrusions into a dwelling or other private places. In our tradition the State is not omnipresent in the home. And there are other spheres of our lives and existence, outside the home, where the State should not be a dominant presence. Freedom extends beyond spatial bounds. Liberty presumes an autonomy of self that includes freedom of thought, belief, expression, and certain intimate conduct. The instant case involves liberty of the person both in its spatial and more transcendent dimensions.

I. The question before the Court is the validity of a Texas statute making it a crime for two persons of the same sex to engage in certain intimate sexual conduct.

In Houston, Texas, officers of the Harris County Police Department were dispatched to a private residence in response to a reported weapons disturbance. They entered an apartment where one of the petitioners, John Geddes Lawrence, resided. The right of the police to enter does not seem to have been questioned. The officers observed Lawrence and another man, Tyron Garner, engaging in a sexual act. The two petitioners were arrested, held in custody over night, and charged and convicted before a Justice of the Peace.

The complaints described their crime as "deviate sexual intercourse, namely anal sex, with a member of the same sex (man)." The applicable state law is Tex. Penal Code Ann. §21.06(a) (2003). It provides: "A person commits an offense if he engages in deviate sexual intercourse with another individual of the same sex." The statute defines "deviate sexual intercourse" as "any contact between any part of the genitals of one person and the mouth or anus of another person; or . . . the penetration of the genitals or the anus of another person with an object." §21.01(1). The petitioners . . . challenged the statute as a violation of the Equal Protection Clause of the Fourteenth Amendment and of a like provision of the Texas Constitution. Tex. Const., Art. 1, §3a. Those contentions were rejected. The petitioners, having entered a plea of *nolo contendere*, were each fined $200 and assessed court costs of $141.25.

The [Texas] Court of Appeals . . . considered the petitioners' federal constitutional arguments under both the Equal Protection and Due Process Clauses of the Fourteenth Amendment [but rejected those] constitutional arguments and affirmed the convictions. The . . . Court of Appeals considered our decision in Bowers v. Hardwick [p. 571] to be controlling on the federal due process aspect of the case. *Bowers* then being authoritative, this was proper. . . .

The petitioners were adults at the time of the alleged offense. Their conduct was in private and consensual.

II. We conclude the case should be resolved by determining whether the petitioners were free as adults to engage in the private conduct in the exercise of their liberty under the Due Process Clause of the Fourteenth Amendment to the Constitution. For this inquiry we deem it necessary to reconsider the Court's holding in *Bowers*.

There are broad statements of the substantive reach of liberty under the Due Process Clause in earlier cases, including Pierce v. Society of Sisters and Meyer v. Nebraska, but the most pertinent beginning point is our decision in Griswold v. Connecticut [p. 518].

In *Griswold* the Court . . . described the protected interest as a right to privacy and placed emphasis on the marriage relation and the protected space of the marital bedroom. After *Griswold* it was established that the right to make certain decisions regarding sexual conduct extends beyond the marital relationship. . . . Eisenstadt v. Baird [p.531, which] invalidated a law prohibiting the distribution of contraceptives to unmarried persons, . . . was decided under the Equal Protection Clause, but with respect to unmarried persons, the Court went on to state the fundamental proposition that the law impaired the exercise of their personal rights[:] "If the right of privacy means anything, it is the right of the *individual*, married or single, to be free from unwarranted governmental intrusion into matters so fundamentally affecting a person as the decision whether to bear or beget a child."

[The Court in Roe v. Wade] recognized the right of a woman to make certain fundamental decisions affecting her destiny and confirmed once more that the protection of liberty under the Due Process Clause has a substantive dimension of fundamental significance in defining the rights of the person. In Carey v. Population Services Int'l, 431 U.S. 678 (1977), the Court [voided] a New York law forbidding sale or distribution of contraceptive devices to persons under 16 years of age. . . . Both *Eisenstadt* and *Carey*, as well as the holding and rationale in *Roe*, confirmed that the reasoning of *Griswold* could not be confined to the protection of rights of married adults. This was the state of the law with respect to some of the most relevant cases when the Court considered Bowers v. Hardwick.

[The Court in *Bowers* framed the issue as] "whether the Federal Constitution confers a fundamental right upon homosexuals to engage in sodomy. . . ." To say that the issue in *Bowers* was simply the right to engage in certain sexual conduct demeans the claim the individual put forward, just as it would demean a married couple were it to be said marriage is simply about the right to have sexual intercourse. The laws involved in *Bowers* and here are, to be sure, statutes that purport to do no more than prohibit a particular sexual act. Their penalties and purposes, though, have more far-reaching consequences, touching upon the most private human conduct, sexual behavior, and in the most private of places, the home. The statutes do seek to control a personal relationship that, whether or not entitled to formal recognition in the law, is within the liberty of persons to choose without being punished as criminals.

This, as a general rule, should counsel against attempts by the State, or a court, to define the meaning of the relationship or to set its boundaries absent injury to a person or abuse of an institution the law protects. . . . When sexuality finds overt expression in intimate conduct with another person, the conduct can be but one element in a personal bond that is more enduring. The liberty protected by the Constitution allows homosexual persons the right to make this choice.

[The *Bowers* Court asserted that proscriptions against sodomy "have ancient roots."] We need not . . . reach a definitive historical judgment, but [at] the outset it should be noted that there is no longstanding history in this country of laws directed at homosexual conduct as a distinct matter. Beginning in colonial times there were prohibitions of sodomy derived from the English criminal laws passed in the first instance by the Reformation Parliament of 1533. The English prohibition was understood to include relations between men and women as well as relations between men and men. See, e.g., King v. Wiseman, 92 Eng. Rep. 774, 775 (K. B. 1718) (interpreting "mankind" in Act of 1533 as including women and girls). Nineteenth-century commentators similarly read American sodomy, buggery, and crime-against-nature statutes as criminalizing certain relations between men and women and between men and men. . . . Thus early American sodomy laws were not directed at homosexuals as such but instead sought to prohibit nonprocreative sexual activity more generally. This does not suggest approval of homosexual conduct. It does tend to show that this particular form of conduct was not thought of as a separate category from like conduct between heterosexual persons.

Laws prohibiting sodomy do not seem to have been enforced against consenting adults acting in private. A substantial number of sodomy prosecutions and convictions for which there are surviving records were for predatory acts against those who could not or did not consent, as in the case of a minor or the victim of an assault. As to these, one purpose for the prohibitions was to ensure there would be no lack of coverage if a predator committed a sexual assault that did not constitute rape as defined by the criminal law. . . . The longstanding criminal prohibition of homosexual sodomy upon which the *Bowers* decision placed such reliance is as consistent with a general condemnation of nonprocreative sex as it is with an established tradition of prosecuting acts because of their homosexual character. . . . But far from possessing "ancient roots," American laws targeting same-sex couples did not develop until the last third of the 20th century. . . . It was not until the 1970's that any State singled out same-sex relations for criminal prosecution, and only nine States have done so. Over the course of the last decades, States with same-sex prohibitions have moved toward abolishing them. In summary, the historical grounds relied upon in *Bowers*. . . , at the very least, are overstated.

It must be acknowledged, of course, that the Court in *Bowers* was making the broader point that for centuries there have been powerful voices to condemn homosexual conduct as immoral. The condemnation has been shaped by religious beliefs, conceptions of right and acceptable behavior, and respect for the traditional family. For many persons these are not trivial concerns but profound and deep convictions accepted as ethical and moral principles to which they aspire and which thus determine the course of their lives. These considerations do not answer the question before us, however. The issue is whether the majority may use the power of the State to enforce these views on the whole society through operation of the criminal law. "Our obligation is to define the liberty of all, not to mandate our own moral code." Planned Parenthood of Southeastern Pa. v. Casey.

... In all events we think that our laws and traditions in the past half century are of most relevance here. These references show an emerging awareness that liberty gives substantial protection to adult persons in deciding how to conduct their private lives in matters pertaining to sex. This emerging recognition should have been apparent when *Bowers* was decided. In 1955 the American Law Institute promulgated the Model Penal Code and made clear that it did not recommend or provide for "criminal penalties for consensual sexual relations conducted in private." [Beginning in 1961 states began to change their] laws to conform to the Model Penal Code. [At the time of the *Bowers* decision] 24 States and the District of Columbia had sodomy laws. . . . A committee advising the British Parliament recommended in 1957 repeal of laws punishing homosexual conduct [and] Parliament enacted the substance of those recommendations 10 years later. Sexual Offences Act 1967, §1. Of even more importance, almost five years before *Bowers* was decided the European Court of Human Rights . . . held that [Northern Ireland's laws proscribing homosexual] conduct were invalid under the European Convention on Human Rights. Dudgeon v. United Kingdom, 45 Eur. Ct. H. R. (1981) P52. Authoritative in all countries that are members of the Council of Europe (21 nations then, 45 nations now), the decision is at odds with the premise in *Bowers* that the claim put forward was insubstantial in our Western civilization.

[The] deficiencies in *Bowers* became even more apparent in the years following its announcement. The 25 States with laws prohibiting the relevant conduct referenced in the *Bowers* decision are reduced now to 13, of which 4 enforce their laws only against homosexual conduct. In those States where sodomy is still proscribed, whether for same-sex or heterosexual conduct, there is a pattern of nonenforcement with respect to consenting adults acting in private. . . . Two principal cases decided after *Bowers* cast its holding into even more doubt. In *Casey*, the Court reaffirmed the substantive force of the liberty protected by the Due Process Clause [and] confirmed that our laws and tradition afford constitutional protection to personal decisions relating to marriage, procreation, contraception, family relationships, child rearing, and education. In explaining the respect the Constitution demands for the autonomy of the person in making these choices, we stated as follows: "These matters, involving the most intimate and personal choices a person may make in a lifetime, choices central to personal dignity and autonomy, are central to the liberty protected by the Fourteenth Amendment. At the heart of liberty is the right to define one's own concept of existence, of meaning, of the universe, and of the mystery of human life. Beliefs about these matters could not define the attributes of personhood were they formed under compulsion of the State." Persons in a homosexual relationship may seek autonomy for these purposes, just as heterosexual persons do. The decision in Bowers would deny them this right.

The second post-*Bowers* case of principal relevance is Romer v. Evans, [where] the Court struck down class-based legislation directed at homosexuals as a violation of the Equal Protection Clause. As an alternative argument in this case, [petitioners] contend that *Romer* provides the basis for declaring the Texas statute invalid under the Equal Protection Clause. That is a tenable argument, but we conclude the instant case requires us to address whether *Bowers* itself has continuing validity. Were we to hold the statute invalid under the Equal Protection Clause some might question whether a prohibition would be valid if drawn differently, say, to prohibit the conduct both between same-sex and different-sex participants. . . . The central holding of *Bowers* has been brought in question by this case, and it should be addressed. Its continuance as precedent demeans the lives of homosexual persons.

The stigma this criminal statute imposes, moreover, is not trivial. The offense, to be sure, is but a class C misdemeanor, a minor offense in the Texas legal system. Still, it remains a criminal offense with all that imports for the dignity of the persons charged. . . . We are advised that if Texas convicted an adult for private, consensual homosexual conduct under the statute here in question the convicted person would come within the [sex offender] registration laws of a least four States were he or she to be subject to their jurisdiction. . . . Furthermore, the Texas criminal conviction carries with it the other collateral consequences always following a conviction, such as notations on job application forms, to mention but one example.

The foundations of *Bowers* have sustained serious erosion from our recent decisions in *Casey* and *Romer*. When our precedent has been thus weakened, criticism from other sources is of greater significance. The courts of five different States have declined to follow it in interpreting provisions in their own state constitutions parallel to the Due Process Clause of the Fourteenth Amendment. To the extent *Bowers* relied on values we share with a wider civilization, it should be noted that the reasoning and holding in *Bowers* have been rejected elsewhere. . . . The right the petitioners seek in this case has been accepted as an integral part of human freedom in many other countries. There has been no showing that in this country the governmental interest in circumscribing personal choice is somehow more legitimate or urgent.

The doctrine of *stare decisis* is essential to the respect accorded to the judgments of the Court and to the stability of the law. It is not, however, an inexorable command. In *Casey* we noted that when a Court is asked to overrule a precedent recognizing a constitutional liberty interest, individual or societal reliance on the existence of that liberty cautions with particular strength against reversing course. The holding in *Bowers*, however, has not induced detrimental reliance comparable to some instances where recognized individual rights are involved. Indeed, there has been no individual or societal reliance on *Bowers* of the sort that could counsel against overturning its holding once there are compelling reasons to do so. *Bowers* itself causes uncertainty, for the precedents before and after its issuance contradict its central holding.

The rationale of *Bowers* does not withstand careful analysis. In his dissenting opinion in *Bowers* Justice Stevens came to these conclusions:

> Our prior cases make two propositions abundantly clear. First, the fact that the governing majority in a State has traditionally viewed a particular practice as immoral is not a sufficient reason for upholding a law prohibiting the practice; neither history nor tradition could save a law prohibiting miscegenation from constitutional attack. Second, individual decisions by married persons, concerning the intimacies of their physical relationship, even when not intended to produce offspring, are a form of 'liberty' protected by the Due Process Clause of the Fourteenth Amendment. Moreover, this protection extends to intimate choices by unmarried as well as married persons."

Justice Stevens'[s] analysis, in our view, should have been controlling in *Bowers* and should control here. *Bowers* was not correct when it was decided, and it is not correct today. It ought not to remain binding precedent. Bowers v. Hardwick should be and now is overruled.

The present case does not involve minors. It does not involve persons who might be injured or coerced or who are situated in relationships where consent might not easily be refused. It does not involve public conduct or prostitution. It does not involve whether the government must give formal recognition to any relationship that homosexual persons seek to enter. The case does involve two adults who, with full and mutual consent from each other, engaged in sexual practices common to a homosexual lifestyle. The petitioners are entitled to respect for their private lives. The State cannot demean their existence or control their destiny by making their private sexual conduct a crime. Their right to liberty under the Due Process Clause gives them the full right to engage in their conduct without intervention of the government. "It is a promise of the Constitution that there is a realm of personal liberty which the government may not enter." The Texas statute furthers no legitimate state interest which can justify its intrusion into the personal and private life of the individual.

[Those] who drew and ratified the Due Process Clauses . . . knew times can blind us to certain truths and later generations can see that laws once thought necessary and proper in fact serve only to oppress. As the Constitution endures, persons in every generation can invoke its principles in their own search for greater freedom.

The judgment of the [Texas] Court of Appeals . . . is reversed, and the case is remanded for further proceedings not inconsistent with this opinion.

JUSTICE O'CONNOR, concurring in the judgment.

. . . I joined *Bowers*, and do not join the Court in overruling it. Nevertheless, I agree with the Court that Texas'[s] statute banning same-sex sodomy is unconstitutional. . . . I base my conclusion on the Fourteenth Amendment's Equal Protection Clause.

. . . We have been most likely to apply rational basis review to hold a law unconstitutional under the Equal Protection Clause where, as here, the challenged legislation inhibits personal relationships. [*Moreno*; *Eisenstadt*; *Cleburne*; *Romer*.] The statute at issue here makes sodomy a crime only if a person "engages in deviate sexual intercourse with another individual of the same sex." Sodomy between opposite-sex partners, however, is not a crime in Texas. That is, Texas treats the same conduct differently based solely on the participants. Those harmed by this law are people who have a same-sex sexual orientation and thus are more likely to engage in [the prohibited] behavior. The Texas statute makes homosexuals unequal in the eyes of the law by making particular conduct — and only that conduct — subject to criminal sanction. [The] effect of Texas'[s] sodomy law is not just limited to the threat of prosecution or consequence of conviction. Texas'[s] sodomy law brands all homosexuals as criminals, thereby making it more difficult for homosexuals to be treated in the same manner as everyone else. Indeed, Texas itself has previously acknowledged . . . that the law "legally sanctions discrimination against [homosexuals] in a variety of ways unrelated to the criminal law," including in the areas of "employment, family issues, and housing."

Texas attempts to justify its law, and the effects of the law, by arguing that the statute satisfies rational basis review because it furthers the legitimate governmental interest of the promotion of morality. [While in Bowers we pointed] to the government's interest in promoting morality, *Bowers* did not hold that moral disapproval of a group is a rational basis under the Equal Protection Clause to criminalize homosexual sodomy when heterosexual sodomy is not punished. This case raises a different issue than *Bowers*: whether, under the Equal Protection Clause, moral disapproval is a legitimate state interest to justify by itself a statute that bans homosexual sodomy, but not heterosexual sodomy. It is not. Moral disapproval of this group, like a bare desire to harm the group, is an interest that is insufficient to satisfy rational basis review under the Equal Protection Clause. [*Moreno*; *Romer*.] Indeed, we have never held that moral disapproval, without any other asserted state interest, is a sufficient rationale under the Equal Protection Clause to justify a law that discriminates among groups of persons.

Moral disapproval of a group cannot be a legitimate governmental interest under the Equal Protection Clause because legal classifications must not be "drawn for the purpose of disadvantaging the group burdened by the law." . . . [Because] Texas so rarely enforces its sodomy law as applied to private, consensual acts, the law serves more as a statement of dislike and disapproval against homosexuals than as a tool to stop criminal behavior. The Texas sodomy law "raises the inevitable inference that the disadvantage imposed is born of animosity toward the class of persons affected."

. . . While it is true that the law applies only to conduct, the conduct targeted by this law is conduct that is closely correlated with being homosexual. Under such circumstances, Texas'[s] sodomy law is targeted at more than conduct. It is instead directed toward gay persons as a class. [In] Romer v. Evans, we refused to sanction a law that singled out homosexuals "for disfavored legal status." The same is true here. . . . A State can of course assign certain consequences to a violation of its criminal law. But the State cannot single out one identifiable class of citizens for punishment that does not apply to everyone else, with moral disapproval as the only asserted state interest for the law. The Texas sodomy statute subjects homosexuals to "a lifelong penalty and stigma. A legislative classification that threatens the creation of an underclass . . . cannot be reconciled with" the Equal Protection Clause. Plyler v. Doe (Powell, J., concurring).

Whether a sodomy law that is neutral both in effect and application would violate the substantive component of the Due Process Clause is an issue that need not be decided today. . . .

That this law as applied to private, consensual conduct is unconstitutional under the Equal Protection Clause does not mean that other laws distinguishing between heterosexuals and homosexuals would similarly fail under rational basis review. Texas cannot assert any legitimate state interest here, such as national security or preserving the traditional institution of marriage. Unlike the moral disapproval of same-sex relations — the asserted state interest in this case — other reasons exist to promote the institution of marriage beyond mere moral disapproval of an excluded group.

A law branding one class of persons as criminal solely based on the State's moral disapproval of that class and the conduct associated with that class runs contrary to the values of the Constitution and the Equal Protection Clause, under any standard of review. I therefore concur in the Court's judgment that Texas'[s] sodomy law banning "deviate sexual intercourse" between consenting adults of the same sex, but not between consenting adults of different sexes, is unconstitutional.

JUSTICE SCALIA, with whom THE CHIEF JUSTICE and JUSTICE THOMAS join, dissenting.

"Liberty finds no refuge in a jurisprudence of doubt." [*Casey*.] That was the Court's sententious response, barely more than a decade ago, to those seeking to overrule Roe v. Wade. The Court's response today, to those who have engaged in a 17-year crusade to overrule Bowers v. Hardwick, is very different. The need for stability and certainty presents no barrier.

Most of the rest of today's opinion has no relevance to its actual holding — that the Texas statute "furthers no legitimate state interest which can justify" its application to petitioners under rational-basis review. Though there is discussion of "fundamental propositions" and "fundamental decisions," nowhere does the Court's opinion declare that homosexual sodomy is a "fundamental right" under the Due Process Clause; nor does it subject the Texas law to the standard of review that would be appropriate (strict scrutiny) if homosexual sodomy *were* a "fundamental right." Thus, while overruling the *outcome* of *Bowers*, the Court leaves strangely untouched its central legal conclusion: "Respondent would have us announce . . . a fundamental right to engage in homosexual sodomy. This we are quite unwilling to do." [*Bowers*.] Instead the Court simply describes petitioners' conduct as "an exercise of their liberty" — which it undoubtedly is — and proceeds to apply an unheard-of form of rational-basis review that will have far-reaching implications beyond this case.

I. . . . I do not myself believe in rigid adherence to *stare decisis* in constitutional cases; but I do believe that we should be consistent rather than manipulative in invoking the doctrine. Today's opinions in support of reversal do not bother to distinguish — or indeed, even bother to mention — the paean to *stare decisis* coauthored by three Members of today's majority in Planned Parenthood v. Casey. There, when *stare decisis* meant preservation of judicially invented abortion rights, the widespread criticism of *Roe* was strong reason to *reaffirm* it. . . . Today, however, the widespread opposition to *Bowers* . . . is offered as a reason in favor of *overruling* it.

. . . The Court's claim that *Casey* "casts some doubt" upon the holding in *Bowers* (or any other case, for that matter) does not withstand analysis. . . . *Casey* provided a *less* expansive right to abortion than did *Roe*, *which was already on the books when Bowers was decided*. . . .

I do not quarrel with the Court's claim that Romer v. Evans "eroded" the "foundations" of *Bowers'*[s] rational-basis holding. But *Roe* and *Casey* have been equally "eroded" by Washington v. Glucksberg, which held that *only* fundamental rights which are " 'deeply rooted in this Nation's history and tradition' " qualify for anything other than rational basis scrutiny under the doctrine of "substantive due process." *Roe* and *Casey*, of course, subjected the restriction of abortion to heightened scrutiny without even attempting to establish that the freedom to abort *was* rooted in this Nation's tradition.

. . . "There has been," the Court says, "no individual or societal reliance on *Bowers* of the sort that could counsel against overturning its holding . . . ." It seems to me that the "societal reliance" on the principles confirmed in *Bowers* and discarded today has been overwhelming. Countless judicial decisions and legislative enactments have relied on the ancient proposition that a governing majority's belief that certain sexual behavior is "immoral and unacceptable" constitutes a rational basis for regulation. . . . We ourselves relied extensively on *Bowers* when we concluded, in Barnes v. Glen Theatre, Inc. that Indiana's public indecency statute furthered "a substantial government interest in protecting order and morality." State laws against bigamy, same-sex marriage, adult incest, prostitution, masturbation, adultery, fornication, bestiality, and obscenity are likewise sustainable only in light of *Bowers'* validation of laws based on moral choices. Every single one of these laws is called into question by today's decision; the Court makes no effort to cabin the scope of its decision to exclude them from its holding. The impossibility of distinguishing homosexuality from other traditional "morals" offenses is precisely why *Bowers* rejected the rational-basis challenge. "The law," it said, "is constantly based on notions of morality, and if all laws representing essentially moral choices are to be invalidated under the Due Process Clause, the courts will be very busy indeed." [*Bowers*.] . . .

II. Having decided that it need not adhere to *stare decisis*, the Court still must establish that *Bowers* was wrongly decided and that the Texas statute, as applied to petitioners, is unconstitutional.

Texas Penal Code Ann. §21.06(a) (2003) undoubtedly imposes constraints on liberty. So do laws prohibiting prostitution, recreational use of heroin, and, for that matter, working more than 60 hours per week in a bakery. But there is no right to "liberty" under the Due Process Clause, though today's opinion repeatedly makes that claim. The Fourteenth Amendment *expressly allows* States to deprive their citizens of "liberty," so long as "due process of law" is provided [and our] opinions applying the doctrine known as "substantive due process" hold that the Due Process Clause prohibits States from infringing *fundamental* liberty interests, unless the infringement is narrowly tailored to serve a compelling state interest. Washington v. Glucksberg. We have held repeatedly, in cases the Court today does not overrule, that *only* fundamental rights qualify for this so-called "heightened scrutiny" protection — that is, rights which are " 'deeply rooted in this Nation's history and tradition.' " All other liberty interests may be abridged or abrogated pursuant to a validly enacted state law if that law is rationally related to a legitimate state interest.

Bowers held, first, that criminal prohibitions of homosexual sodomy are not subject to heightened scrutiny because they do not implicate a "fundamental right" under the Due Process Clause. . . . The Court today does not overrule this holding. Not once does it describe homosexual sodomy as a "fundamental right" or a "fundamental liberty interest," nor does it subject the Texas statute to strict scrutiny. Instead, having failed to establish that the right to homosexual sodomy is " 'deeply rooted in this Nation's history and tradition,' " the Court concludes that the application of Texas's statute to petitioners' conduct fails the rational-basis test, and overrules *Bowers*' holding to the contrary[:] "The Texas statute furthers no legitimate state interest which can justify its intrusion into the personal and private life of the individual." I shall address that rational-basis holding presently. First, however, I address some aspersions that the Court casts upon *Bowers'* conclusion that homosexual sodomy is not a "fundamental right" — even though, as I have said, the Court does not have the boldness to reverse that conclusion.

III. The Court's description of "the state of the law" at the time of *Bowers* only confirms that *Bowers* was right. The Court points to *Griswold*, [but] that case *expressly disclaimed* any reliance on the doctrine of "substantive due process," and grounded the so-called "right to privacy" in penumbras of constitutional provisions *other than* the Due Process Clause. *Eisenstadt* likewise had nothing to do with "substantive due process"; it invalidated a Massachusetts law prohibiting the distribution of contraceptives to unmarried persons solely on the basis of the Equal Protection Clause. Of course *Eisenstadt* contains well known dictum relating to the "right to privacy," but this referred to the right recognized in *Griswold* — a right penumbral to the *specific* guarantees in the *Bill of Rights*, and not a "substantive due process" right. Roe v. Wade recognized that the right to abort an unborn child was a "fundamental right" protected by the Due Process Clause. The *Roe* Court, however, made no attempt to establish that this right was " 'deeply rooted in this Nation's history and tradition' "; instead, it based its conclusion that "the Fourteenth Amendment's concept of personal liberty . . . is broad enough to encompass a woman's decision whether or not to terminate her pregnancy" on its own normative judgment that anti-abortion laws were undesirable. We have since rejected *Roe*'s holding that regulations of abortion must be narrowly tailored to serve a compelling state interest, [*Casey*] — and thus, by logical implication, *Roe*'s holding that the right to abort an unborn child is a "fundamental right."

After discussing the history of antisodomy laws, the Court proclaims that, "it should be noted that there is no longstanding history in this country of laws directed at homosexual conduct as a distinct matter." . . . It is (as *Bowers* recognized) entirely irrelevant whether the laws in our long national tradition criminalizing homosexual sodomy were "directed at homosexual conduct as a distinct matter."

Whether homosexual sodomy was prohibited by a law targeted at same-sex sexual relations or by a more general law prohibiting both homosexual and heterosexual sodomy, the only relevant point is that it *was* criminalized — which suffices to establish that homosexual sodomy is not a right "deeply rooted in our Nation's history and tradition." The Court today agrees that homosexual sodomy was criminalized and thus does not dispute the facts on which *Bowers actually* relied.

[The Court states:] "We think that our laws and traditions in the past half century are of most relevance here. These references show *an emerging awareness* that liberty gives substantial protection to adult persons in deciding how to conduct their private lives *in matters pertaining to sex*." (emphasis added). Apart from the fact that such an "emerging awareness" does not establish a "fundamental right," the statement is factually false. States continue to prosecute all sorts of crimes by adults "in matters pertaining to sex": prostitution, adult incest, adultery, obscenity, and child pornography. Sodomy laws, too, have been enforced "in the past half century," in which there have been 134 reported cases involving prosecutions for consensual, adult, homosexual sodomy. In relying, for evidence of an "emerging recognition," upon the American Law Institute's 1955 recommendation not to criminalize " 'consensual sexual relations conducted in private,' " the Court ignores the fact that this recommendation was "a point of resistance in most of the states that considered adopting the Model Penal Code." In any event, an "emerging awareness" is by definition not "deeply rooted in this Nation's history and traditions," as we have said "fundamental right" status requires. Constitutional entitlements do not spring into existence because some States choose to lessen or eliminate criminal sanctions on certain behavior. Much less do they spring into existence, as the Court seems to believe, because *foreign nations* decriminalize conduct. The *Bowers* majority opinion *never* relied on "values we share with a wider civilization," but rather rejected the claimed right to sodomy on the ground that such a right was not " 'deeply rooted in *this Nation's* history and tradition,' " (emphasis added). . . . The Court's discussion of these foreign views (ignoring, of course, the many countries that have retained criminal prohibitions on sodomy) is therefore meaningless dicta. Dangerous dicta, however, since "this Court . . . should not impose foreign moods, fads, or fashions on Americans."

IV. I turn now to the ground on which the Court squarely rests its holding: the contention that there is no rational basis for the law here under attack. This proposition is so out of accord with our jurisprudence — indeed, with the jurisprudence of *any* society we know — that it requires little discussion.

The Texas statute undeniably seeks to further the belief of its citizens that certain forms of sexual behavior are "immoral and unacceptable" — the same interest furthered by criminal laws against fornication, bigamy, adultery, adult incest, bestiality, and obscenity. *Bowers* held that this *was* a legitimate state interest. The Court today reaches the opposite conclusion. The Texas statute, it says, "furthers *no legitimate state interest* which can justify its intrusion into the personal and private life of the individual" (emphasis added). The Court embraces instead Justice Stevens' declaration in his *Bowers* dissent, that "the fact that the governing majority in a State has traditionally viewed a particular practice as immoral is not a sufficient reason for upholding a law prohibiting the practice." This effectively decrees the end of all morals legislation. If, as the Court asserts, the promotion of majoritarian sexual morality is not even a *legitimate* state interest, none of the above-mentioned laws can survive rational-basis review.

V. Finally, I turn to petitioners' equal-protection challenge, which no Member of the Court save Justice O'Connor embraces. [The Texas law] does distinguish between the sexes insofar as concerns the partner with whom the sexual acts are performed: men can violate the law only with other men, and women only with other women. . . .

The objection is made, however, that the antimiscegenation laws invalidated in Loving v. Virginia, 388 U.S. 1 (1967), similarly were applicable to whites and blacks alike, and only distinguished between the races insofar as the *partner* was concerned. In *Loving*, however, we correctly applied heightened scrutiny . . . because the Virginia statute was "designed to maintain White Supremacy." A racially discriminatory purpose is always sufficient to subject a law to strict scrutiny, even a facially neutral law that makes no mention of race. No purpose to discriminate against men or women as a class can be gleaned from the Texas law, so rational-basis review applies. That review is readily satisfied here by the same rational basis that satisfied it in *Bowers* — society's belief that certain forms of sexual behavior are "immoral and unacceptable." This is the same justification that supports many other laws regulating sexual behavior that make a distinction based upon the identity of the partner — for example, laws against adultery, fornication, and adult incest, and laws refusing to recognize homosexual marriage.

Justice O'Connor argues that the discrimination in this law [is] "directed toward gay persons as a class." . . . Even if the Texas law *does* deny equal protection to "homosexuals as a class," that denial *still* does not need to be justified by anything more than a rational basis, which our cases show is satisfied by the enforcement of traditional notions of sexual morality.

Justice O'Connor simply decrees application of "a more searching form of rational basis review" to the Texas statute. . . . Nor does Justice O'Connor explain precisely what her "more searching form" of rational-basis review consists of. It must at least mean, however, that laws exhibiting " 'a . . . desire to harm a politically unpopular group' " are invalid *even though* there may be a conceivable rational basis to support them.

This reasoning leaves on pretty shaky grounds state laws limiting marriage to opposite-sex couples. Justice O'Connor seeks to preserve them by the conclusory statement that "preserving the traditional institution of marriage" is a legitimate state interest. But "preserving the traditional institution of marriage" is just a kinder way of describing the State's *moral disapproval* of same-sex couples. Texas's interest in §21.06 could be recast in similarly euphemistic terms: "preserving the traditional sexual mores of our society." In the jurisprudence Justice O'Connor has seemingly created, judges can validate laws by characterizing them as "preserving the traditions of society" (good); or invalidate them by characterizing them as "expressing moral disapproval" (bad). . . .

Today's opinion is the product of a Court, which is the product of a law-profession culture, that has largely signed on to the so-called homosexual agenda, by which I mean the agenda promoted by some homosexual activists directed at eliminating the moral opprobrium that has traditionally attached to homosexual conduct. . . .

One of the most revealing statements in today's opinion is the Court's grim warning that the criminalization of homosexual conduct is "an invitation to subject homosexual persons to discrimination both in the public and in the private spheres." It is clear from this that the Court has taken sides in the culture war, departing from its role of assuring, as neutral observer, that the democratic rules of engagement are observed. Many Americans do not want persons who openly engage in homosexual conduct as partners in their business, as scoutmasters for their children, as teachers in their children's schools, or as boarders in their home. They view this as protecting themselves and their families from a lifestyle that they believe to be immoral and destructive. The Court views it as "discrimination" which it is the function of our judgments to deter. So imbued is the Court with the law profession's anti-anti-homosexual culture, that it is seemingly unaware that the attitudes of that culture are not obviously "mainstream"; that in most States what the Court calls "discrimination" against those who engage in homosexual acts is perfectly legal; that proposals to ban such "discrimination" under Title VII have repeatedly been rejected by Congress; that in some cases such "discrimination" is *mandated* by federal statute; and that in some cases such "discrimination" is a constitutional right [Boy Scouts of America v. Dale.]

Let me be clear that I have nothing against homosexuals, or any other group, promoting their agenda through normal democratic means. Social perceptions of sexual and other morality change over time, and every group has the right to persuade its fellow citizens that its view of such matters is the best. That homosexuals have achieved some success in that enterprise is attested to by the fact that Texas is one of the few remaining States that criminalize private, consensual homosexual acts. But persuading one's fellow citizens is one thing, and imposing one's views in absence of democratic majority will is something else. I would no more *require* a State to criminalize homosexual acts — or, for that matter, display *any* moral disapprobation of them — than I would *forbid* it to do so. What Texas has chosen to do is well within the range of traditional democratic action, and its hand should not be stayed through the invention of a brand-new "constitutional right" by a Court that is impatient of democratic change. It is indeed true that "later generations can see that laws once thought necessary and proper in fact serve only to oppress;" and when that happens, later generations can repeal those laws. But it is the premise of our system that those judgments are to be made by the people, and not imposed by a governing caste that knows best.

One of the benefits of leaving regulation of this matter to the people rather than to the courts is that the people, unlike judges, need not carry things to their logical conclusion. The people may feel that their disapprobation of homosexual conduct is strong enough to disallow homosexual marriage, but not strong enough to criminalize private homosexual acts — and may legislate accordingly. [The] Court says that the present case "does not involve whether the government must give formal recognition to any relationship that homosexual persons seek to enter." Do not believe it. More illuminating than this bald, unreasoned disclaimer is the progression of thought displayed by an earlier passage in the Court's opinion, which notes the constitutional protections afforded to "personal decisions relating to *marriage*, procreation, contraception, family relationships, child rearing, and education," and then declares that "persons in a homosexual relationship may seek autonomy for these purposes, just as heterosexual persons do." (Emphasis added.) Today's opinion dismantles the structure of constitutional law that has permitted a distinction to be made between heterosexual and homosexual unions, insofar as formal recognition in marriage is concerned. If moral disapprobation of homosexual conduct is "no legitimate state interest" for purposes of proscribing that conduct; and if, as the Court coos (casting aside all pretense of neutrality), "when sexuality finds overt expression in intimate conduct with another person, the conduct can be but one element in a personal bond that is more enduring"; what justification could there possibly be for denying the benefits of marriage to homosexual couples exercising "the liberty protected by the Constitution"? Surely not the encouragement of procreation, since the sterile and the elderly are allowed to marry. This case "does not involve" the issue of homosexual marriage only if one entertains the belief that principle and logic have nothing to do with the decisions of this Court. Many will hope that, as the Court comfortingly assures us, this is so.

The matters appropriate for this Court's resolution are only three: Texas's prohibition of sodomy neither infringes a "fundamental right" (which the Court does not dispute), nor is unsupported by a rational relation to what the Constitution considers a legitimate state interest, nor denies the equal protection of the laws. I dissent.

JUSTICE THOMAS, dissenting.

. . . I write separately to note that the law before the Court today "is . . . uncommonly silly." [*Griswold* (Stewart, J., dissenting).] If I were a member of the Texas Legislature, I would vote to repeal it. Punishing someone for expressing his sexual preference through noncommercial consensual conduct with another adult does not appear to be a worthy way to expend valuable law enforcement resources.

Notwithstanding this, I recognize that as a member of this Court [my duty] is to "decide cases 'agreeably to the Constitution and laws of the United States.' " And, just like Justice Stewart, I "can find [neither in the Bill of Rights nor any other part of the Constitution a] general right of privacy," or as the Court terms it today, the "liberty of the person both in its spatial and more transcendent dimensions."

f. Other Asserted Privacy or Autonomy Interests

Page 604: Insert at the very end of the chapter:

In Connecticut Department of Public Safety v. Doe, 538 U.S. 1 (2003), the Court declined to reach the question of whether any fundamental liberty interest was infringed by a Connecticut law that required convicted sex offenders to register and disclose publicly their whereabouts after release from custody. Note that *Whalen* and *Casey* upheld against privacy challenges various forms of governmental data collection in which the identity of the people involved was not available for public disclosure. Does the public disclosure of the identity and residence of convicted sex offenders implicate a fundamental liberty interest? If so, how would you state that interest, bearing in mind the Court's admonition in *Glucksberg* that it is essential to make a "careful description" of claimed fundamental liberty interests? If not, do sex offender registration and disclosure laws nonetheless violate substantive due process under the rationale of Lawrence v. Texas?

Chapter 7

Economic Rights: The Takings and Contracts Clauses

A. The Takings Clause

Page 630: Insert the following after the note and immediately before subsection 3:

The Uneasy Line Between Lucas *and* Penn Central. Although *Lucas* purported to establish a bright-line rule denominating as takings all regulations that deprive the property owner of all economically viable use of his property, the application of *Lucas* often turns on characterization of the property interest affected by the regulation. Does a property owner lack any reasonable expectation of investment return if he acquires property subject to existing regulations that would, if applied to him after acquisition of the property, constitute a taking? Has a property owner lost all economically viable use of his property if regulations absolutely forbid any development or use for a protracted period of time, albeit not forever?

In Palazzolo v. Rhode Island, 533 U.S. 606 (2001), the Court rejected the idea that a landowner may not assert that any regulations in effect at the time he acquires title constitute a taking. Such a rule would immunize extreme and unreasonable regulations against attack by future generations. Moreover, the application of such a rule would prove capricious, permitting older owners or those with the will and means to hold property for a long time to challenge regulations but deny that ability to younger owners or those who have recently arrived in a locality and acquired property. The rejected rule would also have the effect of denying to in-place owners the ability to transfer to others the same title they had. The Court concluded that the regulations did not deny to Palazzolo all economically viable use of his property and so remanded the case to the Rhode Island Supreme Court for a determination of whether the regulations effected a taking under the *Penn Central* balancing test. In a concurrence, Justice O'Connor suggested that regulations in place at the time an owner acquires property are relevant to the *Penn Central* issue of the owner's reasonable investment-backed expectations.

TAHOE-SIERRA PRESERVATION COUNCIL, INC. v. TAHOE REGIONAL PLANNING AGENCY

535 U.S. 302 (2002)

JUSTICE STEVENS delivered the opinion of the Court.

The question presented is whether a moratorium on development imposed during the process of devising a comprehensive land-use plan constitutes a *per se* taking of property requiring compensation. . . . [Tahoe Regional Planning Agency (TRPA) imposed two moratoria, totaling 32 months from 1981 to 1984, on development in the Lake Tahoe Basin while formulating a comprehensive land-use plan for the area designed to address the threat of pollution of Lake Tahoe from increasing residential development in the Lake Tahoe Basin. Petitioners, real estate owners affected by the moratoria and an association representing such owners, filed parallel suits, later consolidated, claiming that TRPA's actions constituted a taking of their property without just compensation.]

I. The relevant facts are undisputed. . . . Lake Tahoe is "uniquely beautiful," [so much so] that Mark Twain aptly described the clarity of its waters as "not *merely* transparent, but dazzlingly, brilliantly so." [M. Twain, Roughing It 174-175 (1872), emphasis added by the Court]. Lake Tahoe's exceptional clarity is attributed to the absence of algae that obscures the waters of most other lakes. Historically, the lack of nitrogen and phosphorous, which nourish the growth of algae, has ensured the transparency of its waters. Unfortunately, the lake's pristine state has deteriorated rapidly over the past 40 years; increased land development in the Lake Tahoe Basin (Basin) has threatened the "noble sheet of blue water" beloved by Twain and countless others. "[D]ramatic decreases in clarity first began to be noted in the [1950s], shortly after development at the lake began in earnest." The lake's unsurpassed beauty, it seems, is the wellspring of its undoing. The upsurge of development in the area has caused "increased nutrient loading of the lake largely because of the increase in impervious coverage of land in the Basin resulting from that development," [a trend that, unless stopped, was predicted to cause the lake to] "lose its clarity and its trademark blue color, becoming green and opaque for eternity."

[The TRPA identified properties with steep slopes and] certain areas near streams or wetlands known as "Stream Environment Zones" (SEZs) [as] especially vulnerable to the impact of development because, in their natural state, they act as filters for much of the debris that runoff carries. [In order to implement an interstate compact concerning the Basin (Compact), TRPA enacted two ordinances to suspend development until it adopted] the permanent plan required by the Compact. . . . In combination, [the two ordinances] effectively prohibited all construction on sensitive lands in California and on all SEZ lands in the entire Basin for 32 months, and on sensitive lands in Nevada (other than SEZ lands) for eight months. It is these two moratoria that are at issue in this case. . . .

II. . . . [The District Court ruled that the moratoria constituted a taking under Lucas v. South Carolina Coastal Council because they temporarily deprived petitioners of all economically viable use of their land. On appeal, the Ninth Circuit reversed, concluding] that because the regulations had only a temporary impact on petitioners' fee interest in the properties, no categorical taking [under *Lucas*] had occurred. It . . . distinguished *Lucas* as applying to the "relatively rare" case in which a regulation denies all productive use of an entire parcel, whereas the moratoria involve only a "temporal 'slice' " of the fee interest. [The Ninth Circuit noted that] "a property interest may include a physical dimension (which describes the size and shape of the property in question), a functional dimension (which describes the extent to which an owner may use or dispose of the property in question), and a temporal dimension (which describes the duration of the property interest)," [and rejected the argument] "that we should conceptually sever each plaintiff's fee interest into discrete segments in at least one of these dimensions — the temporal one — and treat each of those segments as separate and distinct property interests for purposes of takings analysis." . . . We now affirm.

III. Petitioners make only a facial attack on [the moratoria]. They contend that the mere enactment of a temporary regulation that, while in effect, denies a property owner all viable economic use of her property gives rise to an unqualified constitutional obligation to compensate her for the value of its use during that period. [They] assert that our opinions in *First English* and *Lucas* have already endorsed their view, and that it is a logical application of the principle that the Takings Clause was "designed to bar Government from forcing some people alone to bear burdens which, in all fairness and justice, should be borne by the public as a whole." Armstrong v. United States, 364 U.S. 40, 49 (1960). [Our] cases do not support their proposed categorical rule. . . . [We] conclude that the circumstances in this case are best analyzed within the *Penn Central* framework.

IV. The text of the Fifth Amendment itself provides a basis for drawing a distinction between physical takings and regulatory takings. Its plain language requires the payment of compensation whenever the government acquires private property for a public purpose, whether the acquisition is the result of a condemnation proceeding or a physical appropriation. But the Constitution contains no comparable reference to regulations that prohibit a property owner from making certain uses of her private property. . . . When the government physically takes possession of an interest in property for some public purpose, it has a categorical duty to compensate the former owner, regardless of whether the interest that is taken constitutes an entire parcel or merely a part thereof. [*Loretto; Causby.*] But a government regulation that . . . bans certain private uses of a portion of an owner's property . . . does not constitute a categorical taking. [Village of Euclid v. Ambler Realty Co.; Keystone Bituminous Coal Ass'n v. DeBenedictis; *Penn Central.*] "The first category of cases requires courts to apply a clear rule; the second necessarily entails complex factual assessments of the purposes and economic effects of government actions." Yee v. Escondido, 503 U.S. 519, 523 (1992).

This longstanding distinction between acquisitions of property for public use, on the one hand, and regulations prohibiting private uses, on the other, makes it inappropriate to treat cases involving physical takings as controlling precedents for the evaluation of a claim that there has been a "regulatory taking." . . . Land-use regulations are ubiquitous and most of them [have an] impact [upon] property values in some tangential way — often in completely unanticipated ways. Treating them all as *per se* takings would transform government regulation into a luxury few governments could afford. By contrast, physical appropriations are relatively rare, easily identified, and usually represent a greater affront to individual property rights.

[Petitioners] rely principally on [*Lucas*] to argue that the *Penn Central* framework is inapplicable here. [But] it was . . . Pennsylvania Coal Co. v. Mahon that gave birth to our regulatory takings jurisprudence [and, after *Mahon*,] even though multiple factors are relevant in the analysis of regulatory takings claims, in such cases we must focus on "the parcel as a whole." [*Penn Central.*] This requirement . . . explains why, for example, a regulation that prohibited commercial transactions in eagle feathers, but did not bar other uses or impose any physical invasion or restraint upon them, was not a taking, [Andrus v. Allard, 444 U.S. 51 (1949), and] clarifies why . . . a requirement that coal pillars be left in place to prevent mine subsidence [was not a taking.] *Keystone.*

[However a regulation is to be determined to be a taking, it is a] separate remedial question of how compensation is measured once a regulatory taking is established. [In First English Evangelical Lutheran Church of Glendale v. County of Los Angeles, 482 U.S. 304 (1987), the Court adopted the principle that] "once a court finds that a police power regulation has effected a 'taking,' the government entity must pay just compensation for the period commencing on the date the regulation first effected the 'taking,' and ending on the date the government entity chooses to rescind or otherwise amend the regulation." [While] nothing that we say today qualifies [*First English*], we did not address in that case the quite different and logically prior question whether the temporary regulation at issue had in fact constituted a taking. . . .

Similarly, [although] *Lucas* endorsed and applied a categorical rule, it was not the one that petitioners propose. . . . *Lucas* states that compensation is required when a regulation deprives an owner of "*all* economically beneficial uses" of his land. . . . Anything less than a "complete elimination of value," or a "total loss," the Court acknowledged, would require the kind of analysis applied in *Penn Central.* [But] our holding that the permanent "obliteration of the value" of a fee simple estate constitutes a categorical taking does not answer the question whether a regulation prohibiting any economic use of land for a 32-month period has the same legal effect. Petitioners seek to bring this case under the rule announced in *Lucas* by arguing that we can effectively sever a 32-month segment from the remainder of each landowner's fee simple estate, and then ask whether that segment has been taken in its entirety by the moratoria. Of course, defining the property interest taken in terms of the very regulation being challenged is circular. With property so divided, every delay would become a total ban; the moratorium and the normal permit process alike would constitute categorical takings. Petitioners' "conceptual severance" argument is unavailing because it ignores *Penn Central*'s admonition that in regulatory takings cases we must focus on "the parcel as a whole."

An interest in real property is defined by the metes and bounds that describe its geographic dimensions and the term of years that describes the temporal aspect of the owner's interest. Both dimensions must be considered if the interest is to be viewed in its entirety. Hence, a permanent deprivation of the owner's use of the entire area is a taking of "the parcel as a whole," whereas a temporary restriction that merely causes a diminution in value is not. Logically, a fee simple estate cannot be rendered valueless by a temporary prohibition on economic use, because the property will recover value as soon as the prohibition is lifted. . . . *Lucas* [and] *First English* . . . make clear that the categorical rule in *Lucas* was carved out for the "extraordinary case" in which a regulation permanently deprives property of all value; the default rule remains that, in the regulatory taking context, we require a more fact specific inquiry.

V. Considerations of "fairness and justice" arguably could [induce us now to] announce a categorical rule that . . . compensation is required whenever government temporarily deprives an owner of all economically viable use of her property, [or to] craft a narrower rule that would cover all temporary land-use restrictions except . . . "normal delays in obtaining building permits, changes in zoning ordinances, variances, and the like," [or] we could adopt a rule . . . that would "allow a short fixed period for deliberations to take place without compensation ." [An] extreme categorical rule that any deprivation of all economic use, no matter how brief, constitutes a compensable taking surely cannot be sustained[, for it] would apply to [such normal matters as] orders temporarily prohibiting access to crime scenes, businesses that violate health codes, fire-damaged buildings, or other [issues] that we cannot now foresee. . . . A rule that required compensation for every delay in the use of property would render routine government processes prohibitively expensive or encourage hasty decisionmaking.

More importantly, for reasons set out at some length by Justice O'Connor in her concurring opinion in [*Palazzolo*], we are persuaded that the better approach to claims that a regulation has effected a temporary taking "requires careful examination and weighing of all the relevant circumstances." [In *Palazzolo* Justice O'Connor observed that because the] "concepts of 'fairness and justice' that underlie the Takings Clause . . . are less than fully determinate . . . we have eschewed any 'set formula' for determining when 'justice and fairness' require that economic injuries caused by public action be compensated by the government, rather than remain disproportionately concentrated on a few persons. . . . Our polestar . . . remains the principles set forth in *Penn Central*." . . . In rejecting petitioners' *per se* rule, we do not hold that the temporary nature of a land-use restriction precludes finding that it effects a taking; we simply recognize that it should not be given exclusive significance one way or the other.

[Moratoria] are used widely among land-use planners to preserve the status quo while formulating a more permanent development strategy [and] are an essential tool of successful development. Yet even the weak version of petitioners' categorical rule would treat these interim measures as takings regardless of the good faith of the planners, the reasonable expectations of the landowners, or the actual impact of the moratorium on property values.

[With] a temporary ban on development there is a lesser risk that individual landowners will be "singled out" to bear a special burden that should be shared by the public as a whole. At least with a moratorium there is a clear "reciprocity of advantage" because it protects the interests of all affected landowners against immediate construction that might be inconsistent with the provisions of the plan that is ultimately adopted. . . . In fact, there is reason to believe property values often will continue to increase despite a moratorium. Such an increase makes sense in this context because property values throughout the Basin can be expected to reflect the added assurance that Lake Tahoe will remain in its pristine state. . . .

It may well be true that any moratorium that lasts for more than one year should be viewed with special skepticism, [but] we could not possibly conclude that every delay of over one year is constitutionally unacceptable. . . . In our view, the duration of the restriction is one of the important factors that a court must consider in the appraisal of a regulatory takings claim, but with respect to that factor as with respect to other factors, the "temptation to adopt what amount to *per se* rules in either direction must be resisted." *Palazzolo,* [O'Connor, J., concurring]. We conclude [that] "fairness and justice" will be best served by relying on the familiar *Penn Central* approach when deciding cases like this, rather than by attempting to craft a new categorical rule.

[Affirmed.]

CHIEF JUSTICE REHNQUIST, with whom JUSTICE SCALIA and JUSTICE THOMAS join, dissenting.

For over half a decade petitioners were prohibited from building homes, or any other structures, on their land. Because the Takings Clause requires the government to pay compensation when it deprives owners of all economically viable use of their land, and because a ban on all development lasting almost six years does not resemble any traditional land-use planning device, I dissent.

I. "A court cannot determine whether a regulation has gone 'too far' unless it knows how far the regulation goes." [Although the Court] relies on the flawed determination of the Court of Appeals that the relevant time period lasted only from August 1981 until April 1984 [in fact, because] respondent caused petitioners' inability to use their land from 1981 through 1987, that is the appropriate period of time from which to consider their takings claim.

II. I now turn to determining whether a ban on all economic development lasting almost six years is a taking. . . . The District Court . . . held that the [moratoria] "did in fact deny the plaintiffs all economically viable use of their land" [and the] Court of Appeals did not overturn this finding. . . . But the Court refuses to apply *Lucas* on the ground that the deprivation was "temporary." Neither the Takings Clause nor our case law supports such a distinction. For one thing, a distinction between "temporary" and "permanent" prohibitions is tenuous. The "temporary" prohibition in this case that the Court finds is not a taking lasted almost six years. The "permanent" prohibition that the Court held to be a taking in *Lucas* lasted less than two years . . . because the law, as it often does, changed. Under the Court's decision today, the takings question turns entirely on the initial label given a regulation, a label that is often without much meaning. There is every incentive for government to simply label any prohibition on development "temporary," or to fix a set number of years. As in this case, this initial designation does not preclude the government from repeatedly extending the "temporary" prohibition into a long-term ban on all development. The Court now holds that such a designation by the government is conclusive even though in fact the moratorium greatly exceeds the time initially specified. . . .

More fundamentally, even if a practical distinction between temporary and permanent deprivations were plausible, to treat the two differently in terms of takings law would be at odds with the justification for the *Lucas* rule, [which is] that a "total deprivation of use is, from the landowner's point of view, the equivalent of a physical appropriation." The regulation in *Lucas* was the "practical equivalence" of a long-term physical appropriation. . . . The "practical equivalence," from the landowner's point of view, of a "temporary" ban on all economic use is a forced leasehold. . . . Surely that leasehold would require compensation. [What] happened in this case is no different than if the government had taken a 6-year lease of their property. . . .

Lucas is implicated when the government deprives a landowner of "all economically beneficial or productive use of land." The District Court found, and the Court agrees, that the moratorium "temporarily" deprived petitioners of " 'all economically viable use of their land.' " [The] "temporary" denial of all viable use of land for six years is a taking.

III. The Court worries that applying *Lucas* here compels finding that an array of traditional, short-term, land-use planning devices are takings. But since the beginning of our regulatory takings jurisprudence, we have recognized that property rights "are enjoyed under an implied limitation." . . . When a regulation merely delays a final land use decision, we have recognized that there are other background principles of state property law that prevent the delay from being deemed a taking. We thus noted in *First English* that our discussion of temporary takings did not apply "in the case of normal delays in obtaining building permits, changes in zoning ordinances, variances, and the like." [The] short-term delays attendant to zoning and permit regimes are a longstanding feature of state property law and part of a landowner's reasonable investment-backed expectations. . . . But a moratorium prohibiting all economic use for a period of six years is not one of the longstanding, implied limitations of state property law. Moratoria [that] prohibit only certain categories of development, such as fast-food restaurants, or all commercial development, . . . do not implicate *Lucas* because they do not deprive landowners of all economically beneficial use of their land. As for moratoria that prohibit all development, these do not have the lineage of permit and zoning requirements and thus it is less certain that property is acquired under the "implied limitation" of a moratorium prohibiting all development. . . .

But this case does not require us to decide as a categorical matter whether moratoria prohibiting all economic use are an implied limitation of state property law, because the duration of this "moratorium" far exceeds that of ordinary moratoria. . . . Because the prohibition on development of nearly six years in this case cannot be said to resemble any "implied limitation" of state property law, it is a taking that requires compensation.

Lake Tahoe is a national treasure and I do not doubt that respondent's efforts at preventing further degradation of the lake were made in good faith in furtherance of the public interest. But, as is the case with most governmental action that furthers the public interest, the Constitution requires that the costs and burdens be borne by the public at large, not by a few targeted citizens.

JUSTICE THOMAS, with whom JUSTICE SCALIA joins, dissenting.

I join the CHIEF JUSTICE's dissent. I write separately to address the majority's conclusion that the temporary moratorium at issue here was not a taking because it was not a "taking of 'the parcel as a whole.' " While this questionable rule has been applied to various alleged regulatory takings, it was, in my view, rejected in the context of *temporal* deprivations of property by *First English*, which held that temporary and permanent takings "are not different in kind" when a landowner is deprived of all beneficial use of his land. I had thought that *First English* put to rest the notion that the "relevant denominator" is land's infinite life. Consequently, a regulation effecting a total deprivation of the use of a so-called "temporal slice" of property is compensable under the Takings Clause unless background principles of state property law prevent it from being deemed a taking. . . .

A taking is exactly what occurred in this case. No one seriously doubts that the land use regulations at issue rendered petitioners' land unsusceptible of *any* economically beneficial use. This was true at the inception of the moratorium, and it remains true today. [The Court's] "logical" assurance that a "temporary restriction . . . merely causes a diminution in value" is cold comfort to the property owners in this case or any other. After all, "*in the long run* we are all dead." John Maynard Keynes, Monetary Reform 88 (1924).

I would hold that regulations prohibiting all productive uses of property are subject to *Lucas' per se* rule, regardless of whether the property so burdened retains theoretical useful life and value if, and when, the "temporary" moratorium is lifted. To my mind, such potential future value bears on the amount of compensation due and has nothing to do with the question whether there was a taking in the first place.

NOTES

1. The End of Conceptual Severance? Conceptual severance, you will recall, is the idea that property affected by a regulation might be conceptually severed into two parcels, one of which bears the full impact of the regulation. By means of conceptual severance, a regulation that absolutely forbids any economically viable use of 30 acres of a 40-acre parcel might result in a conclusion that the regulation is a taking of the conceptually severed parcel, consisting of the affected 30 acres. Does *Tahoe-Sierra* bury conceptual severance, or does it apply only to the narrower issue of applying conceptual severance to a temporal severance — the precise issue involved in the moratoria at issue in the case?

2. The Meaning of Just Compensation. At issue in Brown v. Legal Foundation of Washington, 538 U.S. 216 (2003), was whether Washington's practice of forcing lawyers and real estate escrow agents to deposit client funds into a pooled interest-bearing trust account, and then taking the interest earned on those accounts to pay for legal services provided by the state to indigents, denied just compensation to the clients whose funds earned the interest. In Phillips v. Washington Legal Foundation, 524 U.S. 156 (1998), the Court had held that the interest earned on such accounts was the property of the owner of the principal, but had not reached the compensation issue. Washington's system required lawyers and escrow agents to deposit client funds into separate, individual interest-bearing trust accounts if the deposited funds would earn interest, net of transaction costs, and to pay the net interest to the principal owner, but required all other client funds to be deposited into pooled trust accounts, with the interest earned to be paid to the Legal Foundation of Washington, a charitable foundation limited to financing legal services for the indigent ("IOLTA" accounts).

A five-justice majority, in an opinion written by Justice Stevens, concluded that no compensation was due to owners of principal whose funds were deposited in pooled accounts, where the interest generated was in amounts so small that they would never be paid to the owners because the costs of computing and paying the interest to the owners would exceed the amount of earned interest. The majority reasoned that no compensation was due to such depositors because their "pecuniary loss" was "zero." Just compensation, said the Court, must be measured by the property owner's "net loss rather than the value of the public's gain."

Justice Scalia, writing for the four dissenters, contended that there was no difference between "the value the owner has lost [and] the value the government has gained." They "have lost the interest that *Phillips* says rightfully belongs to them — which is precisely what the government has gained. . . . The State could satisfy its obligation to pay just compensation by simply returning [the property owner's] money to the IOLTA account from which it was seized, leaving others to incur the accounting costs in the event [the property owners] seek to extract their interest from the account." Justice Scalia noted that the Court in *Phillips* had illustrated its holding by observing that "[t]he government may not seize rents received by the owner of a building simply because it can prove that the costs incurred in collecting the rents exceed the amount collected."

Chapter 8

Equal Protection

C. Strict Scrutiny and Suspect Classifications: Race and Ethnicity

4. Affirmative Action

Page 750: Insert the following immediately before subsection C.5:

Race and Admissions to Public Universities

While it is now clear that strict scrutiny applies to racial preferences in admissions to public universities, until the 2002 Term it was far from clear whether the use of race to achieve a diverse student body is a compelling government interest or, if so, when the use of race is narrowly tailored to the accomplishment of such diversity. Nor was it entirely clear what is meant by diversity. Consider how much clarity was brought to these issues by the following two cases.

GRUTTER v. BOLLINGER
539 U.S. 306 (2003)

JUSTICE O'CONNOR delivered the opinion of the Court.

This case requires us to decide whether the use of race as a factor in student admissions by the University of Michigan Law School (Law School) is unlawful.

I. The Law School ranks among the Nation's top law schools. It receives more than 3,500 applications each year for a class of around 350 students. Seeking to "admit a group of students who individually and collectively are among the most capable," the Law School looks for individuals with "substantial promise for success in law school" and "a strong likelihood of succeeding in the practice of law and contributing in diverse ways to the well-being of others." More broadly, the Law School seeks "a mix of students with varying backgrounds and experiences who will respect and learn from each other." [The] written admissions policy to implement these goals [focuses] on academic ability coupled with a flexible assessment of applicants' talents, experiences, and potential "to contribute to the learning of those around them." The policy requires admissions officials to evaluate each applicant based on all the information available in the file, including a personal statement, letters of recommendation, and an essay describing the ways in which the applicant will contribute to the life and diversity of the Law School. In reviewing an applicant's file, admissions officials must consider the applicant's undergraduate grade point average (GPA) and Law School Admissions Test (LSAT) score because they are important (if imperfect) predictors of academic success in law school. The policy stresses that "no applicant should be admitted unless we expect that applicant to do well enough to graduate with no serious academic problems."

[The] policy requires admissions officials to look beyond grades and test scores to other criteria that are important to the Law School's educational objectives. So-called "'soft' variables" such as "the enthusiasm of recommenders, the quality of the undergraduate institution, the quality of the applicant's essay, and the areas and difficulty of undergraduate course selection" are all brought to bear in assessing an "applicant's likely contributions to the intellectual and social life of the institution." The policy aspires to "achieve that diversity which has the potential to enrich everyone's education and thus make a law school class stronger than the sum of its parts." The policy does not restrict the types of diversity contributions eligible for "substantial weight" in the admissions process, but instead recognizes "many possible bases for diversity admissions." The policy does, however, reaffirm the Law School's longstanding commitment to "one particular type of diversity," that is, "racial and ethnic diversity with special reference to the inclusion of students from groups which have been historically discriminated against, like African-Americans, Hispanics and Native Americans, who without this commitment might not be represented in our student body in meaningful numbers." By enrolling a " 'critical mass' of [underrepresented] minority students," the Law School seeks to "ensure their ability to make unique contributions to the character of the Law School." . . .

Petitioner Barbara Grutter is a white Michigan resident who applied to the Law School in 1996 with a 3.8 grade point average and 161 LSAT score. [After the Law School rejected her, Grutter filed suit in federal district court, alleging that the Law School had] discriminated against her on the basis of race in violation of the Fourteenth Amendment. . . . [Grutter] alleged that her application was rejected because the Law School uses race as a "predominant" factor, giving applicants who belong to certain minority groups "a significantly greater chance of admission than students with similar credentials from disfavored racial groups," [and that the Law School] "had no compelling interest to justify [its] use of race in the admissions process." . . .

[Following a 15-day court trial, the district judge ruled that "the Law School's use of race as a factor in admissions decisions was unlawful" because the Law School's "asserted interest in assembling a diverse student body was not compelling" and that, even if it was a compelling interest, "the Law School had not narrowly tailored its use of race to further that interest." The trial record indicated that the Law School's admissions director consulted "so-called 'daily reports' that kept track of the racial and ethnic composition of the class . . . to ensure that a critical mass of underrepresented minority students would be reached so as to realize the educational benefits of a diverse student body. Other Law School officials testified that "critical mass" means "meaningful numbers" or "meaningful representation," numbers sufficient to encourage minority students to participate in the classroom and not feel isolated, and that a "critical mass of underrepresented minority students could not be enrolled if admissions decisions were based primarily on undergraduate GPAs and LSAT scores." The Law School's Dean admitted that in some cases the race of an applicant was a "determinative" factor in the admissions decision. Another Law School official testified that the admissions policy was designed to include students "from groups which have been historically discriminated against" but that the policy did not include Asians and Jews, groups who have experienced discrimination, because they "were already being admitted to the Law School in significant numbers." A former Law School faculty member testified that the educational benefit of a "critical mass" of minority students is that "racial stereotypes lose their force because nonminority students learn there is no 'minority viewpoint' but rather a variety of viewpoints among minority students. Grutter's expert testified that race "is an extremely strong factor in the decision for acceptance," and that racial minorities favored by the Law School's admission policy "are given an extremely large allowance for admission" as compared to applicants who are members of nonfavored groups. The Law School's expert testified "that if race were not considered . . . underrepresented minority students would have comprised 4 percent of the entering class in 2000 instead of the actual figure of 14.5 percent.]

Sitting en banc, the Court of Appeals reversed the District Court's judgment. . . . We granted certiorari to resolve the disagreement among the Courts of Appeals on a question of national importance: Whether diversity is a compelling interest that can justify the narrowly tailored use of race in selecting applicants for admission to public universities.

II. We last addressed the use of race in public higher education over 25 years ago [in] *Bakke*. . . . Since this Court's splintered decision in *Bakke*, Justice Powell's opinion announcing the judgment of the Court has served as the touchstone for constitutional analysis of race-conscious admissions policies. Public and private universities across the Nation have modeled their own admissions programs on Justice Powell's views on permissible race-conscious policies. . . .

Justice Powell [applied strict scrutiny and rejected as insufficiently compelling all but one of the interests asserted by the university]. Justice Powell approved the university's use of race to further only one interest: "the attainment of a diverse student body." With the important proviso that "constitutional limitations protecting individual rights may not be disregarded," Justice Powell grounded his analysis in the academic freedom that "long has been viewed as a special concern of the First Amendment." . . . In seeking the "right to select those students who will contribute the most to the 'robust exchange of ideas,' " a university seeks "to achieve a goal that is of paramount importance in the fulfillment of its mission." . . . Justice Powell was, however, careful to emphasize that in his view race "is only one element in a range of factors a university properly may consider in attaining the goal of a heterogeneous student body." For Justice Powell, "it is not an interest in simple ethnic diversity, in which a specified percentage of the student body is in effect guaranteed to be members of selected ethnic groups," that can justify the use of race. Rather, "the diversity that furthers a compelling state interest encompasses a far broader array of qualifications and characteristics of which racial or ethnic origin is but a single though important element." [For] the reasons set out below, today we endorse Justice Powell's view that student body diversity is a compelling state interest that can justify the use of race in university admissions.

holding diversity = compelling state interest

. . . Because the Fourteenth Amendment "protects *persons*, not *groups*," all "governmental action based on race — a *group* classification long recognized as in most circumstances irrelevant and therefore prohibited — should be subjected to detailed judicial inquiry to ensure that the *personal* right to equal protection of the laws has not been infringed." [Adarand Constructors, Inc. v. Pena.] It follows from that principle that "government may treat people differently because of their race only for the most compelling reasons." [All] racial classifications imposed by government "must be analyzed by a reviewing court under strict scrutiny." This means that such classifications are constitutional only if they are narrowly tailored to further compelling governmental interests. . . . Strict scrutiny is not "strict in theory, but fatal in fact." Although all governmental uses of race are subject to strict scrutiny, not all are invalidated by it. . . . When race-based action is necessary to further a compelling governmental interest, such action does not violate the constitutional guarantee of equal protection so long as the narrow-tailoring requirement is also satisfied.

Context matters when reviewing race-based governmental action under the Equal Protection Clause. . . . In *Adarand Constructors* we made clear that strict scrutiny must take " 'relevant differences' into account." . . . Not every decision influenced by race is equally objectionable and strict scrutiny is designed to provide a framework for carefully examining the importance and the sincerity of the reasons advanced by the governmental decisionmaker for the use of race in that particular context.

III. With these principles in mind, we turn to the question whether the Law School's use of race is justified by a compelling state interest. [The Law School asserts] only one justification for [its] use of race in the admissions process: obtaining "the educational benefits that flow from a diverse student body." [The] Law School asks us to recognize, in the context of higher education, a compelling state interest in student body diversity.

We first wish to dispel the notion that the Law School's argument has been foreclosed, either expressly or implicitly, by our affirmative-action cases decided since *Bakke*. It is true that some language in those opinions might be read to suggest that remedying past discrimination is the only permissible justification for race-based governmental action. But we have never held that the only governmental use of race that can survive strict scrutiny is remedying past discrimination. Nor, since *Bakke*, have we directly addressed the use of race in the context of public higher education. Today, we hold that the Law School has a compelling interest in attaining a diverse student body.

The Law School's educational judgment that such diversity is essential to its educational mission is one to which we defer. . . . Our scrutiny of the interest asserted by the Law School is no less strict for taking into account complex educational judgments in an area that lies primarily within the expertise of the university. . . . We have long recognized that, given the important purpose of public education and the expansive freedoms of speech and thought associated with the university environment, universities occupy a special niche in our constitutional tradition. In announcing the principle of student body diversity as a compelling state interest, Justice Powell invoked our cases recognizing a constitutional dimension, grounded in the First Amendment, of educational autonomy: "The freedom of a university to make its own judgments as to education includes the selection of its student body.". . . Our conclusion that the Law School has a compelling interest in a diverse student body is informed by our view that attaining a diverse student body is at the heart of the Law School's proper institutional mission, and that "good faith" on the part of a university is "presumed" absent "a showing to the contrary."

. . . The Law School's interest is not simply "to assure within its student body some specified percentage of a particular group merely because of its race or ethnic origin." That would amount to outright racial balancing, which is patently unconstitutional. Rather, the Law School's concept of critical mass is defined by reference to the educational benefits that diversity is designed to produce. These benefits are substantial. [The] Law School's admissions policy promotes "cross-racial understanding," helps to break down racial stereotypes, and "enables [students] to better understand persons of different races." These benefits are "important and laudable," because "classroom discussion is livelier, more spirited, and simply more enlightening and interesting" when the students have "the greatest possible variety of backgrounds."

The Law School's claim of a compelling interest is further bolstered by its *amici*, who point to the educational benefits that flow from student body diversity. [Numerous] studies show that student body diversity promotes learning outcomes, and "better prepares students for an increasingly diverse workforce and society, and better prepares them as professionals." These benefits are not theoretical but real, as major American businesses have made clear that the skills needed in today's increasingly global marketplace can only be developed through exposure to widely diverse people, cultures, ideas, and viewpoints. What is more, high-ranking retired officers and civilian leaders of the United States military assert that, "based on [their] decades of experience," a "highly qualified, racially diverse officer corps . . . is essential to the military's ability to fulfill its principle [sic] mission to provide national security." The primary sources for the Nation's officer corps are the service academies and the Reserve Officers Training Corps (ROTC), the latter comprising students already admitted to participating colleges and universities. At present, "the military cannot achieve an officer corps that is *both* highly qualified *and* racially diverse unless the service academies and the ROTC used limited race-conscious recruiting and admissions policies." To fulfill its mission, the military "must be selective in admissions for training and education for the officer corps, *and* it must train and educate a highly qualified, racially diverse officer corps in a racially diverse setting." We agree that "it requires only a small step from this analysis to conclude that our country's other most selective institutions must remain both diverse and selective."

We have repeatedly acknowledged the overriding importance of preparing students for work and citizenship, describing education as pivotal to "sustaining our political and cultural heritage" with a fundamental role in maintaining the fabric of society. Plyler v. Doe. This Court has long recognized that "education . . . is the very foundation of good citizenship." Brown v. Board of Education. For this reason, the diffusion of knowledge and opportunity through public institutions of higher education must be accessible to all individuals regardless of race or ethnicity. . . . Effective participation by members of all racial and ethnic groups in the civic life of our Nation is essential if the dream of one Nation, indivisible, is to be realized. Moreover, universities, and in particular, law schools, represent the training ground for a large number of our Nation's leaders. . . . In order to cultivate a set of leaders with legitimacy in the eyes of the citizenry, it is necessary that the path to leadership be visibly open to talented and qualified individuals of every race and ethnicity. All members of our heterogeneous society must have confidence in the openness and integrity of the educational institutions that provide this training. . . .

Even in the limited circumstance when drawing racial distinctions is permissible to further a compelling state interest, [the] means chosen to accomplish the [government's] asserted purpose must be specifically and narrowly framed to accomplish that purpose." The purpose of the narrow tailoring requirement is to ensure that "the means chosen 'fit' . . . the compelling goal so closely that there is little or no possibility that the motive for the classification was illegitimate racial prejudice or stereotype." Richmond v. J. A. Croson Co., (plurality opinion).

Since *Bakke*, we have had no occasion to define the contours of the narrow-tailoring inquiry with respect to race-conscious university admissions programs. That inquiry must be calibrated to fit the distinct issues raised by the use of race to achieve student body diversity in public higher education. . . . To be narrowly tailored, a race-conscious admissions program cannot use a quota system — it cannot "insulate each category of applicants with certain desired qualifications from competition with all other applicants." Instead, a university may consider race or ethnicity only as a " 'plus' in a particular applicant's file," without "insulating the individual from comparison with all other candidates for the available seats." In other words, an admissions program must be "flexible enough to consider all pertinent elements of diversity in light of the particular qualifications of each applicant, and to place them on the same footing for consideration, although not necessarily according them the same weight."

We find that the Law School's admissions program bears the hallmarks of a narrowly tailored plan. As Justice Powell made clear in *Bakke*, truly individualized consideration demands that race be used in a flexible, nonmechanical way. It follows from this mandate that universities cannot establish quotas for members of certain racial groups or put members of those groups on separate admissions tracks. Nor can universities insulate applicants who belong to certain racial or ethnic groups from the competition for admission. Universities can, however, consider race or ethnicity more flexibly as a "plus" factor in the context of individualized consideration of each and every applicant.

We are satisfied that the Law School's admissions program, like the Harvard plan described by Justice Powell, does not operate as a quota. [A] "quota" is a program in which a certain fixed number or proportion of opportunities are "reserved exclusively for certain minority groups." [*Croson.*] . . . The Law School's goal of attaining a critical mass of underrepresented minority students does not transform its program into a quota. [There] is of course "some relationship between numbers and achieving the benefits to be derived from a diverse student body, and between numbers and providing a reasonable environment for those students admitted." [But, "some] attention to numbers," without more, does not transform a flexible admissions system into a rigid quota. [Moreover,] the number of African-American, Latino, and Native-American students in each class at the Law School varied from 13.5 to 20.1 percent, a range inconsistent with a quota.

That a race-conscious admissions program does not operate as a quota does not, by itself, satisfy the requirement of individualized consideration. When using race as a "plus" factor in university admissions, a university's admissions program must remain flexible enough to ensure that each applicant is evaluated as an individual and not in a way that makes an applicant's race or ethnicity the defining feature of his or her application. The importance of this individualized consideration in the context of a race-conscious admissions program is paramount. Here, the Law School engages in a highly individualized, holistic review of each applicant's file, giving serious consideration to all the ways an applicant might contribute to a diverse educational environment. . . . Unlike the program at issue in Gratz v. Bollinger, the Law School awards no mechanical, predetermined diversity "bonuses" based on race or ethnicity. . . .

We also find that . . . the Law School's race-conscious admissions program adequately ensures that all factors that may contribute to student body diversity are meaningfully considered alongside race in admissions decisions. With respect to the use of race itself, all underrepresented minority students admitted by the Law School have been deemed qualified. By virtue of our Nation's struggle with racial inequality, such students are both likely to have experiences of particular importance to the Law School's mission, and less likely to be admitted in meaningful numbers on criteria that ignore those experiences. . . .

What is more, the Law School actually gives substantial weight to diversity factors besides race. The Law School frequently accepts nonminority applicants with grades and test scores lower than underrepresented minority applicants (and other nonminority applicants) who are rejected. This shows that the Law School seriously weighs many other diversity factors besides race that can make a real and dispositive difference for nonminority applicants as well.

[Grutter argues] that the Law School's plan is not narrowly tailored because race-neutral means exist to obtain the educational benefits of student body diversity that the Law School seeks. We disagree. Narrow tailoring does not require exhaustion of every conceivable race-neutral alternative. Nor does it require a university to choose between maintaining a reputation for excellence or fulfilling a commitment to provide educational opportunities to members of all racial groups. Narrow tailoring does, however, require serious, good faith consideration of workable race-neutral alternatives that will achieve the diversity the university seeks. We agree with the Court of Appeals that the Law School sufficiently considered workable race-neutral alternatives. The District Court took the Law School to task for failing to consider race-neutral alternatives such as "using a lottery system" or "decreasing the emphasis for all applicants on undergraduate GPA and LSAT scores." But these alternatives would require a dramatic sacrifice of diversity, the academic quality of all admitted students, or both. . . .

We acknowledge that "there are serious problems of justice connected with the idea of preference itself." Narrow tailoring, therefore, requires that a race-conscious admissions program not unduly harm members of any racial group. Even remedial race-based governmental action generally "remains subject to continuing oversight to assure that it will work the least harm possible to other innocent persons competing for the benefit." To be narrowly tailored, a race-conscious admissions program must not "unduly burden individuals who are not members of the favored racial and ethnic groups." We are satisfied that the Law School's admissions program does not. Because the Law School considers "all pertinent elements of diversity," it can (and does) select nonminority applicants who have greater potential to enhance student body diversity over underrepresented minority applicants. . . . We agree that, in the context of its individualized inquiry into the possible diversity contributions of all applicants, the Law School's race-conscious admissions program does not unduly harm nonminority applicants.

We are mindful, however, that "[a] core purpose of the Fourteenth Amendment was to do away with all governmentally imposed discrimination based on race." Palmore v. Sidoti. Accordingly, race-conscious admissions policies must be limited in time. This requirement reflects that racial classifications, however compelling their goals, are potentially so dangerous that they may be employed no more broadly than the interest demands. Enshrining a permanent justification for racial preferences would offend this fundamental equal protection principle. We see no reason to exempt race-conscious admissions programs from the requirement that all governmental use of race must have a logical end point. The Law School, too, concedes that all "race-conscious programs must have reasonable durational limits." In the context of higher education, the durational requirement can be met by sunset provisions in race-conscious admissions policies and periodic reviews to determine whether racial preferences are still necessary to achieve student body diversity. . . . The requirement that all race-conscious admissions programs have a termination point "assures all citizens that the deviation from the norm of equal treatment of all racial and ethnic groups is a temporary matter, a measure taken in the service of the goal of equality itself." . . . We take the Law School at its word that it would "like nothing better than to find a race-neutral admissions formula" and will terminate its race-conscious admissions program as soon as practicable. It has been 25 years since Justice Powell first approved the use of race to further an interest in student body diversity in the context of public higher education. Since that time, the number of minority applicants with high grades and test scores has indeed increased.

We expect that 25 years from now, the use of racial preferences will no longer be necessary to further the interest approved today.

IV. In summary, the Equal Protection Clause does not prohibit the Law School's narrowly tailored use of race in admissions decisions to further a compelling interest in obtaining the educational benefits that flow from a diverse student body. . . . The judgment of the Court of Appeals for the Sixth Circuit, accordingly, is affirmed.

CHIEF JUSTICE REHNQUIST, with whom JUSTICE SCALIA, JUSTICE KENNEDY, and JUSTICE THOMAS join, dissenting.

I agree with the Court that, "in the limited circumstance when drawing racial distinctions is permissible," the government must ensure that its means are narrowly tailored to achieve a compelling state interest. I do not believe, however, that the University of Michigan Law School's (Law School) means are narrowly tailored to the interest it asserts. The Law School claims it must take the steps it does to achieve a " 'critical mass' " of underrepresented minority students. But its actual program bears no relation to this asserted goal. Stripped of its "critical mass" veil, the Law School's program is revealed as a naked effort to achieve racial balancing. . . . Although the Court recites the language of our strict scrutiny analysis, its application of that review is unprecedented in its deference.

[The] asserted justification for the Law School's use of race in the admissions process is "obtaining 'the educational benefits that flow from a diverse student body,' " [which benefits can only be obtained by enrolling] a "critical mass" of underrepresented minorities . . . . In practice, the Law School's program bears little or no relation to its asserted goal of achieving "critical mass." Respondents explain that the Law School seeks to accumulate a "critical mass" of *each* underrepresented minority group. But the record demonstrates that the Law School's admissions practices with respect to these groups differ dramatically and cannot be defended under any consistent use of the term "critical mass."

From 1995 through 2000, the Law School admitted between 1,130 and 1,310 students. Of those, between 13 and 19 were Native American, between 91 and 108 were African-Americans, and between 47 and 56 were Hispanic. If the Law School is admitting between 91 and 108 African-Americans in order to achieve "critical mass," thereby preventing African-American students from feeling "isolated or like spokespersons for their race," one would think that a number of the same order of magnitude would be necessary to accomplish the same purpose for Hispanics and Native Americans. Similarly, even if all of the Native American applicants admitted in a given year matriculate, which the record demonstrates is not at all the case, how can this possibly constitute a "critical mass" of Native Americans in a class of over 350 students? In order for this pattern of admission to be consistent with the Law School's explanation of "critical mass," one would have to believe that the objectives of "critical mass" offered by respondents are achieved with only half the number of Hispanics and one-sixth the number of Native Americans as compared to African-Americans. But respondents offer no race-specific reasons for such disparities. Instead, they simply emphasize the importance of achieving "critical mass," without any explanation of why that concept is applied differently among the three underrepresented minority groups.

These different numbers, moreover, come only as a result of substantially different treatment among the three underrepresented minority groups, as is apparent in an example offered by the Law School and highlighted by the Court: The school asserts that it "frequently accepts nonminority applicants with grades and test scores lower than underrepresented minority applicants (and other nonminority applicants) who are rejected." Specifically, the Law School states that "sixty-nine minority applicants were rejected between 1995 and 2000 with at least a 3.5 [Grade Point Average (GPA)] and a [score of] 159 or higher on the [Law School Admissions Test (LSAT)]" while a number of Caucasian and Asian-American applicants with similar or lower scores were admitted. Review of the record reveals only 67 such individuals. Of these 67 individuals, *56* were Hispanic, while only 6 were African-American, and only 5 were Native American. This discrepancy reflects a consistent practice. For example, in 2000, 12 Hispanics who scored between a 159-160 on the LSAT and earned a GPA of 3.00 or higher applied for admission and only 2 were admitted. App. 200-201. Meanwhile, 12 African-Americans in the same range of qualifications applied for admission and all 12 were admitted. *Id.*, at 198. Likewise, that same year, 16 Hispanics who scored between a 151-153 on the LSAT and earned a 3.00 or higher applied for admission and only 1 of those applicants was admitted. Twenty-three similarly qualified African-Americans applied for admission and 14 were admitted.

These statistics have a significant bearing on petitioner's case. Respondents have *never* offered any race-specific arguments explaining why significantly more individuals from one underrepresented minority group are needed in order to achieve "critical mass" or further student body diversity. They certainly have not explained why Hispanics, who they have said are among "the groups most isolated by racial barriers in our country," should have their admission capped out in this manner. [The] the Law School's disparate admissions practices with respect to these minority groups demonstrate that its alleged goal of "critical mass" is simply a sham. . . .

Only when the "critical mass" label is discarded does a likely explanation for these numbers emerge. The Court states that the Law School's goal of attaining a "critical mass" of underrepresented minority students is not an interest in merely " 'assuring within its student body some specified percentage of a particular group merely because of its race or ethnic origin.' " The Court recognizes that such an interest "would amount to outright racial balancing, which is patently unconstitutional." The Court concludes, however, that the Law School's use of race in admissions . . . only pays " 'some attention to numbers.' " But the correlation between the percentage of the Law School's pool of applicants who are members of the three minority groups and the percentage of the admitted applicants who are members of these same groups is far too precise to be dismissed as merely the result of the school paying "some attention to [the] numbers." As the tables below show, from 1995 through 2000 the percentage of admitted applicants who were members of these minority groups closely tracked the percentage of individuals in the school's applicant pool who were from the same groups.

Table 1						
Year	Number of law school applicants	Number of African-American applicants	% of applicants who were African-American	Number of applicants admitted by the law school	Number of African-American applicants admitted	% of admitted applicants who were African-American
1995	4147	404	9.7%	1130	106	9.4%
1996	3677	342	9.3%	1170	108	9.2%
1997	3429	320	9.3%	1218	101	8.3%
1998	3537	304	8.6%	1310	103	7.9%
1999	3400	247	7.3%	1280	91	7.1%
2000	3432	259	7.5%	1249	91	7.3%

Table 2						
Year	Number of law school applicants	Number of Hispanic applicants	% of applicants who were Hispanic	Number of applicants admitted by the law school	Number of Hispanic applicants admitted	% of admitted applicants who were Hispanic
1995	4147	213	5.1%	1130	56	5.0%
1996	3677	186	5.1%	1170	54	4.6%
1997	3429	163	4.8%	1218	47	3.9%
1998	3537	150	4.2%	1310	55	4.2%
1999	3400	152	4.5%	1280	48	3.8%
2000	3432	168	4.9%	1249	53	4.2%

Table 3						
Year	Number of law school applicants	Number of Native American applicants	% of applicants who were Native American	Number of applicants admitted by the law school	Number of Native American applicants admitted	% of admitted applicants who were Native American
1995	4147	45	1.1%	1130	14	1.2%
1996	3677	31	0.8%	1170	13	1.1%
1997	3429	37	1.1%	1218	19	1.6%
1998	3537	40	1.1%	1310	18	1.4%
1999	3400	25	0.7%	1280	13	1.0%
2000	3432	35	1.0%	1249	14	1.1%

For example, in 1995, when 9.7% of the applicant pool was African-American, 9.4% of the admitted class was African-American. By 2000, only 7.5% of the applicant pool was African-American, and 7.3% of the admitted class was African-American. This correlation is striking. Respondents themselves emphasize that the number of underrepresented minority students admitted to the Law School would be significantly smaller if the race of each applicant were not considered. But, as the examples above illustrate, the measure of the decrease would differ dramatically among the groups. The tight correlation between the percentage of applicants and admittees of a given race, therefore, must result from careful race based planning by the Law School. It suggests a formula for admission based on the aspirational assumption that all applicants are equally qualified academically, and therefore that the proportion of each group admitted should be the same as the proportion of that group in the applicant pool.

[The] Law School cannot precisely control which of its admitted applicants decide to attend the university. But it can and, as the numbers demonstrate, clearly does employ racial preferences in extending offers of admission. Indeed, the ostensibly flexible nature of the Law School's admissions program that the Court finds appealing appears to be, in practice, a carefully managed program designed to ensure proportionate representation of applicants from selected minority groups.

I do not believe that the Constitution gives the Law School such free rein in the use of race. The Law School has offered no explanation for its actual admissions practices and, unexplained, we are bound to conclude that the Law School has managed its admissions program, not to achieve a "critical mass," but to extend offers of admission to members of selected minority groups in proportion to their statistical representation in the applicant pool. But this is precisely the type of racial balancing that the Court itself calls "patently unconstitutional."

Finally, I believe that the Law School's program fails strict scrutiny because it is devoid of any reasonably precise time limit on the Law School's use of race in admissions. We have emphasized that we will consider "the planned duration of the remedy" in determining whether a race-conscious program is constitutional. *Fullilove* (Powell, J. concurring); United States v. Paradise. Our previous cases have required some limit on the duration of programs such as this because discrimination on the basis of race is invidious. The Court suggests a possible 25-year limitation on the Law School's current program. Respondents, on the other hand, remain more ambiguous, [identifying] "such a limit in the Law School's resolve to cease considering race when genuine race-neutral alternatives become available." These discussions of a time limit are the vaguest of assurances. In truth, they permit the Law School's use of racial preferences on a seemingly permanent basis. Thus, an important component of strict scrutiny — that a program be limited in time — is casually subverted. The Court, in an unprecedented display of deference under our strict scrutiny analysis, upholds the Law School's program despite its obvious flaws. We have said that when it comes to the use of race, the connection between the ends and the means used to attain them must be precise. But here the flaw is deeper than that; it is not merely a question of "fit" between ends and means. Here the means actually used are forbidden by the Equal Protection Clause of the Constitution.

JUSTICE KENNEDY, dissenting.

. . . The Court . . . does not apply strict scrutiny. By trying to say otherwise, it undermines both the test and its own controlling precedents. Justice Powell's approval of the use of race in university admissions reflected a tradition, grounded in the First Amendment, of acknowledging a university's conception of its educational mission. Our precedents provide a basis for the Court's acceptance of a university's considered judgment that racial diversity among students can further its educational task, when supported by empirical evidence. . . . Having approved the use of race as a factor in the admissions process, the majority proceeds to nullify the essential safeguard Justice Powell insisted upon as the precondition of the approval. The safeguard was rigorous judicial review, with strict scrutiny as the controlling standard. . . . The Court confuses deference to a university's definition of its educational objective with deference to the implementation of this goal. In the context of university admissions the objective of racial diversity can be accepted based on empirical data known to us, but deference is not to be given with respect to the methods by which it is pursued. Preferment by race, when resorted to by the State, can be the most divisive of all policies, containing within it the potential to destroy confidence in the Constitution and in the idea of equality. The majority today refuses to be faithful to the settled principle of strict review designed to reflect these concerns.

The Court, in a review that is nothing short of perfunctory, accepts the University of Michigan Law School's assurances that its admissions process meets with constitutional requirements. The majority fails to confront the reality of how the Law School's admissions policy is implemented. The dissenting opinion by the Chief Justice, which I join in full, demonstrates beyond question why the concept of critical mass is a delusion used by the Law School to mask its attempt to make race an automatic factor in most instances and to achieve numerical goals indistinguishable from quotas. An effort to achieve racial balance among the minorities the school seeks to attract is, by the Court's own admission, "patently unconstitutional." It remains to point out how critical mass becomes inconsistent with individual consideration in some more specific aspects of the admissions process.

About 80 to 85 percent of the places in the entering class are given to applicants in the upper range of Law School Admissions Test scores and grades. An applicant with these credentials likely will be admitted without consideration of race or ethnicity. With respect to the remaining 15 to 20 percent of the seats, race is likely outcome determinative for many members of minority groups. That is where the competition becomes tight and where any given applicant's chance of admission is far smaller if he or she lacks minority status. At this point the numerical concept of critical mass has the real potential to compromise individual review.

The Law School has not demonstrated how individual consideration is, or can be, preserved at this stage of the application process given the instruction to attain what it calls critical mass. In fact the evidence shows otherwise. There was little deviation among admitted minority students during the years from 1995 to 1998. The percentage of enrolled minorities fluctuated only by 0.3%, from 13.5% to 13.8%. The number of minority students to whom offers were extended varied by just a slightly greater magnitude of 2.2%, from the high of 15.6% in 1995 to the low of 13.4% in 1998.

The District Court relied on this uncontested fact to draw an inference that the Law School's pursuit of critical mass mutated into the equivalent of a quota. Admittedly, there were greater fluctuations among enrolled minorities in the preceding years, 1987-1994, by as much as 5 or 6%. The percentage of minority offers, however, at no point fell below 12%, historically defined by the Law School as the bottom of its critical mass range. The greater variance during the earlier years, in any event, does not dispel suspicion that the school engaged in racial balancing. The data would be consistent with an inference that the Law School modified its target only twice, in 1991 (from 13% to 19%), and then again in 1995 (back from 20% to 13%). The intervening year, 1993, when the percentage dropped to 14.5%, could be an aberration, caused by the school's [admitted] miscalculation as to how many applicants with offers would accept or by its redefinition, made in April 1992, of which minority groups were entitled to race-based preference.

Year	Percentage of enrolled minority students
1987	12.3%
1988	13.6%
1989	14.4%
1990	13.4%
1991	19.1%
1992	19.8%
1993	14.5%
1994	20.1%
1995	13.5%
1996	13.8%
1997	13.6%
1998	13.8%

The narrow fluctuation band raises an inference that the Law School subverted individual determination, and strict scrutiny requires the Law School to overcome the inference. . . . The Law School has the burden of proving, in conformance with the standard of strict scrutiny, that it did not utilize race in an unconstitutional way. At the very least, the constancy of admitted minority students and the close correlation between the racial breakdown of admitted minorities and the composition of the applicant pool, require the Law School either to produce a convincing explanation or to show it has taken adequate steps to ensure individual assessment. The Law School does neither.

The obvious tension between the pursuit of critical mass and the requirement of individual review increased by the end of the admissions season. Most of the decisions where race may decide the outcome are made during this period. The admissions officers consulted the daily reports which indicated the composition of the incoming class along racial lines. As Dennis Shields, Director of Admissions from

1991 to 1996, stated, "the further [he] went into the [admissions] season the more frequently [he] would want to look at these [reports] and see the change from day-to-day." These reports would "track exactly where [the Law School] stood at any given time in assembling the class," and so would tell the admissions personnel whether they were short of assembling a critical mass of minority students. Shields generated these reports because the Law School's admissions policy told him the racial make-up of the entering class was "something [he] needed to be concerned about," and so he had "to find a way of tracking what's going on." The consultation of daily reports during the last stages in the admissions process suggests there was no further attempt at individual review save for race itself. The admissions officers could use the reports to recalibrate the plus factor given to race depending on how close they were to achieving the Law School's goal of critical mass. The bonus factor of race would then become divorced from individual review; it would be premised instead on the numerical objective set by the Law School.

The Law School made no effort to guard against this danger. It provided no guidelines to its admissions personnel on how to reconcile individual assessment with the directive to admit a critical mass of minority students. The admissions program could have been structured to eliminate at least some of the risk that the promise of individual evaluation was not being kept. The daily consideration of racial breakdown of admitted students is not a feature of affirmative-action programs used by other institutions of higher learning. The Little Ivy League colleges, for instance, do not keep ongoing tallies of racial or ethnic composition of their entering students. See Brief for Amherst College et al. as *Amici Curiae* 10.

To be constitutional, a university's compelling interest in a diverse student body must be achieved by a system where individual assessment is safeguarded through the entire process. There is no constitutional objection to the goal of considering race as one modest factor among many others to achieve diversity, but an educational institution must ensure, through sufficient procedures, that each applicant receives individual consideration and that race does not become a predominant factor in the admissions decisionmaking. The Law School failed to comply with this requirement, and by no means has it carried its burden to show otherwise by the test of strict scrutiny.

The Court's refusal to apply meaningful strict scrutiny will lead to serious consequences. By deferring to the law schools' choice of minority admissions programs, the courts will lose the talents and resources of the faculties and administrators in devising new and fairer ways to ensure individual consideration. Constant and rigorous judicial review forces the law school faculties to undertake their responsibilities as state employees in this most sensitive of areas with utmost fidelity to the mandate of the Constitution. Dean Allan Stillwagon, who directed the Law School's Office of Admissions from 1979 to 1990, explained the difficulties he encountered in defining racial groups entitled to benefit under the School's affirmative action policy. He testified that faculty members were "breathtakingly cynical" in deciding who would qualify as a member of underrepresented minorities. An example he offered was faculty debate as to whether Cubans should be counted as Hispanics: One professor objected on the grounds that Cubans were

Republicans. . . . This is not to suggest the faculty at Michigan or other law schools do not pursue aspirations they consider laudable and consistent with our constitutional traditions. It is but further evidence of the necessity for scrutiny that is real, not feigned, where the corrosive category of race is a factor in decisionmaking. Prospective students, the courts, and the public can demand that the State and its law schools prove their process is fair and constitutional in every phase of implementation. . . .

If universities are given the latitude to administer programs that are tantamount to quotas, they will have few incentives to make the existing minority admissions schemes transparent and protective of individual review. The unhappy consequence will be to perpetuate the hostilities that proper consideration of race is designed to avoid. The perpetuation, of course, would be the worst of all outcomes. . . .

It is regrettable the Court's important holding allowing racial minorities to have their special circumstances considered in order to improve their educational opportunities is accompanied by a suspension of the strict scrutiny which was the predicate of allowing race to be considered in the first place. . . . The Constitution cannot confer the right to classify on the basis of race even in this special context absent searching judicial review. For these reasons, though I reiterate my approval of giving appropriate consideration to race in this one context, I must dissent in the present case.

JUSTICE SCALIA, with whom JUSTICE THOMAS joins, concurring in part and dissenting in part.

I join the opinion of the Chief Justice. As he demonstrates, the University of Michigan Law School's mystical "critical mass" justification for its discrimination by race challenges even the most gullible mind. The admissions statistics show it to be a sham to cover a scheme of racially proportionate admissions.

I also join Parts I through VII of Justice Thomas's opinion. [Part VII of Justice Thomas's opinion describes the portions of the Court's opinion in which Justices Thomas and Scalia concurred.] I find particularly unanswerable his central point: that the allegedly "compelling state interest" at issue here is not the incremental "educational benefit" that emanates from the fabled "critical mass" of minority students, but rather Michigan's interest in maintaining a "prestige" law school whose normal admissions standards disproportionately exclude blacks and other minorities. If that is a compelling state interest, everything is.

I add the following: The "educational benefit" that the University of Michigan seeks to achieve by racial discrimination consists, according to the Court, of " 'cross-racial understanding,' " and " 'better prepar[ation of] students for an increasingly diverse workforce and society,' " all of which is necessary not only for work, but also for good "citizenship." This is not, of course, an "educational benefit" on which students will be graded on their Law School transcript (Works and Plays Well with Others: B+) or tested by the bar examiners (Q: Describe in 500 words or less your cross-racial understanding). For it is a lesson of life rather than law — essentially the same lesson taught to (or rather learned by, for it cannot be "taught" in the usual sense) people three feet shorter and twenty years younger than the full-grown adults at the University of Michigan Law School, in institutions ranging from Boy Scout troops to public-school kindergartens. If properly considered an "educational benefit" at all, it is surely not one that is either uniquely relevant to law school or uniquely "teachable" in a formal educational setting. And therefore: If it is appropriate for the University of Michigan Law School to use racial discrimination for the purpose of putting together a "critical mass" that will convey generic lessons in socialization and good citizenship, surely it is no less appropriate — indeed, *particularly* appropriate — for the civil service system of the State of Michigan to do so. There, also, those exposed to "critical masses" of certain races will presumably become better Americans, better Michiganders, better civil servants. And surely private employers cannot be criticized — indeed, should be praised — if they also "teach" good citizenship to their adult employees through a patriotic, all-American system of racial discrimination in hiring. The nonminority individuals who are deprived of a legal education, a civil service job, or any job at all by reason of their skin color will surely understand.

Unlike a clear constitutional holding that racial preferences in state educational institutions are impermissible, or even a clear anticonstitutional holding that racial preferences in state educational institutions are OK, today's *Grutter-Gratz* split double header seems perversely designed to prolong the controversy and the litigation. Some future lawsuits will presumably focus on whether the discriminatory scheme in question contains enough evaluation of the applicant "as an individual," and sufficiently avoids "separate admissions tracks" to fall under *Grutter* rather than *Gratz*. Some will focus on whether a university has gone beyond the bounds of a " 'good faith effort' " and has so zealously pursued its "critical mass" as to make it an unconstitutional *de facto* quota system, rather than merely " 'a permissible goal.' " Other lawsuits may focus on whether, in the particular setting at issue, any educational benefits flow from racial diversity. (That issue was not contested in *Grutter*; and while the opinion accords "a degree of deference to a university's academic decisions," [it is also clear that] "deference does not imply abandonment or abdication of judicial review." Still other suits may challenge the bona fides of the institution's expressed commitment to the educational benefits of diversity that immunize the discriminatory scheme in *Grutter*. (Tempting targets, one would suppose, will be those universities that talk the talk of multiculturalism and racial diversity in the courts but walk the walk of tribalism and racial segregation on their campuses — through minority-only student organizations, separate minority housing opportunities, separate minority student centers, even separate minority-only graduation ceremonies.) And still other suits may claim that the institution's racial preferences have gone below or above the mystical *Grutter*-approved "critical mass." Finally, litigation can be expected on behalf of minority groups intentionally short changed in the institution's composition of its generic minority "critical mass." I do not look forward to any of these cases. The Constitution proscribes government discrimination on the basis of race, and state-provided education is no exception.

JUSTICE THOMAS, with whom JUSTICE SCALIA joins as to Parts I-VII, concurring in part and dissenting in part.

Frederick Douglass, speaking to a group of abolitionists almost 140 years ago, delivered a message lost on today's majority:

> In regard to the colored people, there is always more that is benevolent, I perceive, than just, manifested towards us. What I ask for the negro is not benevolence, not pity, not sympathy, but simply *justice*. The American people have always been anxious to know what they shall do with us . . . . I have had but one answer from the beginning. Do nothing with us! Your doing with us has already played the mischief with us. Do nothing with us! If the apples will not remain on the tree of their own strength, if they are worm-eaten at the core, if they are early ripe and disposed to fall, let them fall! . . . And if the negro cannot stand on his own legs, let him fall also. All I ask is, give him a chance to stand on his own legs! Let him alone! . . . Your interference is doing him positive injury.

What the Black Man Wants: An Address Delivered in Boston, Massachusetts, on 26 January 1865, reprinted in 4 The Frederick Douglass Papers 59, 68 (J. Blassingame & J. McKivigan eds. 1991) (emphasis in original).

Like Douglass, I believe blacks can achieve in every avenue of American life without the meddling of university administrators. Because I wish to see all students succeed whatever their color, I share, in some respect, the sympathies of those who sponsor the type of discrimination advanced by the University of Michigan Law School (Law School). The Constitution does not, however, tolerate institutional devotion to the status quo in admissions policies when such devotion ripens into racial discrimination. Nor does the Constitution countenance the unprecedented deference the Court gives to the Law School, an approach inconsistent with the very concept of "strict scrutiny."

No one would argue that a university could set up a lower general admission standard and then impose heightened requirements only on black applicants. Similarly, a university may not maintain a high admission standard and grant exemptions to favored races. The Law School, of its own choosing, and for its own purposes, maintains an exclusionary admissions system that it knows produces racially disproportionate results. Racial discrimination is not a permissible solution to the self-inflicted wounds of this elitist admissions policy.

The majority upholds the Law School's racial discrimination not by interpreting the people's Constitution, but by responding to a faddish slogan of the cognoscenti. Nevertheless, I concur in part in the Court's opinion. First, I agree with the Court insofar as its decision, which approves of only one racial classification, confirms that further use of race in admissions remains unlawful. Second, I agree with the Court's holding that racial discrimination in higher education admissions will be illegal in 25 years. I respectfully dissent from the remainder of the Court's opinion and the judgment, however, because I believe that the Law School's current use of race violates the Equal Protection Clause and that the Constitution means the same thing today as it will in 300 months.

I. The majority agrees that the Law School's racial discrimination should be subjected to strict scrutiny. . . . The Constitution abhors classifications based on race, not only because those classifications can harm favored races or are based on illegitimate motives, but also because every time the government places citizens on racial registers and makes race relevant to the provision of burdens or benefits, it demeans us all.

II. Unlike the majority, I seek to define with precision the interest being asserted by the Law School before determining whether that interest is so compelling as to justify racial discrimination. The Law School maintains that it wishes to obtain "educational benefits that flow from student body diversity." This statement must be evaluated carefully, because it implies that both "diversity" and "educational benefits" are components of the Law School's compelling state interest. . . . The Law School . . . believes that only a racially mixed student body can lead to the educational benefits it seeks. . . . The Law School's argument, as facile as it is, can only be understood in one way: Classroom [racial] aesthetics yields educational benefits, racially discriminatory admissions policies are required to achieve the right racial mix, and therefore the policies are required to achieve the educational benefits. It is the *educational benefits* that are the end, or allegedly compelling state interest, not "diversity."

. . . The Law School adamantly disclaims any race-neutral alternative that would reduce "academic selectivity," which would in turn "require the Law School to become a very different institution, and to sacrifice a core part of its educational mission." In other words, the Law School seeks to improve marginally the education it offers without sacrificing too much of its exclusivity and elite status. The proffered interest that the majority vindicates today, then, is not simply "diversity." Instead the Court upholds the use of racial discrimination as a tool to advance the Law School's interest in offering a marginally superior education while maintaining an elite institution. Unless each constituent part of this state interest is of pressing public necessity, the Law School's use of race is unconstitutional. I find each of them to fall far short of this standard.

III. Under the proper standard, there is no pressing public necessity in maintaining a public law school at all and, it follows, certainly not an elite law school. Likewise, marginal improvements in legal education do not qualify as a compelling state interest. While legal education at a public university may be good policy or otherwise laudable, it is obviously not a pressing public necessity . . . . As the foregoing makes clear, Michigan has no compelling interest in having a law school at all, much less an *elite* one. Still, even assuming that a State may, under appropriate circumstances, demonstrate a cognizable interest in having an elite law school, Michigan has failed to do so here. . . .

The only cognizable state interests vindicated by operating a public law school are . . . the education of that State's citizens and the training of that State's lawyers. . . . The Law School today, however, does precious little training of those attorneys who will serve the citizens of Michigan. In 2002, graduates of the University of Michigan Law School made up less than 6% of applicants to the Michigan bar, even though the Law School's graduates constitute nearly 30% of all law students graduating in Michigan. Less than 16% of the Law School's graduating class elects to stay in Michigan after law school. . . . In sum, the Law School trains few Michigan residents and overwhelmingly serves students, who, as lawyers, leave the State of Michigan. By contrast, Michigan's other public law school, Wayne State University Law School, sends 88% of its graduates on to serve the people of Michigan. . . . The Law School's decision to be an elite institution does little to advance the welfare of the people of Michigan or any cognizable interest of the State of Michigan. . . .

IV. . . . The Court never explicitly holds that the Law School's desire to retain the status quo in "academic selectivity" is itself a compelling state interest, and, as I have demonstrated, it is not. Therefore, the Law School should be forced to choose between its classroom aesthetic and its exclusionary admissions system — it cannot have it both ways.

The Court bases its unprecedented deference to the Law School — a deference antithetical to strict scrutiny — on an idea of "educational autonomy" grounded in the First Amendment. In my view, there is no basis for a right of public universities to do what would otherwise violate the Equal Protection Clause.

The constitutionalization of "academic freedom" began with the concurring opinion of Justice Frankfurter in Sweezy v. New Hampshire, 354 U.S. 234 (1957), [in which Justice Frankfurter] asserted that a "free society" depends on "free universities" and "this means the exclusion of governmental intervention in the intellectual life of a university, [including] who may be admitted to study." . . . The only source for the Court's conclusion that public universities are entitled to deference even within the confines of strict scrutiny is Justice Powell's opinion in *Bakke*. Justice Powell . . . relied only on Justice Frankfurter's opinion in *Sweezy* and the Court's decision in Keyishian v. Board of Regents of Univ. of State of N.Y., 385 U.S. 589 (1967), to support his view that the First Amendment somehow protected a public university's use of race in admissions. [In *Keyishian*,] however, the Court did not relax any independent constitutional restrictions on public universities. I doubt that when Justice Frankfurter spoke of governmental intrusions into the independence of universities, he was thinking of the Constitution's ban on racial discrimination. The majority's broad deference to [the Law School] finds no basis in the Constitution or decisions of this Court.

The Court relies heavily on social science evidence to justify its deference [but] never acknowledges . . . the growing evidence that racial (and other sorts) of heterogeneity actually impairs learning among black students. See, e.g., Flowers & Pascarella, Cognitive Effects of College Racial Composition on African American Students After 3 Years of College, 40 J. of College Student Development 669, 674 (1999) (concluding that black students experience superior cognitive development at Historically Black Colleges (HBCs) and that, even among blacks, "a substantial diversity moderates the cognitive effects of attending an HBC"). . . . The majority grants deference to the Law School's "assessment that diversity will, in fact, yield educational benefits." It follows, therefore, that an HBC's assessment that racial homogeneity will yield educational benefits would similarly be given deference. An HBC's rejection of white applicants in order to maintain racial homogeneity seems permissible, therefore, under the majority's view of the Equal Protection Clause. Contained within today's majority opinion is the seed of a new constitutional justification for a concept I thought long and rightly rejected — racial segregation.

Moreover one would think, in light of the Court's decision in United States v. Virginia, that before being given license to use racial discrimination, the Law School would be required to radically reshape its admissions process, even to the point of sacrificing some elements of its character. In *Virginia*, a majority of the Court, without a word about academic freedom, accepted the all-male Virginia Military Institute's (VMI) representation that some changes in its "adversative" method of education would be required with the admission of women, but did not defer to VMI's judgment that these changes would be too great. Instead, the Court concluded that they were "manageable." That case involved sex discrimination, which is subjected to intermediate, not strict, scrutiny. So in *Virginia*, where the standard of review dictated that greater flexibility be granted to VMI's educational policies than the Law School deserves here, this Court gave no deference. . . .

Virginia is also notable for the fact that the Court relied on the "experience" of formerly single-sex institutions, such as the service academies, to conclude that admission of women to VMI would be "manageable." Today, however, the majority ignores the "experience" of those institutions that have been forced to abandon explicit racial discrimination in admissions. The sky has not fallen at Boalt Hall at the University of California, Berkeley, for example. Prior to Proposition 209's adoption of Cal. Const., Art. 1, §31(a), which bars the State from "granting preferential treatment . . . on the basis of race . . . in the operation of . . . public education," Boalt Hall enrolled 20 blacks and 28 Hispanics in its first-year class for 1996. In 2002, without deploying express racial discrimination in admissions, Boalt's entering class enrolled 14 blacks and 36 Hispanics. Total underrepresented minority student enrollment at Boalt Hall now exceeds 1996 levels. Apparently the Law School cannot be counted on to be as resourceful. . . .

V. . . .

[No] modern law school can claim ignorance of the poor performance of blacks, relatively speaking, on the Law School Admissions Test (LSAT). Nevertheless, law schools continue to use the test and then attempt to "correct" for black underperformance by using racial discrimination in admissions so as to obtain their aesthetic student body. The Law School's continued adherence to measures it knows produce racially skewed results is not entitled to deference by this Court. . . . Having decided to use the LSAT, the Law School must accept the constitutional burdens that come with this decision. The Law School may freely continue to employ the LSAT and other allegedly merit-based standards in whatever fashion it likes. What the Equal Protection Clause forbids, but the Court today allows, is the use of these standards hand-in-hand with racial discrimination. An infinite variety of admissions methods are available to the Law School. Considering all of the radical thinking that has historically occurred at this country's universities, the Law School's intractable approach toward admissions is striking. The Court will not even deign to make the Law School try other methods, however, preferring instead to grant a 25-year license to violate the Constitution. . . .

VI. The absence of any articulated legal principle supporting the majority's principal holding suggests another rationale. I believe what lies beneath the Court's decision today are the benighted notions that one can tell when racial discrimination benefits (rather than hurts) minority groups, and that racial discrimination is necessary to remedy general societal ills. This Court's precedents supposedly settled both issues, but clearly the majority still cannot commit to the principle that racial classifications are *per se* harmful and that almost no amount of benefit in the eye of the beholder can justify such classifications.

. . . I must contest the notion that the Law School's discrimination benefits those admitted as a result of it. . . . The Law School is not looking for those students who, despite a lower LSAT score or undergraduate grade point average, will succeed in the study of law. The Law School seeks only a facade — it is sufficient that the class looks right, even if it does not perform right.

The Law School tantalizes unprepared students with the promise of a University of Michigan degree and all of the opportunities that it offers. These overmatched students take the bait, only to find that they cannot succeed in the cauldron of competition. . . . Indeed, to cover the tracks of the aestheticists, this cruel farce of racial discrimination must continue — in selection for the Michigan Law Review, see University of Michigan Law School Student Handbook 2002-2003, pp. 39-40 (noting the presence of a "diversity plan" for admission to the review), and in hiring at law firms and for judicial clerkships — until the "beneficiaries" are no longer tolerated. . . .

It is uncontested that each year, the Law School admits a handful of blacks who would be admitted in the absence of racial discrimination. Who can differentiate between those who belong and those who do not? The majority of blacks are admitted to the Law School because of discrimination, and because of this policy all are tarred as undeserving. . . . When blacks take positions in the highest places of government, industry, or academia, it is an open question today whether their skin color played a part in their advancement. The question itself is the stigma — because either racial discrimination did play a role, in which case the person may be deemed "otherwise unqualified," or it did not, in which case asking the question itself unfairly marks those blacks who would succeed without discrimination. Is this what the Court means by "visibly open"?

VII. As the foregoing makes clear, I believe the Court's opinion to be, in most respects, erroneous. I do, however, find two points on which I agree. . . .

I join the Court's opinion insofar as it confirms that . . . the Law School may not discriminate in admissions between similarly situated blacks and Hispanics, or between whites and Asians. This is so because preferring black to Hispanic applicants, for instance, does nothing to further the interest recognized by the majority today. Indeed, the majority describes such racial balancing as "patently unconstitutional."

The Court also holds that racial discrimination in admissions should be given another 25 years before it is deemed no longer narrowly tailored to the Law School's fabricated compelling state interest. While I agree that in 25 years the practices of the Law School will be illegal, they are, for the reasons I have given, illegal now. . . .

For the immediate future, however, the majority has placed its imprimatur on a practice that can only weaken the principle of equality embodied in the Declaration of Independence and the Equal Protection Clause. "Our Constitution is color-blind, and neither knows nor tolerates classes among citizens." Plessy v. Ferguson (Harlan, J., dissenting). It has been nearly 140 years since Frederick Douglass asked the intellectual ancestors of the Law School to "do nothing with us!" and the Nation adopted the Fourteenth Amendment. Now we must wait another 25 years to see this principle of equality vindicated. I therefore respectfully dissent from the remainder of the Court's opinion and the judgment.

GRATZ v. BOLLINGER

539 U.S. 244 (2003)

CHIEF JUSTICE REHNQUIST delivered the opinion of the Court.

We granted certiorari in this case to decide whether "the University of Michigan's use of racial preferences in undergraduate admissions violates the Equal Protection Clause of the Fourteenth Amendment, Title VI of the Civil Rights Act of 1964 (42 U.S.C. §2000d), or 42 U.S.C. §1981." Because we find that the manner in which the University considers the race of applicants in its undergraduate admissions guidelines violates these constitutional and statutory provisions, we reverse that portion of the District Court's decision upholding the guidelines.

I. Petitioners Jennifer Gratz and Patrick Hamacher both applied for admission to the University of Michigan's (University) College of Literature, Science, and the Arts (LSA) as residents of the State of Michigan. Both petitioners are Caucasian. Gratz [was denied admission to the LSA and] enrolled in the University of Michigan at Dearborn, from which she graduated in the spring of 1999. Hamacher applied for admission to the LSA for the fall of 1997 [was denied] and he enrolled at Michigan State University. . . .

Gratz and Hamacher filed a lawsuit in [federal court against the University and its officers, on behalf of a class] of "those individuals who applied for and were not granted admission to the College of Literature, Science and the Arts of the University of Michigan for all academic years from 1995 forward and who are members of those racial or ethnic groups, including Caucasian, that defendants treated less favorably on the basis of race in considering their application for admission."

The University has changed its admissions guidelines a number of times during the period relevant to this litigation, and we summarize the most significant of these changes briefly. The University's Office of Undergraduate Admissions (OUA) oversees the LSA admissions process. In order to promote consistency in the review of the large number of applications received, the OUA uses written guidelines for each academic year. Admissions counselors make admissions decisions in accordance with these guidelines. OUA considers a number of factors in making admissions decisions, including high school grades, standardized test scores, high school quality, curriculum strength, geography, alumni relationships, and leadership. OUA also considers race. During all periods relevant to this litigation, the University has considered African-Americans, Hispanics, and Native Americans to be "underrepresented minorities," and it is undisputed that the University admits "virtually every qualified . . . applicant" from these groups.

During 1995 and 1996, OUA counselors evaluated applications according to grade point average combined with what were referred to as the "SCUGA" factors. These factors included the quality of an applicant's high school (S), the strength of an applicant's high school curriculum (C), an applicant's unusual circumstances (U), an applicant's geographical residence (G), and an applicant's alumni relationships (A). After these scores were combined to produce an applicant's "GPA 2" score, the reviewing admissions counselors referenced a set of "Guidelines" tables, which listed GPA 2 ranges on the vertical axis, and American College Test/Scholastic Aptitude Test (ACT/SAT) scores on the horizontal axis. Each table was divided into cells that included one or more courses of action to be taken, including admit, reject, delay for additional information, or postpone for reconsideration.

In both years, applicants with the same GPA 2 score and ACT/SAT score were subject to different admissions outcomes based upon their racial or ethnic status. For example, as a Caucasian in-state applicant, Gratz's GPA 2 score and ACT score placed her within a cell calling for a postponed decision on her application. An in-state or out-of-state minority applicant with Gratz's scores would have fallen within a cell calling for admission.

In 1997, the University modified its admissions procedure. Specifically, the formula for calculating an applicant's GPA 2 score was restructured to include additional point values under the "U" category in the SCUGA factors. Under this new system, applicants could receive points for underrepresented minority status, socioeconomic disadvantage, or attendance at a high school with a predominantly underrepresented minority population, or underrepresentation in the unit to which the student was applying (for example, men who sought to pursue a career in nursing). Under the 1997 procedures, Hamacher's GPA 2 score and ACT score placed him in a cell on the in-state applicant table calling for postponement of a final admissions decision. An underrepresented minority applicant placed in the same cell would generally have been admitted.

Beginning with the 1998 academic year, the OUA dispensed with the Guidelines tables and the SCUGA point system in favor of a "selection index," on which an applicant could score a maximum of 150 points. This index was divided linearly into ranges generally calling for admissions dispositions as follows: 100-150 (admit); 95-99 (admit or postpone); 90-94 (postpone or admit); 75-89 (delay or postpone); 74 and below (delay or reject).

Each application received points based on high school grade point average, standardized test scores, academic quality of an applicant's high school, strength or weakness of high school curriculum, in-state residency, alumni relationship, personal essay, and personal achievement or leadership. Of particular significance here, under a "miscellaneous" category, an applicant was entitled to 20 points based upon his or her membership in an underrepresented racial or ethnic minority group.

The University explained that the " 'development of the selection index for admissions in 1998 changed only the mechanics, not the substance of how race and ethnicity were considered in admissions.' "

In all application years from 1995 to 1998, the guidelines provided that qualified applicants from underrepresented minority groups be admitted as soon as possible in light of the University's belief that such applicants were more likely to enroll if promptly notified of their admission. Also from 1995 through 1998, the University carefully managed its rolling admissions system to permit consideration of certain applications submitted later in the academic year through the use of "protected seats." Specific groups — including athletes, foreign students, ROTC candidates, and underrepresented minorities — were "protected categories" eligible for these seats. A committee called the Enrollment Working Group (EWG) projected how many applicants from each of these protected categories the University was likely to receive after a given date and then paced admissions decisions to permit full consideration of expected applications from these groups. If this space was not filled by qualified candidates from the designated groups toward the end of the admissions season, it was then used to admit qualified candidates remaining in the applicant pool, including those on the waiting list.

During 1999 and 2000, the OUA used the selection index, under which every applicant from an underrepresented racial or ethnic minority group was awarded 20 points. Starting in 1999, however, the University established an Admissions Review Committee (ARC), to provide an additional level of consideration for some applications. Under the new system, counselors may, in their discretion, "flag" an application for the ARC to review after determining that the applicant (1) is academically prepared to succeed at the University, (2) has achieved a minimum selection index score, and (3) possesses a quality or characteristic important to the University's composition of its freshman class, such as high class rank, unique life experiences, challenges, circumstances, interests or talents, socioeconomic disadvantage, and underrepresented race, ethnicity, or geography. After reviewing "flagged" applications, the ARC determines whether to admit, defer, or deny each applicant. . . .

II. As they have throughout the course of this litigation, petitioners contend that the University's consideration of race in its undergraduate admissions decisions violates . . . the Equal Protection Clause of the Fourteenth Amendment. [Petitioners] argue that even if the University's interest in diversity can constitute a compelling state interest, the District Court erroneously concluded that the University's use of race in its current freshman admissions policy is narrowly tailored to achieve such an interest. Petitioners argue that the guidelines the University began using in 1999 do not "remotely resemble the kind of consideration of race and ethnicity that Justice Powell endorsed in *Bakke*." Respondents reply that . . . their program "hews closely" to both the admissions program described by Justice Powell as well as the Harvard College admissions program that he endorsed. Specifically, respondents contend that the LSA's policy provides the individualized consideration that "Justice Powell considered a hallmark of a constitutionally appropriate admissions program." For the reasons set out below, we do not agree.

It is by now well established that "all racial classifications reviewable under the Equal Protection Clause must be strictly scrutinized." . . . To withstand our strict scrutiny analysis, respondents must demonstrate that the University's use of race in its current admission program employs "narrowly tailored measures that further compelling governmental interests." . . . We find that the University's policy, which automatically distributes 20 points, or one-fifth of the points needed to guarantee admission, to every single "underrepresented minority" applicant solely because of race, is not narrowly tailored to achieve the interest in educational diversity that respondents claim justifies their program. . . .

Justice Powell's opinion in *Bakke* emphasized the importance of considering each particular applicant as an individual, assessing all of the qualities that individual possesses, and in turn, evaluating that individual's ability to contribute to the unique setting of higher education. The admissions program Justice Powell described, however, did not contemplate that any single characteristic automatically ensured a specific and identifiable contribution to a university's diversity. . . . Instead, under the approach Justice Powell described, each characteristic of a particular applicant was to be considered in assessing the applicant's entire application.

The current LSA policy does not provide such individualized consideration. The LSA's policy automatically distributes 20 points to every single applicant from an "underrepresented minority" group, as defined by the University. The only consideration that accompanies this distribution of points is a factual review of an application to determine whether an individual is a member of one of these minority groups. Moreover, unlike Justice Powell's example, where the race of a "particular black applicant" could be considered without being decisive, the LSA's automatic distribution of 20 points has the effect of making "the factor of race . . . decisive" for virtually every minimally qualified underrepresented minority applicant.

Also instructive in our consideration of the LSA's system is the example provided in the description of the Harvard College Admissions Program, which Justice Powell both discussed in, and attached to, his opinion in *Bakke*. The example was included to "illustrate the kind of significance attached to race" under the Harvard College program. It provided as follows:

> The Admissions Committee, with only a few places left to fill, might find itself forced to choose between A, the child of a successful black physician in an academic community with promise of superior academic performance, and B, a black who grew up in an inner-city ghetto of semi-literate parents whose academic achievement was lower but who had demonstrated energy and leadership as well as an apparently abiding interest in black power. If a good number of black students much like A but few like B had already been admitted, the Committee might prefer B; and vice versa. If C, a white student with extraordinary artistic talent, were also seeking one of the remaining places, his unique quality might give him an edge over both A and B. Thus, the critical criteria are often individual qualities or experience *not dependent upon race but sometimes associated with it.* (Emphasis added.)

This example further demonstrates the problematic nature of the LSA's admissions system. Even if student C's "extraordinary artistic talent" rivaled that of Monet or Picasso, the applicant would receive, at most, five points under the LSA's system. At the same time, every single underrepresented minority applicant, including students A and B, would automatically receive 20 points for submitting an application. Clearly, the LSA's system does not offer applicants the individualized selection process described in Harvard's example. Instead of considering how the differing backgrounds, experiences, and characteristics of students A, B, and C might benefit the University, admissions counselors reviewing LSA applications would simply award both A and B 20 points because their applications indicate that they are African-American, and student C would receive up to 5 points for his "extraordinary talent."

Respondents emphasize the fact that the LSA has created the possibility of an applicant's file being flagged for individualized consideration by the ARC. We think that the flagging program only emphasizes the flaws of the University's system as a whole when compared to that described by Justice Powell. Again, students A, B, and C illustrate the point. First, student A would never be flagged. This is because, as the University has conceded, the effect of automatically awarding 20 points is that virtually every qualified underrepresented minority applicant is admitted. Student A, an applicant "with promise of superior academic performance," would certainly fit this description. Thus, the result of the automatic distribution of 20 points is that the University would never consider student A's individual background, experiences, and characteristics to assess his individual "potential contribution to diversity." Instead, every applicant like student A would simply be admitted. It is possible that students B and C would be flagged and considered as individuals. This assumes that student B was not already admitted because of the automatic 20-point distribution, and that student C could muster at least 70 additional points. But the fact that the "review committee can look at the applications individually and ignore the points," once an application is flagged is of little comfort under our strict scrutiny analysis. The record does not reveal precisely how many applications are flagged for this individualized consideration, but it is undisputed that such consideration is the exception and not the rule in the operation of the LSA's admissions program. Additionally, this individualized review is only provided *after* admissions counselors automatically distribute the University's version of a "plus" that makes race a decisive factor for virtually every minimally qualified underrepresented minority applicant.

Respondents contend that "the volume of applications and the presentation of applicant information make it impractical for [LSA] to use the . . . admissions system" upheld by the Court today in *Grutter*. But the fact that the implementation of a program capable of providing individualized consideration might present administrative challenges does not render constitutional an otherwise problematic system. Nothing in Justice Powell's opinion in *Bakke* signaled that a university may employ whatever means it desires to achieve the stated goal of diversity without regard to the limits imposed by our strict scrutiny analysis.

We conclude, therefore, that because the University's use of race in its current freshman admissions policy is not narrowly tailored to achieve respondents' asserted compelling interest in diversity, the admissions policy violates the Equal Protection Clause of the Fourteenth Amendment.[1] We further find that the admissions policy also violates Title VI and 42 U.S.C. §1981. Accordingly, we reverse that portion of the District Court's decision granting respondents summary judgment with respect to liability and remand the case for proceedings consistent with this opinion.

JUSTICE SOUTER, with whom JUSTICE GINSBURG joins, dissenting.

The cases now contain two pointers toward the line between the valid and the unconstitutional in race-conscious admissions schemes. *Grutter* reaffirms the permissibility of individualized consideration of race to achieve a diversity of students, at least where race is not assigned a preordained value in all cases. On the other hand, Justice Powell's opinion in [*Bakke*] rules out a racial quota or set-aside, in which race is the sole fact of eligibility for certain places in a class. Although the freshman admissions system here is subject to argument on the merits, I think it is closer to what *Grutter* approves than to what *Bakke* condemns, and should not be held unconstitutional on the current record.

The record does not describe a system with a quota like the one struck down in *Bakke*, which "insulated" all nonminority candidates from competition from certain seats. The *Bakke* plan "focused *solely* on ethnic diversity" and effectively told nonminority applicants that "no matter how strong their qualifications, quantitative and extracurricular, including their own potential for contribution to educational diversity, they are never afforded the chance to compete with applicants from the preferred groups for the [set-aside] special admissions seats."

The plan here, in contrast, lets all applicants compete for all places and values an applicant's offering for any place not only on grounds of race, but on grades, test scores, strength of high school, quality of course of study, residence, alumni relationships, leadership, personal character, socioeconomic disadvantage, athletic ability, and quality of a personal essay. A nonminority applicant who scores highly in these other categories can readily garner a selection index exceeding that of a minority applicant who gets the 20-point bonus. . . .

The Court nonetheless finds fault with a scheme that "automatically" distributes 20 points to minority applicants because "the only consideration that accompanies

---

1. Justice Ginsburg in her dissent observes that "one can reasonably anticipate . . . that colleges and universities will seek to maintain their minority enrollment . . . whether or not they can do so in full candor through adoption of affirmative action plans of the kind here at issue." She goes on to say that "if honesty is the best policy, surely Michigan's accurately described, fully disclosed College affirmative action program is preferable to achieving similar numbers through winks, nods, and disguises." These observations are remarkable for two reasons. First, they suggest that universities — to whose academic judgment we are told in Grutter v. Bollinger we should defer — will pursue their affirmative-action programs whether or not they violate the United States Constitution. Second, they recommend that these violations should be dealt with, not by requiring the universities to obey the Constitution, but by changing the Constitution so that it conforms to the conduct of the universities.

this distribution of points is a factual review of an application to determine whether an individual is a member of one of these minority groups." The objection goes to the use of points to quantify and compare characteristics, or to the number of points awarded due to race, but on either reading the objection is mistaken.

The very nature of a college's permissible practice of awarding value to racial diversity means that race must be considered in a way that increases some applicants' chances for admission. Since college admission is not left entirely to inarticulate intuition, it is hard to see what is inappropriate in assigning some stated value to a relevant characteristic, whether it be reasoning ability, writing style, running speed, or minority race. Justice Powell's plus factors necessarily are assigned some values. The college simply does by a numbered scale what the law school accomplishes in its "holistic review;" the distinction does not imply that applicants to the undergraduate college are denied individualized consideration or a fair chance to compete on the basis of all the various merits their applications may disclose.

Nor is it possible to say that the 20 points convert race into a decisive factor comparable to reserving minority places as in *Bakke*. Of course we can conceive of a point system in which the "plus" factor given to minority applicants would be so extreme as to guarantee every minority applicant a higher rank than every nonminority applicant in the university's admissions system. But petitioners do not have a convincing argument that the freshman admissions system operates this way. The present record obviously shows that nonminority applicants may achieve higher selection point totals than minority applicants owing to characteristics other than race, and the fact that the university admits "virtually every qualified underrepresented minority applicant" may reflect nothing more than the likelihood that very few qualified minority applicants apply, as well as the possibility that self-selection results in a strong minority applicant pool. It suffices for me, as it did for the District Court, that there are no *Bakke*-like set-asides and that consideration of an applicant's whole spectrum of ability is no more ruled out by giving 20 points for race than by giving the same points for athletic ability or socioeconomic disadvantage.

JUSTICE GINSBURG, with whom JUSTICE SOUTER joins, and with whom JUSTICE BREYER joins as to Part I, dissenting.

I. Educational institutions, the Court acknowledges, are not barred from any and all consideration of race when making admissions decisions. But the Court once again maintains that the same standard of review controls judicial inspection of all official race classifications. This insistence on "consistency" would be fitting were our Nation free of the vestiges of rank discrimination long reinforced by law. But we are not far distant from an overtly discriminatory past, and the effects of centuries of law-sanctioned inequality remain painfully evident in our communities and schools.

In the wake "of a system of racial caste only recently ended" large disparities endure. Unemployment, poverty, and access to health care vary disproportionately by race. Neighborhoods and schools remain racially divided. African-American and

Hispanic children are all too often educated in poverty-stricken and underperforming institutions. Adult African-Americans and Hispanics generally earn less than whites with equivalent levels of education. Equally credentialed job applicants receive different receptions depending on their race. Irrational prejudice is still encountered in real estate markets and consumer transactions. "Bias both conscious and unconscious, reflecting traditional and unexamined habits of thought, keeps up barriers that must come down if equal opportunity and nondiscrimination are ever genuinely to become this country's law and practice."

The Constitution instructs all who act for the government that they may not "deny to any person . . . the equal protection of the laws." In implementing this equality instruction, as I see it, government decisionmakers may properly distinguish between policies of exclusion and inclusion. Actions designed to burden groups long denied full citizenship stature are not sensibly ranked with measures taken to hasten the day when entrenched discrimination and its after effects have been extirpated. Our jurisprudence ranks race a "suspect" category, "not because [race] is inevitably an impermissible classification, but because it is one which usually, to our national shame, has been drawn for the purpose of maintaining racial inequality." But where race is considered "for the purpose of achieving equality" no automatic proscription is in order. For, as insightfully explained, "the Constitution is both color blind and color conscious. To avoid conflict with the equal protection clause, a classification that denies a benefit, causes harm, or imposes a burden must not be based on race. In that sense, the Constitution is color blind. But the Constitution is color conscious to prevent discrimination being perpetuated and to undo the effects of past discrimination."

The mere assertion of a laudable governmental purpose, of course, should not immunize a race-conscious measure from careful judicial inspection. Close review is needed "to ferret out classifications in reality malign, but masquerading as benign," and to "ensure that preferences are not so large as to trammel unduly upon the opportunities of others or interfere too harshly with legitimate expectations of persons in once-preferred groups."

II. Examining in this light the admissions policy employed by the University of Michigan's College of Literature, Science, and the Arts (College) . . . I see no constitutional infirmity. . . . The racial and ethnic groups to which the College accords special consideration (African-Americans, Hispanics, and Native-Americans) historically have been relegated to inferior status by law and social practice; their members continue to experience class-based discrimination to this day. There is no suggestion that the College adopted its current policy in order to limit or decrease enrollment by any particular racial or ethnic group, and no seats are reserved on the basis of race. Nor has there been any demonstration that the College's program unduly constricts admissions opportunities for students who do not receive special consideration based on race. . . .

The stain of generations of racial oppression is still visible in our society, and the determination to hasten its removal remains vital. One can reasonably anticipate, therefore, that colleges and universities will seek to maintain their minority enrollment — and the networks and opportunities thereby opened to minority graduates

— whether or not they can do so in full candor through adoption of affirmative action plans of the kind here at issue. Without recourse to such plans, institutions of higher education may resort to camouflage. For example, schools may encourage applicants to write of their cultural traditions in the essays they submit, or to indicate whether English is their second language. Seeking to improve their chances for admission, applicants may highlight the minority group associations to which they belong, or the Hispanic surnames of their mothers or grandparents. In turn, teachers' recommendations may emphasize who a student is as much as what he or she has accomplished. If honesty is the best policy, surely Michigan's accurately described, fully disclosed College affirmative action program is preferable to achieving similar numbers through winks, nods, and disguises.[2]

NOTES AND PROBLEM

1. *The Meaning of Diversity as a Compelling Interest.* What is meant by diversity or, more precisely, what kind of diversity qualifies as a compelling interest? Is it a variety of socio-economic backgrounds, interests, life experiences, ethnicity, and viewpoints? Is it simply racial diversity? Is it limited to inclusion of specific historically disadvantaged racial minorities? If diversity means racial diversity, whether broadly or narrowly conceived, which of the following statements better captures the essence of the Court's decisions in *Grutter* and *Gratz*?

(a) Under the Court's equal protection jurisprudence the use of race is presumptively void, but in public university admissions the presence of multiple racial groups in the student body is a compelling interest that can only be achieved by using race; thus, racial discrimination in public university admissions is justified and constitutionally valid so long as such discrimination is practiced subjectively (and thus obscured from view) rather than objectively (and thus open to public scrutiny).

(b) Under the Court's equal protection jurisprudence the use of race is presumptively void, but in public university admissions the presence of multiple racial groups in the student body is a compelling interest that can only be achieved by using race and courts will defer to university administrators regarding the method of racial discrimination that is needed to achieve that objective unless the chosen method permits admissions officers to avoid individualized assessment of the importance of race to the particular admission decision.

2. *The Meaning of Narrow Tailoring.* What satisfies the requirement of narrow tailoring? Is individualized assessment of the importance of race to each particular admission decision satisfactory? If so, suppose the University of Michigan changes its undergraduate admissions system to require that each application be read and a range of points assigned by the reader for such things as grades, test scores, activi-

---

2. Contrary to the Court's contention, I do not suggest "changing the Constitution so that it conforms to the conduct of the universities." In my view, the Constitution, properly interpreted, permits government officials to respond openly to the continuing importance of race. Among constructionally permissible options, those that candidly disclose their consideration of race seem to me preferable to those that conceal it.

ties, race, recommendations, and personal essay. Instead of the automatic 20 point boost given to "underrepresented racial minorities" under the plan invalidated in *Gratz* the new system permits a reader to grant zero to 20 points for race. Does this hypothetical admissions system meet the narrow tailoring requirement? If so, would your conclusion remain the same if it turned out that 95% of all "underrepresented" racial minority applicants received 20 points? What if only 65% of such applicants received 20 points?

3. *Problem.* You are the admissions director of a selective public university. Your university receives about 30,000 applications per year for 3,000 spaces in the entering freshman class. Your budget does not permit hiring enough staff to conduct detailed individualized reading and appraisal of every application, and the university President has told you that there is a "less than zero" chance that your budget will be increased. Nevertheless, the President has informed you that a diverse student body is "absolutely critical," and has made it clear that while diversity may mean a number of things it must include "significant" representation of historically disadvantaged minorities, particularly Americans of African, Hispanic, or aboriginal ancestry. The President has also told you that she is "not interested in litigation," and has instructed you to devise an admissions policy that will comply with current standards of constitutional law. Do so.

E. Intermediate Scrutiny: Sex and Illegitimacy

Page 795: Insert as a second note following the VMI *case, immediately before the Note on Illegitimate Children:*

"Real" Differences, Stereotypes, and the Standard of Review after **VMI.** In Nguyen v. Immigration and Naturalization Service, 533 U.S. 53 (2001), the Supreme Court upheld provisions of federal citizenship law that confer American citizenship automatically on a child born overseas outside marriage to a U.S. citizen mother and a noncitizen father but that require U.S. citizen fathers of such children born to a noncitizen mother to take affirmative steps to acknowledge their fatherhood in order for the child to obtain American citizenship. Under 8 U.S.C. §1409, a child born abroad and out of wedlock acquires at birth the nationality status of a citizen mother who meets a specified residency requirement, but when the father is the citizen parent, §1409(a)(4) makes American citizenship dependent on the father taking one of three actions before the child turns 18: legitimization, a declaration of paternity under oath by the father, or a court order of paternity. In addition, §1409(a)(1) required "clear and convincing" evidence of any child's status as the child of an American citizen, whether the citizen be father or mother.

The Court applied intermediate scrutiny due to the differential treatment based on the sex of the parent but concluded that the scheme did not violate equal protection because it served important governmental objectives and the discriminatory means employed were substantially related to the achievement of those objectives. The Court cited United States v. Virginia, p. 781, for this standard of review. Writing for the Court, Justice Kennedy concluded that the sex classification at issue was substantially related to two important government objectives:

> The first governmental interest to be served is the importance of assuring that a biological parent-child relationship exists. In the case of the mother, the relation is verifiable from the birth itself [but in] the case of the father, the uncontestable fact is that he need not be present at the birth [and if] he is present [that] circumstance is not incontrovertible proof of fatherhood. Fathers and mothers are not similarly situated with regard to the proof of biological parenthood. . . . Just as neutral terms can mask discrimination that is unlawful, gender specific terms can mark a permissible distinction. The equal protection question is whether the distinction is lawful. Here, the use of gender specific terms takes into account a biological difference between the parents. The differential treatment is inherent in a sensible statutory scheme, given the unique relationship of the mother to the event of birth.
>
> The second important governmental interest furthered in a substantial manner by [the scheme is ensuring] that the child and the citizen parent have some demonstrated opportunity or potential to develop [a] relationship that . . . consists of the real, everyday ties that provide a connection between child and citizen parent and, in turn, the United States. In the case of a citizen mother and a child born overseas, the opportunity for a meaningful relationship between citizen parent and child inheres in the very event of birth, an event so often critical to our constitutional and statutory understandings of citizenship. The mother knows that the child is in being and is hers and has an initial point of contact with him. There is at least an opportunity for mother and child to develop a real, meaningful relationship. The same opportunity does not result from the event of birth, as a matter of biological inevitability, in the case of the unwed father. [It] is not always certain that a father will know that a child was conceived, nor is it always clear that even the mother will be sure of the father's identity. . . . Principles of equal protection do not require Congress to ignore this reality. . . .
>
> Petitioners [argue] that, rather than fulfilling an important governmental interest, §1409 merely embodies a gender-based stereotype. [On the contrary], §1409 addresses an undeniable difference in the circumstance of the parents at the time a child is born, [and that] difference does not result from some stereotype, defined as a frame of mind resulting from irrational or uncritical analysis.

The Court concluded that the differential treatment was substantially related to the two identified important objectives:

> First, it should be unsurprising that Congress decided to require that an opportunity for a parent-child relationship occur during the formative years of the child's minority. . . . Second, petitioners argue that §1409(a)(4) is not effective [because] although a mother will know of her child's birth, "knowledge that one is a parent, no matter how it is acquired, does not guarantee a relationship with one's child." They thus maintain that the imposition of the additional requirements of §1409(a)(4) only on the children of citizen fathers must reflect a stereotype that women are more likely than men to actually establish a relationship with their children.

> This line of argument misconceives the nature of both the governmental interest at issue and the manner in which we examine statutes alleged to violate equal protection. As to the former, . . . Congress enacted an easily administered scheme to promote the . . . substantial interest of ensuring at least an *opportunity* for a parent-child relationship to develop [emphasis added].
>
> Even if one conceives of the interest Congress pursues as the establishment of a real, practical relationship of considerable substance between parent and child in every case, as opposed simply to ensuring the potential for the relationship to begin, petitioners' misconception of the nature of the equal protection inquiry is fatal to their argument. . . . None of our gender-based classification equal protection cases have required that the statute under consideration must be capable of achieving its ultimate objective in every instance. In this difficult context of conferring citizenship on vast numbers of persons, the means adopted by Congress are in substantial furtherance of important governmental objectives. The fit between the means and the important end is "exceedingly persuasive." [*VMI*].

JUSTICE O'CONNOR, joined by JUSTICES SOUTER, GINSBURG, and BREYER dissented:

> The Court recites the governing substantive standard for heightened scrutiny of sex-based classifications but departs from the guidance of our precedents concerning such classifications in several ways. For example, the majority . . . fails adequately to inquire into the actual purposes of §1409(a)(4). . . . The majority also . . . casually dismisses the relevance of available sex-neutral alternatives. [And] the fit between the means and ends of §1409(a)(4) is far too attenuated for the provision to survive heightened scrutiny. In all, the majority opinion represents far less than the rigorous application of heightened scrutiny that our precedents require.

[The dissent argued that the asserted ends could be adequately achieved by reliance on modern DNA testing rather than the three means of establishing paternity specified in §1409(a)(4). With respect to the second important interest identified by the Court, the dissent thought that the Court had failed]

> to demonstrate that this was Congress' actual purpose in enacting §1409(a)(4). The majority's focus on "some demonstrated opportunity or potential to develop . . . real, everyday ties," in fact appears to be the type of hypothesized rationale that is insufficient under heightened scrutiny. [But assuming] that Congress was actually concerned about ensuring a "demonstrated opportunity" for a relationship, it is questionable whether such an opportunity qualifies as an "important" governmental interest apart from the existence of an actual relationship. [It] is difficult to see how, in this citizenship-conferral context, anyone profits from a "demonstrated opportunity" for a relationship in the absence of the fruition of an actual tie. [It] is the actual relationship that does all the work in rendering appropriate a grant of citizenship, regardless of when and how the opportunity for that relationship arose. . . .
>
> The claim that §1409(a)(4) substantially relates to the achievement of the goal of a "real, practical relationship" [finds] support not in biological differences but instead in a stereotype — *i.e.*, "the generalization that mothers are significantly more likely than fathers . . . to develop caring relationships with their children." [In] denying [that]

§1409(a)(4) rests on stereotypes, the majority articulates a misshapen notion of "stereotype." [The] majority asserts that a "stereotype" is "defined as a frame of mind resulting from irrational or uncritical analysis," [but this] Court has long recognized that an impermissible stereotype may enjoy empirical support and thus be in a sense "rational." [J. E. B. v. Alabama, p. 780]. Indeed, the stereotypes that underlie a sex-based classification "may hold true for many, even most, individuals." But in numerous cases where a measure of truth has inhered in the generalization, "the Court has rejected official actions that classify unnecessarily and overbroadly by gender when more accurate and impartial functional lines can be drawn." [The] hallmark of a stereotypical sex-based classification under this Court's precedents is not whether the classification is insulting, but whether it "relies upon the simplistic, outdated assumption that gender could be used as a 'proxy for other, more germane bases of classification.' "

F. Fundamental Rights: Strict Scrutiny Redux

2. Voting: Denial and Dilution

Page 814: Insert the following immediately before subsection F.3:

BUSH v. GORE

531 U.S. 98 (2000)

PER CURIAM. [The Court held that the Florida Supreme Court's ordered manual recount of all ballots cast in the Florida 2000 presidential election that had failed to register a choice for President in the machine tally (so-called undervotes) violated equal protection.]

The individual citizen has no federal constitutional right to vote for electors for the President of the United States unless and until the state legislature chooses a statewide election as the means to implement its power to appoint members of the Electoral College. U.S. Const., Art. II, §1. This is the source for the statement in McPherson v. Blacker, 146 U.S. 1 (1892), that the State legislature's power to select the manner for appointing electors is plenary; it may, if it so chooses, select the electors itself, which indeed was the manner used by State legislatures in several States for many years after the Framing of our Constitution. History has now favored the voter, and in each of the several States the citizens themselves vote for Presidential electors. When the state legislature vests the right to vote for President in its people, the right to vote as the legislature has prescribed is fundamental; and one source of its fundamental nature lies in the equal weight accorded to each vote and the equal dignity owed to each voter. The State, of course, after granting the franchise in the special context of Article II, can take back the power to appoint electors. [But the] right to vote is protected in more than the initial allocation of the franchise. Equal protection applies as well to the manner of its exercise. Having once granted the right to vote on equal terms, the State may not, by later arbitrary and disparate treatment, value one person's vote over that of another. [Harper v. Virginia Bd. of Elections, p. 808] . . . It must be remembered that "the right of suffrage can be denied by a debasement or dilution of the weight of a citizen's vote just as effectively as by wholly prohibiting the free exercise of the franchise." Reynolds v. Sims, [p. 805].

There is no difference between the two sides of the present controversy on these basic propositions. . . . The question before us, however, is whether the recount procedures the Florida Supreme Court has adopted are consistent with its obligation to avoid arbitrary and disparate treatment of the members of its electorate.

Much of the controversy seems to revolve around ballot cards designed to be perforated by a stylus but which, either through error or deliberate omission, have not been perforated with sufficient precision for a machine to count them. In some cases a piece of the card — a chad — is hanging, say by two corners. In other cases there is no separation at all, just an indentation. The Florida Supreme Court has ordered that the intent of the voter be discerned from such ballots, [but the] recount mechanisms implemented in response to [its] decisions [do] not satisfy the minimum requirement for non-arbitrary treatment of voters necessary to secure the fundamental right. Florida's basic command for the count of legally cast votes is to consider the "intent of the voter." This is unobjectionable as an abstract proposition and a starting principle. The problem inheres in the absence of specific standards to ensure its equal application. The formulation of uniform rules to determine intent based on these recurring circumstances is practicable and, we conclude, necessary.

The law does not refrain from searching for the intent of the actor in a multitude of circumstances; and in some cases the general command to ascertain intent is not susceptible to much further refinement. In this instance, however, the question is not whether to believe a witness but how to interpret the marks or holes or scratches on an inanimate object, a piece of cardboard or paper which, it is said, might not have registered as a vote during the machine count. The factfinder confronts a thing, not a person. The search for intent can be confined by specific rules designed to ensure uniform treatment.

The want of those rules here has led to unequal evaluation of ballots in various respects. As seems to have been acknowledged at oral argument, the standards for accepting or rejecting contested ballots might vary not only from county to county but indeed within a single county from one recount team to another. The record provides some examples. A monitor in Miami-Dade County testified at trial that he observed that three members of the county canvassing board applied different standards in defining a legal vote. And testimony at trial also revealed that at least one county changed its evaluative standards during the counting process. Palm Beach County, for example, began the process with a 1990 guideline which precluded counting completely attached chads, switched to a rule that considered a vote to be legal if any light could be seen through a chad, changed back to the 1990 rule, and then abandoned any pretense of a *per se* rule, only to have a court order that the county consider dimpled chads legal. This is not a process with sufficient guarantees of equal treatment. . . .

The [Florida] Supreme Court ratified this uneven treatment. It mandated that the recount totals from two counties, Miami-Dade and Palm Beach, be included in the certified total. The court also appeared to hold *sub silentio* that the recount totals from Broward County, which were not completed until after the original November 14 certification by the Secretary of State, were to be considered part of the new certified vote totals even though the county certification was not contested by Vice President Gore. Yet each of the counties used varying standards to determine what was a legal vote. Broward County used a more forgiving standard than Palm Beach County, and uncovered almost three times as many new votes, a result markedly disproportionate to the difference in population between the counties.

In addition, the recounts in these three counties were not limited to so-called undervotes but extended to all of the ballots. The distinction has real consequences. A manual recount of all ballots identifies not only those ballots which show no vote but also those which contain more than one, the so-called overvotes. Neither category will be counted by the machine. This is not a trivial concern. At oral argument, respondents estimated there are as many as 110,000 overvotes statewide. As a result, the citizen whose ballot was not read by a machine because he failed to vote for a candidate in a way readable by a machine may still have his vote counted in a manual recount; on the other hand, the citizen who marks two candidates in a way discernable by the machine will not have the same opportunity to have his vote count, even if a manual examination of the ballot would reveal the requisite indicia of intent. Furthermore, the citizen who marks two candidates, only one of which is discernable by the machine, will have his vote counted even though it should have been read as an invalid ballot. . . .

That brings the analysis to yet a further equal protection problem. The votes certified by the court included a partial total from one county, Miami-Dade. The Florida Supreme Court's decision thus gives no assurance that the recounts included in a final certification must be complete. Indeed, it is respondent's submission that it would be consistent with the rules of the recount procedures to include whatever partial counts are done by the time of final certification, and we interpret the Florida Supreme Court's decision to permit this. This accommodation no doubt results from the truncated contest period established by the Florida Supreme Court [at] respondents' own urging. The press of time does not diminish the constitutional concern. A desire for speed is not a general excuse for ignoring equal protection guarantees.

In addition to these difficulties the actual process by which the votes were to be counted under the Florida Supreme Court's decision raises further concerns. That order did not specify who would recount the ballots. The county canvassing boards were forced to pull together ad hoc teams comprised of judges [who] had no previous training in handling and interpreting ballots. Furthermore, while others were permitted to observe, they were prohibited from objecting during the recount.

The recount process, in its features here described, is inconsistent with the minimum procedures necessary to protect the fundamental right of each voter in the special instance of a statewide recount under the authority of a single state judicial officer. Our consideration is limited to the present circumstances, for the problem of equal protection in election processes generally presents many complexities. The question before the Court is not whether local entities, in the exercise of their expertise, may develop different systems for implementing elections. Instead, we are presented with a situation where a state court with the power to assure uniformity has ordered a statewide recount with minimal procedural safeguards. When a court orders a statewide remedy, there must be at least some assurance that the rudimentary requirements of equal treatment and fundamental fairness are satisfied.

JUSTICE STEVENS, joined by JUSTICES GINSBURG and BREYER, dissenting.

The failure of the Florida Supreme Court to specify in detail the precise manner in which the "intent of the voter" is to be determined [does not rise] to the level of a constitutional violation. [While] the use of differing substandards for determining voter intent in different counties employing similar voting systems may raise serious concerns, [those] concerns are alleviated — if not eliminated — by the fact that a single impartial magistrate will ultimately adjudicate all objections arising from the recount process. [If] it were otherwise, Florida's decision to leave to each county the determination of what balloting system to employ — despite enormous differences in accuracy — might run afoul of equal protection. So, too, might the similar decisions of the vast majority of state legislatures to delegate to local authorities certain decisions with respect to voting systems and ballot design.

JUSTICE SOUTER, joined by JUSTICE BREYER, dissenting.

Petitioners have raised an equal protection claim [in] the charge that unjustifiably disparate standards are applied in different electoral jurisdictions to otherwise identical facts. It is true that the Equal Protection Clause does not forbid the use of a variety of voting mechanisms within a jurisdiction, even though different mechanisms will have different levels of effectiveness in recording voters' intentions; local variety can be justified by concerns about cost, the potential value of innovation, and so on. But evidence in the record here suggests that a different order of disparity obtains under rules for determining a voter's intent that have been applied (and could continue to be applied) to identical types of ballots used in identical brands of machines and exhibiting identical physical characteristics (such as "hanging" or "dimpled" chads). . . . I can conceive of no legitimate state interest served by these differing treatments of the expressions of voters' fundamental rights. The differences appear wholly arbitrary. . . . I would therefore remand the case to the courts of Florida with instructions to establish uniform standards for evaluating the several types of ballots that have prompted differing treatments, to be applied within and among counties when passing on such identical ballots in any further recounting (or successive recounting) that the courts might order.

NOTE

The Scope of Bush v. Gore*'s Equal Protection.* The Court expressly indicated that its ruling was confined to "the present circumstances, . . . where a state court with the power to assure uniformity has ordered a statewide recount with minimal procedural safeguards" and disclaimed any applicability of the decision to the question of "whether local entities, in the exercise of their expertise, may develop different systems for implementing elections." But can it be so neatly cabined? *Harper* and its kin dealt with formal obstacles to voting (e.g., the poll tax), *Reynolds* and its progeny dealt with structural defects in voting (e.g., ill apportioned electoral districts), and Bush v. Gore deals with the actual mechanism of counting the ballots. Is this latest extension of equal protection workable? What standard can be used to detect when various methods of ascertaining the electorate's preferences are sufficiently disparate to violate equal protection? What differences in such methods are relevant to that inquiry? Are differences in accuracy enough? What if one method produces significantly more spoiled ballots than another method? What does it mean in this context to have "equally weighted" votes?

Is there a meaningful difference between disparities produced by differing mechanical or electronic methods of tabulation and disparities produced by human judgment in recounts, especially when those human actors know in advance the consequences of their judgments? Is it fair to say that there is less reason to be troubled about disparate machine counts than disparate human counts? If so, does your answer change if there is proof that the disparate machine counts were produced by intentional actions of election officials that were designed to produce a partisan advantage?

3. Voting: Gerrymanders

Page 816: Insert the following as the first note in the "NOTES" after Davis v. Bandemer:

The Uncertain Future of *Bandemer*. In Vieth v. Jubelirer, 124 S. Ct. 1769 (2004), a plurality of four justices would have overturned *Bandemer* and declared the question of the validity of political gerrymanders to be a non-justiciable political question. Following the 2000 census, Pennsylvania's legislature, dominated by Republicans, adopted a congressional redistricting plan, which was attacked as a violation of equal protection because the plan "ignored all traditional redistricting criteria . . . solely for the sake of partisan advantage." Justice Scalia, joined by Chief Justice Rehnquist and Justices O'Connor and Thomas, concluded that there are "no judicially discernible and manageable standards for adjudicating political gerrymandering claims."

First, the plurality concluded that *Bandemer*'s standard was neither discernible nor manageable. Although "intentional discrimination against an identifiable political group" is easy enough to prove, the plurality thought that judicial assessment of proof of "an actual discriminatory effect on that group" was well-nigh impossible. The plurality noted that "the legacy of [this] test is one long record of puzzlement and consternation." Second, the plurality rejected a proposed test focusing on "predominant intent" and specific effect. The problem with the "predominant intent" prong of the test was the near impossibility of proving that "partisan advantage was the predominant motivation" for the district boundaries. The "effects prong" of the proposed test would have required proof of (1) systematic "packing"[1] and "cracking"[2] of "the rival party's voters," and (2) a totality of circumstances that establishes that the gerrymander " 'thwart[s] the plaintiffs' ability to translate a majority of votes into a majority of seats.' " The plurality thought this prong was neither discernible nor manageable. First, because "[p]olitical affiliation is not an immutable characteristic, [it is] impossible to assess the effects of partisan gerrymandering, to fashion a standard for evaluating a violation, and finally to craft a remedy."[3] Second, the proposed effects standard was not "judicially discernible in the sense of being relevant to some constitutional violation" because it "rests upon the principle that [political] groups have a right to proportional representation, [and] the Constitution contains no such principle." Finally, the proposed standard was "not judicially manageable" because it is virtually impossible to "identify a majority party" with certainty,[4] and even more difficult to assure that the "majority" party wins a majority of seats, if only because voters remain maddeningly independent of party affiliation when it comes time to cast ballots.

Justice Kennedy concurred in the judgment, concluding that the claim presented in *Vieth* was non-justiciable but was unwilling to conclude that all such claims are non-justiciable: "I would not foreclose all possibility of judicial relief if some limited and precise rationale were found to correct an established violation of the Constitution in some redistricting cases." Justice Kennedy saw two problems with judicial resolution of political gerrymander claims: " the lack of comprehensive and neutral principles for drawing electoral boundaries" and "the absence of rules to limit and confine judicial intervention." The first problem results from the fact there is no commonly agreed "substantive definition of fairness in districting . . . . A de-

---

1. "Packing" is the practice of drawing district boundaries to include supermajorities of a given party's voters.

2. "Cracking" is the practice of drawing district boundaries to split a party's voters among a number of districts, in order to leave that party's voters in the minority in all the districts to which they have been distributed.

3. The plurality cited, as a "delicious illustration" of its conclusion, a case in which a trial judge had concluded that North Carolina's system of electing judges "had resulted in Republican candidates experiencing a consistent and pervasive lack of success and exclusion from the electoral process as a whole and that these effects were likely to continue unabated into the future." Five days later, every Republican candidate for superior court judge in North Carolina was victorious.

4. In Pennsylvania in 2000 Democratic candidates received more votes for President and auditor general and Republicans garnered more votes for United States senator, attorney general, and treasurer. Or consider Massachusetts, in which a succession of Republican governors have presided along with a solidly Democratic legislature and a monolithically Democratic congressional delegation.

termination that a gerrymander violates the law must rest on . . . a conclusion that the [political] classifications, though generally permissible, were applied in an invidious manner or in a way unrelated to any legitimate legislative objective, [and the lack] of any agreed upon model of fair and effective representation makes this analysis difficult to pursue." As to the second problem, Justice Kennedy thought that "we have no basis on which to define clear, manageable, and politically neutral standards for measuring the particular burden a given partisan classification imposes on representational rights." However, Justice Kennedy thought that simply because no judicially discernible and manageable

> standard has emerged in this case should not be taken to prove that none will emerge in the future. . . . The First Amendment may be the more relevant constitutional provision in future cases that allege unconstitutional partisan gerrymandering [because] these allegations involve the First Amendment interest of not burdening or penalizing citizens because of their participation in the electoral process, their voting history, their association with a political party, or their expression of political views. . . . First Amendment concerns arise where a State enacts a law that has the purpose and effect of subjecting a group of voters or their party to disfavored treatment by reason of their views. In the context of partisan gerrymandering, that means that First Amendment concerns arise where an apportionment has the purpose and effect of burdening a group of voters' representational rights. . . . Of course, all this depends first on courts' having available a manageable standard by which to measure the effect of the apportionment and so to conclude that the State did impose a burden or restriction on the rights of a party's voters.

Justice Stevens concurred in the judgment on standing grounds, but noted his belief that political gerrymandering claims at the individual district level are justiciable. He likened political gerrymanders to racial gerrymanders, an analogy disputed by Justice Scalia: "[S]etting out to segregate voters by race is unlawful[;] setting out to segregate them by political affiliation is lawful . . . . A purpose to discriminate on the basis of race receives the strictest scrutiny under the Equal Protection Clause, while a similar purpose to discriminate on the basis of politics does not."

Justice Souter, joined by Justice Ginsburg, dissented, concluding that the case was justiciable and proposing a new, complicated, multi-factor test to assess the substance of a political gerrymander claim. The point of the proposed test would be to identify such an "extremity of unfairness" in gerrymandering that equal protection is violated, a goal that the plurality derided as "utterly unhelpful" because it does not illuminate "the precise constitutional deprivation [the] test is designed to identify and prevent."

Justice Breyer also dissented, contending that statewide political gerrymanders are justiciable when "the *unjustified* use of political factors . . . entrench a minority in power. By entrenchment I mean a situation in which a party that enjoys only minority support among the populace has nonetheless contrived to take, and hold, legislative power. By *unjustified* entrenchment I mean that the minority's hold on power is purely the result of partisan manipulation and not other factors." The plurality tartly dismissed this approach by noting that it requires the judiciary to "assess whether a group (somehow defined) has achieved a level of political power (somehow defined) commensurate with that to which they would be entitled absent *unjustified* political machinations (whatever that means)."

Page 823: Insert as note 3 following Shaw v. Reno *and immediately before subsection F.4:*

3. A Change in Direction? Following Shaw v. Hunt, North Carolina again redrew the boundaries of its Twelfth Congressional District and a federal district court concluded, in a summary judgment, that the new boundaries had again been created with racial considerations dominating all others. In Hunt v. Cromartie (Hunt I), 526 U.S. 541 (1999), the Court reversed, finding that there was a genuine issue of material fact whether the boundaries were drawn with an impermissible race-based objective or to accomplish the constitutionally acceptable objective of creating a safe Democratic seat. On remand the district court ruled, after trial, that the boundaries were drawn with racial considerations foremost, relying on four findings: the district's shape, its splitting of towns and counties, its heavily African-American voting population, and the legislative intention to draw the boundaries by collecting precincts with a high racial, rather than political, identification. In Hunt v. Cromartie (*Hunt II*), 532 U.S. 234 (2001), the Court reversed, ruling that these findings were clearly erroneous. Justice Breyer wrote for a five-justice majority that included Justices Stevens, O'Connor, Souter, and Ginsburg:

> The issue in this case is evidentiary. We must determine whether there is adequate support for the District Court's . . . ultimate finding that the legislature's motive was predominantly racial, not political. [The] evidence taken together [does] not show that racial considerations predominated in the drawing of District 12's boundaries . . . because race in this case correlates closely with political behavior. The basic question is whether the legislature drew District 12's boundaries because of race *rather than* because of political behavior. [Given] the fact that the party attacking the legislature's decision bears the burden of proving that racial considerations are "dominant and controlling," given the "demanding" nature of that burden of proof, and given the sensitivity, the "extraordinary caution," that district courts must show to avoid treading upon legislative prerogatives, the attacking party has not successfully shown that race, rather than politics, predominantly accounts for the result. [Where] majority-minority districts (or the approximate equivalent) are at issue and where racial identification correlates highly with political affiliation, the party attacking the legislatively drawn boundaries must show at the least that the legislature could have achieved its legitimate political objectives in alternative ways that are comparably consistent with traditional districting principles. That party must also show that those districting alternatives would have brought about significantly greater racial balance. Appellees failed to make any such showing here.

Justice Thomas, joined by Chief Justice Rehnquist and Justices Scalia and Kennedy, dissented. They argued that the standard of review employed by the Court was in fact stricter than "clear error" review and that such strict review was neither warranted by precedent or the circumstances of the case. On the merits, and applying what the dissenters said was a "clear error" standard, Justice Thomas concluded that the District Court had not erred: "[R]acial gerrymandering offends the Constitution whether the motivation is malicious or benign. It is not a defense that the legislature merely may have drawn the district based on the stereotype that blacks are reliable Democratic voters."

Does *Hunt II* suggest that although the underlying constitutional standards have not changed, their application in terms of evidentiary burdens of proof may prove to be more lenient toward the creation of "majority-minority" districts? On the other hand, if Justice Thomas is correct to say that the Constitution is offended when legislatures indulge in the assumption that race is a proxy for political preferences, must legislatures as a practical matter do more than lump black voters together and claim that the reason was to create a Democratic district?

Chapter 9

Free Expression of Ideas

B. Content-Based Regulation of Speech

1. Incitement of Immediate Crime

Page 876: Insert the following immediately before subsection B.2:

d. The Related Problem of True Threats

As suggested in the notes following *Brandenburg*, the problem of a true threat, in which the speaker threatens to commit criminal harm to another, is a variant of criminal incitement, in which the speaker urges others to commit criminal acts. In *Watts* the Court used the context of the remarks to distinguish between an unprotected true threat and protected political hyperbole. The Court has returned to the problem of true threats in Virginia v. Black, 538 U.S. 343 (2003), discussed following R.A.V. v. St. Paul and Wisconsin v. Mitchell, because the specific form in which the putative threat was manifested — a burning cross — involves issues of hate speech and symbolic conduct that are also presented in those cases.

In Virginia v. Black, the Court said that true threats "encompass those statements where the speaker means to communicate a serious expression of an intent to commit an act of unlawful violence to a particular individual or group of individuals." It is not, however, always easy to separate the unprotected true threat from protected, albeit uncivil, speech. Nor is it entirely clear what the speaker must intend. In Virginia v. Black, the Court noted that the "speaker need not intend to carry out the threat," so long as the speaker intends to place "the victim in fear of bodily harm or death." This follows, said the Court, from the fact that "a prohibition on true threats 'protects individuals from the fear of violence' and 'from the disruption that fear engenders,' in addition to protecting people 'from the possibility that the threatened violence will occur.' "

A year prior to Virginia v. Black, the Ninth Circuit decided Planned Parenthood of the Columbia/Willamette, Inc. v. American Coalition of Life Activists, 290 F.3d 1058 (9th Cir. 2002). The American Coalition of Life Activists (ACLA), an anti-abortion group, created and distributed posters bearing the names and addresses of the plaintiff physicians and identifying them as abortion providers. The posters proclaimed that the physicians were "guilty" of "crimes against humanity." ACLA also provided information to the operator of an Internet website, the "Nuremberg Files," which condemned abortion as akin to the Nazi war crimes and listed names of physicians and others who provide or support abortion. The posters contained no explicit threats against the physicians, but the physicians knew that similar publicity had preceded murders and clinic violence in the past. Specifically, three other "wanted" posters displaying the names and addresses of physicians providing abortions (made and distributed by unknown third parties, *not* ACLA) had preceded the murders of the three physicians. ACLA thus stripped the physician plaintiffs of their anonymity and "gave violent anti-abortion activists the information to find them."

The physicians brought suit in federal court under the Freedom of Access to Clinics Entrances Act (FACE), 18 U.S.C. §248, which gives aggrieved persons a right of action against whoever by "threat of force . . . intentionally . . . intimidates . . . any person because that person is or has been . . . providing reproductive health services." A jury awarded damages and the trial court permanently enjoined the defendants from threatening, with the specific intent to do so, any of the plaintiffs in violation of FACE. A panel of the Court of Appeals reversed this judgment on free speech grounds, but the Court of Appeals, *en banc*, reinstated the judgment (except for punitive damages).

Judge Rymer, writing for the majority *en banc*, concluded that a true threat occurs when "a reasonable person would foresee that the statement would be interpreted by those to whom the maker communicates the statement as a serious expression of intent to harm or assault." Judge Rymer added that "[i]t is not necessary that the defendant intend to, or be able to carry out his threat; the only intent requirement for a true threat is that the defendant intentionally or knowingly communicate the threat." The majority concluded that the posters constituted a threat because of the "poster pattern — poster followed by murder." The majority conceded that "the language itself is not what is threatening"; rather, threat inhered in the fact that ACLA knew the pattern of "poster followed by murder," knew that such posters "were intimidating and caused fear of serious harm to those named on them," and published them anyway. While the posters were "publicly distributed," they were "personally targeted."

> [No one] participating in selecting these particular abortion providers for such a poster or publishing it could possibly believe anything other than that each would be seriously worried about being next in line to be shot and killed. And they were seriously worried. As a direct result, [the] physicians wore bullet-proof vests and took other extraordinary security measures to protect themselves and their families. [This] fear did not simply happen; ACLA intended to intimidate them from doing what they do.

Judge Reinhardt dissented because "the majority rejects the concept that speech made in a political forum on issues of public concern warrants heightened scrutiny.

. . . It is a fundamental tenet of First Amendment jurisprudence that political speech in a public arena is different from purely private speech directed at an individual."

Judge Kozinski also dissented:

> Where the speaker is engaged in public political speech, the public statements themselves cannot be the sole proof that they were true threats, unless the speech directly threatens actual injury to identifiable individuals. Absent such an unmistakable, specific threat, there must be evidence *aside from the political statements themselves* showing that the public speaker would himself or in conspiracy with others inflict unlawful harm. The majority cites not a scintilla of evidence — other than the posters themselves — that plaintiffs or someone associated with them would carry out the threatened harm. Given this lack of evidence, the posters can be viewed, at most, as a call to arms for *other* abortion protesters to harm plaintiffs. However, the Supreme Court made it clear that under *Brandenburg*, encouragement or even advocacy of violence is protected by the First Amendment. . . .

Judge Berzon authored a third dissent, in which she attempted to devise "standards that, like the constitutional defamation standards that vary with the strength of the protection of the communication, rely not on a unitary 'true threats' standard . . . but on considerations that lessen the danger of mistaken court verdicts and resulting self-censorship to a greater or lesser degree depending upon the nature of the speech in question and the role of speech of that nature in the scheme of the First Amendment." Judge Berzon thought that two criteria were critical: "the public nature of the presentation and content addressing a public issue." Thus, she fashioned a test "for proscribable threats in the public protest context" that would require that the speaker "subjectively intended the specific victims to understand the communication as an unequivocal threat that the speaker or his agents or coconspirators would physically harm them." She noted that the subjective intent requirement "comports with Supreme Court precedent," such as *Brandenburg* [p. 872], *Watts* [p. 875], and *Hess* [p. 874]. "The First Amendment protects advocacy statements that are likely to produce imminent violent action, so long as the statements are not directed at producing such action. To do otherwise would be to endanger the First Amendment protection accorded advocacy of political change by holding speakers responsible for an impact they did not intend." Judge Berzon noted that " 'unequivocal' means . . . unambiguous, given the context. As such, the requirement is essentially a heightened burden of proof, requiring that a threatening meaning be clearly and convincingly apparent." She would also dispense with any requirement that the threatened injury be immediate or imminent because "the harms of apprehension and disruption" are inflicted regardless of whether the threat "proves bluster or not and whether the injury is threatened to be immediate or delayed."

Of the various opinions in *American Coalition of Life Activists*, which is closest to applicable Supreme Court precedent, specifically *Brandenburg* and Virginia v. Black? Which approach, including those taken by the Supreme Court, is the best way of identifying the proscribable true threat? Might your answer depend on your characterization of the interests served by exiling true threats from the First Amendment? Consider that true threats might be proscribable because of the fear of harm they induce in the recipient, or they might be proscribable because of the genuine likelihood of future criminality they proclaim.

Is threatening speech like defamation? Consider that threats, like defamation, are of no intrinsic value to free expression, but some threats must be protected to provide breathing space for the speech that does matter — angry, even rhetorically violent, commentary on matters of public discourse. On this view, the task in this area would be to separate the proscribable true threat from the protected not-quite-true threat. The actual malice test performs this function with respect to defamation; what should the test be for threatening speech?

3. Fighting Words and Hate Speech

Page 916: Insert after the notes and immediately before subsection 4:

VIRGINIA v. BLACK
538 U.S. 343 (2003)

JUSTICE O'CONNOR announced the judgment of the Court and delivered the opinion of the Court with respect to Parts I, II, and III, and an opinion with respect to Parts IV and V in which CHIEF JUSTICE REHNQUIST, JUSTICE STEVENS, and JUSTICE BREYER joined.

[We] consider whether . . . Virginia's statute banning cross burning with "an intent to intimidate a person or group of persons" violates the First Amendment. We conclude that while a State . . . may ban cross burning carried out with the intent to intimidate, the provision in the Virginia statute treating any cross burning as prima facie evidence of intent to intimidate renders the statute unconstitutional in its current form.

I. Respondents Barry Black, Richard Elliott, and Jonathan O'Mara were convicted separately of violating Virginia's cross-burning statute, [which] provides:

> "It shall be unlawful for any person or persons, with the intent of intimidating any person or group of persons, to burn, or cause to be burned, a cross on the property of another, a highway or other public place. . . . Any such burning of a cross shall be prima facie evidence of an intent to intimidate a person or group of persons." [Va. Code Ann. §18.2-423 (1996).]

Black led a Ku Klux Klan rally [attended by 25 to 30 people], which occurred on private property with the permission of the owner . . . . [The rally lasted over an hour. Klansmen spoke about "what they were" and "what they believed in." One observer stated that they "talked real bad about the blacks and the Mexicans," including a statement by one speaker that "he would love to take a .30/.30 and just randomly shoot the blacks." The rally culminated in the ignition of a 25 to 30 foot high cross, located about 300 to 350 yards from the public road, and the playing of "Amazing Grace" over loudspeakers.]

Black was charged with burning a cross with the intent of intimidating a person or group of persons. . . . At his trial, the jury was instructed that "intent to intimidate means the motivation to intentionally put a person or a group of persons in fear of bodily harm. Such fear must arise from the willful conduct of the accused rather than from some mere temperamental timidity of the victim." The trial court also instructed the jury that "the burning of a cross by itself is sufficient evidence from which you may infer the required intent." . . . The jury found Black guilty, and fined him $2,500. The Court of Appeals of Virginia affirmed Black's conviction.

Richard Elliott and Jonathan O'Mara . . . attempted to burn a cross on the yard of James Jubilee, . . . an African-American, [who] was Elliott's next-door neighbor. . . . Before the cross burning, Jubilee spoke to Elliott's mother to inquire about shots being fired from behind the Elliott home. Elliott's mother explained to Jubilee that her son shot firearms as a hobby, and that he used the backyard as a firing range. [Elliott and O'Mara, who "were not affiliated with the Klan,"] drove a truck onto Jubilee's property, planted a cross, and set it on fire, [apparently] to "get back" at Jubilee for complaining about the shooting in the backyard. . . . After seeing the cross, Jubilee was "very nervous" because . . . "a cross burned in your yard . . . tells you that it's just the first round." Elliott and O'Mara were charged with attempted cross burning and conspiracy to commit cross burning. O'Mara pleaded guilty to both counts, reserving the right to challenge the constitutionality of the cross-burning statute, [and was sentenced to 45 days in jail and fined $1,500.] At Elliott's trial, the judge . . . instructed the jury that [Virginia] must prove that "the defendant intended to commit cross burning," that "the defendant did a direct act toward the commission of the cross burning," and that "the defendant had the intent of intimidating any person or group of persons." The court did not instruct the jury on the meaning of the word "intimidate," nor on the prima facie evidence provision of §18.2-423. The jury found Elliott guilty of attempted cross burning and acquitted him of conspiracy to commit cross burning. It sentenced Elliott to 90 days in jail and a $2,500 fine. The Court of Appeals of Virginia affirmed the convictions of both Elliott and O'Mara. . . .

The Supreme Court of Virginia consolidated all three cases, and held that the statute is unconstitutional on its face, [as] "analytically indistinguishable from the ordinance found unconstitutional in [R.A.V. v. St. Paul]." The Virginia statute, the court held, discriminates on the basis of content since it "selectively chooses only cross burning because of its distinctive message." . . . Three justices dissented, concluding that the Virginia cross-burning statute passes constitutional muster because it proscribes only conduct that constitutes a true threat. The justices noted that unlike the ordinance found unconstitutional in R.A.V. v. St. Paul, "the Virginia statute applies to any individual who burns a cross for any reason provided the cross is burned with the intent to intimidate." . . . We granted certiorari.

II. Cross burning originated in the 14th century as a means for Scottish tribes to signal each other. . . . Cross burning in this country, however, long ago became unmoored from its Scottish ancestry. Burning a cross in the United States is inextricably intertwined with the history of the Ku Klux Klan. The first Ku Klux Klan [started as a social club] in Pulaski, Tennessee, in the spring of 1866 [but] soon changed into something far different. The Klan fought Reconstruction and the corresponding drive to allow freed blacks to participate in the political process [by imposing] "a veritable reign of terror" throughout the South [through] tactics such as whipping, threatening to burn people at the stake, and murder. The Klan's victims included blacks, southern whites who disagreed with the Klan, and "carpetbagger" northern whites. The activities of the Ku Klux Klan prompted legislative action at the national level. . . . Congress passed what is now known as the Ku Klux Klan Act. . . . 17 Stat. 13 (now codified at 42 U.S.C. §§1983, 1985, and 1986). President Grant used these new powers to suppress the Klan in South Carolina, the effect of which severely curtailed the Klan in other States as well. By the end of Reconstruction in 1877, the first Klan no longer existed.

The genesis of the second Klan began in 1905, with the publication of Thomas Dixon's The Clansmen: An Historical Romance of the Ku Klux Klan. Dixon's book was a sympathetic portrait of the first Klan, depicting the Klan as a group of heroes "saving" the South from blacks and the "horrors" of Reconstruction. Although the first Klan never actually practiced cross burning, Dixon's book depicted the Klan burning crosses to celebrate the execution of former slaves. Cross burning thereby became associated with the first Ku Klux Klan. When D. W. Griffith turned Dixon's book into the movie The Birth of a Nation in 1915, the association between cross burning and the Klan became indelible. . . . Soon thereafter, in November 1915, the second Klan began.

From the inception of the second Klan, cross burnings have been used to communicate both threats of violence and messages of shared ideology. . . . Klan members took their oaths of loyalty [by the light of a 40-foot high burning cross, and] a Georgia mob celebrated the lynching of Leo Frank by burning a "gigantic cross" on Stone Mountain that was "visible throughout" Atlanta. The new Klan's ideology did not differ much from that of the first Klan. [Both were committed to white supremacy.] Violence was also an elemental part of this new Klan, [including murders, floggings, and tar-and-featherings]. Often, the Klan used cross burnings as a tool of intimidation and a threat of impending violence. . . .

The Klan continued to use cross burnings to intimidate after World War II, [prompting] Virginia to enact its first version of the cross-burning statute in 1950. The decision of this Court in Brown v. Board of Education, along with the civil rights movement of the 1950s and 1960s, sparked another outbreak of Klan violence. These acts of violence included bombings, beatings, shootings, stabbings, and mutilations. Members of the Klan burned crosses on the lawns of those associated with the civil rights movement, assaulted the Freedom Riders, bombed churches, and murdered blacks as well as whites whom the Klan viewed as sympathetic toward the civil rights movement.

Throughout the history of the Klan, cross burnings have also remained potent symbols of shared group identity and ideology. The burning cross became a symbol of the Klan itself and a central feature of Klan gatherings. According to the Klan constitution (called the kloran), the "fiery cross" was the "emblem of that sincere, unselfish devotedness of all klansmen to the sacred purpose and principles we have espoused." And the Klan has often published its newsletters and magazines under the name The Fiery Cross. At Klan gatherings across the country, cross burning became the climax of the rally or the initiation. . . . Throughout the Klan's history, the Klan continued to use the burning cross in their ritual ceremonies. . . . In short, a burning cross has remained a symbol of Klan ideology and of Klan unity.

To this day, regardless of whether the message is a political one or whether the message is also meant to intimidate, the burning of a cross is a "symbol of hate." And while cross burning sometimes carries no intimidating message, at other times the intimidating message is the *only* message conveyed. [The] history of violence associated with the Klan shows that the possibility of injury or death is not just hypothetical. . . . Indeed, as the cases of respondents Elliott and O'Mara indicate, individuals without Klan affiliation who wish to threaten or menace another person sometimes use cross burning because of this association between a burning cross and violence.

In sum, while a burning cross does not inevitably convey a message of intimidation, often the cross burner intends that the recipients of the message fear for their lives. And when a cross burning is used to intimidate, few if any messages are more powerful.

III. A. . . . The hallmark of the protection of free speech is to allow "free trade in ideas" — even ideas that the overwhelming majority of people might find distasteful or discomforting. [*Abrams*, (Holmes, J., dissenting)]. Thus, the First Amendment "ordinarily" denies a State "the power to prohibit dissemination of social, economic and political doctrine which a vast majority of its citizens believes to be false and fraught with evil consequence." [*Whitney*, (Brandeis, J., dissenting)]. The First Amendment affords protection to symbolic or expressive conduct as well as to actual speech. [*R.A.V., O'Brien*, Texas v. Johnson.]

The protections afforded by the First Amendment, however, are not absolute, and we have long recognized that the government may regulate certain categories of expression consistent with the Constitution. [The First Amendment] permits a State to ban a "true threat." "True threats" encompass those statements where the speaker means to communicate a serious expression of an intent to commit an act of unlawful violence to a particular individual or group of individuals. [See] Watts v. United States, [holding that] "political hyberbole" is not a true threat. The speaker need not actually intend to carry out the threat. Rather, a prohibition on true threats "protects individuals from the fear of violence" and "from the disruption that fear engenders," in addition to protecting people "from the possibility that the threatened violence will occur." Intimidation in the constitutionally proscribable sense of the word is a type of true threat, where a speaker directs a threat to a person or group of persons with the intent of placing the victim in fear of bodily harm or death. [The] history of cross burning in this country shows that cross burning is often intimidating, intended to create a pervasive fear in victims that they are a target of violence.

B. The Supreme Court of Virginia ruled that in light of *R.A.V.*, even if it is constitutional to ban cross burning in a content-neutral manner, the Virginia cross-burning statute is unconstitutional because it discriminates on the basis of content and viewpoint. It is true . . . that the burning of a cross is symbolic expression. . . . Individuals burn crosses as opposed to other means of communication because cross burning carries a message in an effective and dramatic manner. The fact that cross burning is symbolic expression, however, does not resolve the constitutional question. . . .

We did not hold in *R.A.V.* that the First Amendment prohibits *all* forms of content-based discrimination within a proscribable area of speech. Rather, we specifically stated that some types of content discrimination did not violate the First Amendment: "When the basis for the content discrimination consists entirely of the very reason the entire class of speech at issue is proscribable, no significant danger of idea or viewpoint discrimination exists. Such a reason, . . . adjudged neutral enough to support exclusion of the entire class of speech from First Amendment protection, is also neutral enough to form the basis of distinction within the class." . . .

Virginia's statute does not run afoul of the First Amendment insofar as it bans cross burning with intent to intimidate. Unlike the statute at issue in *R.A.V.*, the Virginia statute does not single out for opprobrium only that speech directed toward "one of the specified disfavored topics." It does not matter whether an individual burns a cross with intent to intimidate because of the victim's race, gender, or religion, or because of the victim's "political affiliation, union membership, or homosexuality." . . . Indeed, in the case of Elliott and O'Mara, it is at least unclear whether the respondents burned a cross due to racial animus [or] "because they were angry that their neighbor had complained about the presence of a firearm shooting range in . . . Elliott's yard." The First Amendment permits Virginia to outlaw cross burnings done with the intent to intimidate because burning a cross is a particularly virulent form of intimidation. Instead of prohibiting all intimidating messages, Virginia may choose to regulate this subset of intimidating messages in light of cross burning's long and pernicious history as a signal of impending violence. Thus, just as a State may regulate only that obscenity which is the most obscene due to its prurient content, so too may a State choose to prohibit only those forms of intimidation that are most likely to inspire fear of bodily harm. A ban on cross burning carried out with the intent to intimidate is fully consistent with our holding in *R.A.V.* and is proscribable under the First Amendment.

IV. [JUSTICE O'CONNOR, joined by CHIEF JUSTICE REHNQUIST and JUSTICES STEVENS and BREYER.] The Supreme Court of Virginia ruled in the alternative that Virginia's cross-burning statute was unconstitutionally overbroad due to its provision stating that "any such burning of a cross shall be prima facie evidence of an intent to intimidate a person or group of persons." . . . The prima facie evidence provision, as interpreted by the jury instruction [given in Black's case, that "burning of a cross, by itself, is sufficient evidence from which you may infer the required intent,"] renders the statute unconstitutional. . . . As construed by the jury instruction, the prima facie provision strips away the very reason why a State may ban cross burning with the intent to intimidate[,] permits the Commonwealth to arrest, prosecute, and convict a person based solely on the fact of cross burning itself[, and] "would create an unacceptable risk of the suppression of ideas." The act of burning a cross may mean that a person is engaging in constitutionally proscribable intimidation. But that same act may mean only that the person is engaged in core political speech. The prima facie evidence provision in this statute blurs the line between these two meanings of a burning cross [and, as interpreted,] chills constitutionally protected political speech because of the possibility that a State will prosecute — and potentially convict — somebody engaging only in lawful political speech at the core of what the First Amendment is designed to protect. [A] burning cross is not always intended to intimidate. Rather, sometimes the cross burning is a statement of ideology, a symbol of group solidarity. . . . Thus, "burning a cross at a political rally would almost certainly be protected expression." Indeed, occasionally a person who burns a cross does not intend to express either a statement of ideology or intimidation. . . .

The prima facie provision makes no effort to distinguish among these different types of cross burnings. It does not distinguish between a cross burning done with the purpose of creating anger or resentment and a cross burning done with the purpose of threatening or intimidating a victim. It does not distinguish between a cross burning at a public rally or a cross burning on a neighbor's lawn. It does not treat the cross burning directed at an individual differently from the cross burning directed at a group of like-minded believers. It allows a jury to treat a cross burning on the property of another with the owner's acquiescence in the same manner as a cross burning on the property of another without the owner's permission. . . .

It may be true that a cross burning, even at a political rally, arouses a sense of anger or hatred among the vast majority of citizens who see a burning cross. But this sense of anger or hatred is not sufficient to ban all cross burnings. . . . The prima facie evidence provision in this case ignores all of the contextual factors that are necessary to decide whether a particular cross burning is intended to intimidate. The First Amendment does not permit such a shortcut.

[We hold] that because of the interpretation of the prima facie evidence provision given by the jury instruction [in Black's case], the provision makes the statute facially invalid at this point. We also recognize the theoretical possibility that the court, on remand, could interpret the provision in a [different] manner . . . in order to avoid the constitutional objections we have described. We leave open that possibility. We also leave open the possibility that the provision is severable, and if so, whether Elliott and O'Mara could be retried under §18.2-423.

V. [Justice O'Connor, joined by Chief Justice Rehnquist and Justices Stevens and Breyer.] With respect to Barry Black, we agree with the Supreme Court of Virginia that his conviction cannot stand, and we affirm the judgment of the Supreme Court of Virginia. With respect to Elliott and O'Mara, we vacate the judgment of the Supreme Court of Virginia, and remand the case for further proceedings.

JUSTICES SOUTER, KENNEDY, and GINSBURG concurred in the judgment with respect to Black; JUSTICE SCALIA concurred in the judgment with respect to Elliott and O'Mara.

JUSTICE THOMAS, dissenting.

. . . Although I agree with the majority's conclusion that it is constitutionally permissible to "ban . . . cross burning carried out with intent to intimidate," I believe that the majority errs in imputing an expressive component to the activity in question.

[The] perception that a burning cross is a threat and a precursor of worse things to come is not limited to blacks. Because the modern Klan expanded the list of its enemies beyond blacks and "radicals," to include Catholics, Jews, most immigrants, and labor unions, a burning cross is now widely viewed as a signal of impending terror and lawlessness. . . . In our culture, cross burning has almost invariably meant lawlessness and understandably instills in its victims well-grounded fear of physical violence.

Virginia's experience has been no exception. [After] a series of cross burnings . . . took place between 1949 and 1952, [Virginia enacted a ban on cross burning for purposes of intimidation. At] the time the statute was enacted, racial segregation was not only the prevailing practice, but also the law in Virginia. . . . It strains credulity to suggest that a state legislature that adopted a litany of segregationist laws self-contradictorily intended to squelch the segregationist message. . . . The ban on cross burning with intent to intimidate demonstrates that even segregationists understood the difference between intimidating and terroristic conduct and racist expression. . . . Accordingly, this statute prohibits only conduct, not expression. And, just as one cannot burn down someone's house to make a political point and then seek refuge in the First Amendment, those who hate cannot terrorize and intimidate to make their point. In light of my conclusion that the statute here addresses only conduct, there is no need to analyze it under any of our First Amendment tests. . .

I respectfully dissent.

JUSTICE SOUTER, with whom JUSTICE KENNEDY and JUSTICE GINSBURG join, concurring in the judgment in part and dissenting in part.

I agree with the majority that the Virginia statute makes a content-based distinction within the category of punishable intimidating or threatening expression, the very type of distinction we considered in R.A.V. v. St. Paul. I disagree that any exception [from the principles established by *R.A.V.*] should save Virginia's law from unconstitutionality under the holding in *R.A.V.*

[The Virginia statute's] specific prohibition of cross burning with intent to intimidate selects a symbol with particular content from the field of all proscribable expression meant to intimidate. To be sure, that content often includes an essentially intimidating message, [but] even when the symbolic act is meant to terrify, a burning cross may carry a further, ideological message of white Protestant supremacy. [The] burning cross can broadcast threat and ideology together, ideology alone, or threat alone. . . .

Because of the burning cross's extraordinary force as a method of intimidation, the *R.A.V.* exception most likely to cover the statute is the . . . exception for content discrimination on a basis that "consists entirely of the very reason the entire class of speech at issue is proscribable." This is the exception the majority speaks of here as covering statutes prohibiting "particularly virulent" proscribable expression.

I do not think that the Virginia statute qualifies for this virulence exception as *R.A.V.* explained it. . . . *R.A.V.* defines the special virulence exception . . . this way: prohibition by subcategory is nonetheless constitutional if it is made "entirely" on the "basis" of "the very reason" that "the entire class of speech at issue is proscribable" at all. The Court explained that when the subcategory is confined to the most obviously proscribable instances, "no significant danger of idea or viewpoint discrimination exists," and the explanation was rounded out with some illustrative examples. None of them, however, resembles the case before us.

The first example of permissible distinction is for a prohibition of obscenity unusually offensive "in its prurience." . . . [D]istinguishing obscene publications on this basis does not suggest discrimination on the basis of the message conveyed. The opposite is true, however, when a general prohibition of intimidation is rejected in favor of a distinct proscription of intimidation by cross burning. The cross may have been selected because of its special power to threaten, but it may also have been singled out because of disapproval of its message of white supremacy, either because a legislature thought white supremacy was a pernicious doctrine or because it found that dramatic, public espousal of it was a civic embarrassment. Thus, there is no kinship between the cross-burning statute and the core prurience example.

Nor does this case present any analogy to the statute prohibiting threats against the President, the second of *R.A.V.*'s examples of the virulence exception. [Threats] against the President are not generally identified by . . . the content of any message that may accompany the threat, let alone any viewpoint. . . . Differential treatment of threats against the President, then, selects nothing but special risks, not special messages. . . .

I thus read *R.A.V.*'s examples of the particular virulence exception as covering prohibitions that are not clearly associated with a particular viewpoint, and that are consequently different from the Virginia statute. . . .

Since no *R.A.V.* exception can save the statute as content based, it can only survive if narrowly tailored to serve a compelling state interest, a stringent test the statute cannot pass; a content-neutral statute banning intimidation would achieve the same object without singling out particular content.

I conclude that the statute under which all three of the respondents were prosecuted violates the First Amendment, since the statute's content-based distinction was invalid at the time of the charged activities, regardless of whether the prima facie evidence provision was given any effect in any respondent's individual case. . . . Accordingly, I concur in the Court's judgment as to respondent Black and dissent as to respondents Elliott and O'Mara.

NOTES

1. Are Categorical Differences Significant? Can *R.A.V.* and *Black* be harmonized by noting that *R.A.V.* involved St. Paul's attempt selectively to ban fighting words on the basis of their content, and that *Black* involved Virginia's attempt selectively to ban true threats on the basis of their content? Is it plausible to say that the St. Paul ban at issue in *R.A.V.* was not for the purpose of preventing immediate breach of the peace (the reason that fighting words are exiled from the First Amendment), but that Virginia's ban on intentionally intimidatory cross burning was for the purpose of preventing the fear and anxiety experienced by the recipient of any true threat (the reason that true threats are constitutionally unprotected)?

2. The Peculiar Potency of Symbolic Expression. What, if anything, should be made of the fact that a burning cross, like the American flag, the Nazi swastika, the hammer and sickle, or a star of David, among other possibilities, are particularly powerful symbols? No matter how they are used, they convey a message — respectively: white supremacy, nationality and patriotism, genocidal (especially anti-Semitic) terror, communism, Judaism or Zionism. Does the fact that a burning cross necessarily conveys a message of white supremacy mean that Justice Souter's dissent is correct in contending that the Virginia law is viewpoint discriminatory? In Texas v. Johnson Texas unsuccessfully sought to justify its prohibition of flag desecration by asserting that it was interested in preventing breach of the peace. In United States v. Eichman the federal government unsuccessfully contended that the lack of any content-based limits in its ban on physical mutilation of the flag justified the prohibition. In both cases the Court thought that the government interest could not be separated from protecting the idea inherent in the symbol, and thus was aimed at suppressing any contrary ideas inherent in destruction or mutilation of the symbol. Does Justice Thomas treat cross burning as the mirror image of the flag-burning cases? As with mirrors, in which the image is reversed, does he invert the symbolic message of the burning cross by converting it from an unalloyed message of white supremacist hate to an unalloyed message of threat and intimidation? Does the majority rationale in *Black* depend on converting the burning cross into a mixed symbol — a message of threat and intimidation as well as one of ideology? Does the majority rationale depend on treating the burning cross as an indiscriminate message of hatred and intimidation, one that extends to Catholics, Jews, racial minorities, and labor unionists, among others? If so, does that mean that a group that keeps its symbolic message of hatred narrowly focused has more free speech protection than one that allows its message to sprawl?

4. Offensive Speech

d. Indecency and the New Mass Media

Page 942: Insert immediately after Reno v. ACLU *and before the notes:*

ASHCROFT v. THE FREE SPEECH COALITION

535 U.S. 234 (2002)

JUSTICE KENNEDY delivered the opinion of the Court.

[The] Child Pornography Prevention Act of 1996 (CPPA) . . . extends the federal prohibition against child pornography to sexually explicit images that appear to depict minors but were produced without using any real children. The statute prohibits, in specific circumstances, possessing or distributing these images, which may be created by using adults who look like minors or by using computer imaging. The new technology . . . makes it possible to create realistic images of children who do not exist.

By prohibiting child pornography that does not depict an actual child, the statute goes beyond New York v. Ferber. . . . Like the law in *Ferber*, the CPPA seeks to reach beyond obscenity, and it makes no attempt to conform to the *Miller* standard. . . . The principal question to be resolved, then, is whether the CPPA is constitutional where it proscribes a significant universe of speech that is neither obscene under *Miller* nor child pornography under *Ferber*.

I. Before 1996, Congress defined child pornography as the type of depictions at issue in *Ferber*, images made using actual minors. The CPPA retains that prohibition [and adds §2256(8)(B), which] prohibits "any visual depiction, including any photograph, film, video, picture, or computer or computer-generated image or picture" that "is, or appears to be, of a minor engaging in sexually explicit conduct." The prohibition on "any visual depiction" does not depend at all on how the image is produced. The section captures a range of depictions, sometimes called "virtual child pornography," which include computer-generated images, as well as images produced by more traditional means. For instance, the literal terms of the statute embrace a Renaissance painting depicting a scene from classical mythology, a "picture" that "appears to be, of a minor engaging in sexually explicit conduct." The statute also prohibits Hollywood movies, filmed without any child actors, if a jury believes an actor "appears to be" a minor engaging in "actual or simulated . . . sexual intercourse." . . .

[Free Speech Coalition], a California trade association for the adult-entertainment industry, . . . Bold Type, Inc., the publisher of a book advocating the nudist lifestyle; Jim Gingerich, a painter of nudes; and Ron Raffaelli, a photographer specializing in erotic images, [challenged the validity of these provisions. A federal district court] granted summary judgment to the Government [and, on appeal, the] Court of Appeals for the Ninth Circuit reversed, [finding] the CPPA invalid on its face. We granted certiorari.

II. [A] law imposing criminal penalties on protected speech is a stark example of speech suppression. The CPPA's penalties are indeed severe. A first offender may be imprisoned for 15 years [and a] repeat offender faces a prison sentence of [5 to] 30 years in prison. [This] case provides a textbook example of why we permit facial challenges to statutes that burden expression. With these severe penalties in force, few legitimate movie producers or book publishers, or few other speakers in any capacity, would risk distributing images in or near the uncertain reach of this law.

The Constitution gives significant protection from overbroad laws that chill [constitutionally protected] speech; . . . the CPPA is unconstitutional on its face if it prohibits a substantial amount of protected expression. [Broadrick v. Oklahoma.]

[While] freedom of speech . . . does not embrace certain categories of speech, including . . . obscenity and pornography produced with real children. . . , none of them includes the speech prohibited by the CPPA.

. . . The CPPA . . . extends to images that appear to depict a minor engaging in sexually explicit activity without regard to the *Miller* requirements. The materials need not appeal to the prurient interest [nor is it necessary] that the image be patently offensive. . . . The CPPA prohibits speech despite its serious literary, artistic, political, or scientific value. The statute proscribes the visual depiction of an idea — that of teenagers engaging in sexual activity — that is a fact of modern society and has been a theme in art and literature throughout the ages. Under the CPPA, images are prohibited so long as the persons appear to be under 18 years of age. This is higher than the legal age for marriage in many States, as well as the age at which persons may consent to sexual relations. . . . Both themes — teenage sexual activity and the sexual abuse of children — have inspired countless literary works. William Shakespeare created the most famous pair of teenage lovers, one of whom is just 13 years of age. See Romeo and Juliet, act I, sc. 2, l. 9 ("She hath not seen the change of fourteen years"). . . . Last year's Academy Awards featured the movie, Traffic, which was nominated for Best Picture, [and which] portrays a teenager, identified as a 16-year-old, who becomes addicted to drugs. The viewer sees the degradation of her addiction, which in the end leads her to a filthy room to trade sex for drugs. The year before, American Beauty won the Academy Award for Best Picture. In the course of the movie, a teenage girl engages in sexual relations with her teenage boyfriend, and another yields herself to the gratification of a middle-aged man. . . .

The Government [argues] that speech prohibited by the CPPA is virtually indistinguishable from child pornography, which may be banned without regard to whether it depicts works of value. [*Ferber.*] Where the images are themselves the product of child sexual abuse, *Ferber* recognized that the State had an interest in stamping it out without regard to any judgment about its content. The production of the work, not its content, was the target of the statute. . . . In contrast to the speech in *Ferber*, . . . the CPPA prohibits speech that records no crime and creates no victims by its production. Virtual child pornography is not "intrinsically related" to the sexual abuse of children, as were the materials in *Ferber*. While the Government asserts that the images can lead to actual instances of child abuse, the causal link is contingent and indirect. The harm does not necessarily follow from the speech, but depends upon some unquantified potential for subsequent criminal acts.

III. . . . The Government . . . says that the possibility of producing images by using computer imaging makes it very difficult for it to prosecute those who produce pornography by using real children. Experts, we are told, may have difficulty in saying whether the pictures were made by using real children or by using computer imaging. The necessary solution, the argument runs, is to prohibit both kinds of images. The argument, in essence, is that protected speech may be banned as a means to ban unprotected speech. This analysis turns the First Amendment upside down. The Government may not suppress lawful speech as the means to suppress unlawful speech. Protected speech does not become unprotected merely because it resembles the latter. The Constitution requires the reverse. . . . The overbreadth doctrine prohibits the Government from banning unprotected speech if a substantial amount of protected speech is prohibited or chilled in the process. . . .

In sum, §2256(8)(B) covers materials beyond the categories recognized in *Ferber* and *Miller*, and the reasons the Government offers in support of limiting the freedom of speech have no justification. . . . The provision abridges the freedom to engage in a substantial amount of lawful speech [and] is overbroad and unconstitutional. . . .

[Affirmed.]

[JUSTICE THOMAS concurred in the judgment of the Court.]

[JUSTICE O'CONNOR concurred in the judgment in part, and dissented in part.]

. . .

CHIEF JUSTICE REHNQUIST, with whom JUSTICE SCALIA joins in part, dissenting.

. . . Congress has a compelling interest in ensuring the ability to enforce prohibitions of actual child pornography, and we should defer to its findings that rapidly advancing technology soon will make it all but impossible to do so. [While] serious First Amendment concerns would arise were the Government ever to prosecute someone for simple distribution or possession of a film with literary or artistic value, such as "Traffic" or "American Beauty," [the CPPA] need not be construed to reach such materials.

We normally do not strike down a statute on First Amendment grounds "when a limiting instruction has been or could be placed on the challenged statute." Other than computer generated images that are virtually indistinguishable from real children engaged in sexually explicitly conduct, the CPPA can be limited [to reach] only the sort of "hard core of child pornography" that we found without protection in *Ferber*. So construed, the CPPA bans visual depictions of youthful looking adult actors engaged in *actual* sexual activity; mere *suggestions* of sexual activity . . . fall outside the purview of the statute. [We] should be loath to construe a statute as banning film portrayals of Shakespearian tragedies, without some indication — from text or legislative history — that such a result was intended. In fact, Congress explicitly instructed that such a reading of the CPPA would be wholly unwarranted. . . . We have looked to legislative history to limit the scope of child pornography statutes in the past, and we should do so here as well.[1]

This narrow reading of "sexually explicit conduct" . . . is exactly how the phrase was understood prior to the broadening gloss the Court gives it today. Indeed, had "sexually explicit conduct" been thought to reach the sort of material the Court says it does, then films such as "Traffic" and "American Beauty" would not have been

1. JUSTICE SCALIA did not join the discussion of the statute's legislative record. — ED.

made the way they were. "Traffic" won its Academy Award in 2001. "American Beauty" won its Academy Award in 2000. But the CPPA has been on the books, and has been enforced, since 1996. The chill felt by the Court has apparently never been felt by those who actually make movies.

. . . I would construe the CPPA in a manner consistent with the First Amendment, reverse the Court of Appeals' judgment, and uphold the statute in its entirety.

Page 943: Insert after note 2, immediately before subsection 5:

3. The Child Online Protection Act. Congress responded to Reno v. American Civil Liberties Union by enacting the Child Online Protection Act (COPA), 47 U.S.C. §231. The COPA prohibits any person from "knowingly and with knowledge of the character of the material, in interstate or foreign commerce by means of the World Wide Web, making any communication for commercial purposes that is available to any minor and that includes material that is harmful to minors." 47 U.S.C. §231(a)(1). The COPA defines "material that is harmful to minors" by incorporating the *Miller* obscenity test. 47 U.S.C. §231(e)(6). In a facial challenge to the COPA, a federal district court enjoined its enforcement. The Court of Appeals for the Third Circuit upheld the injunction on the ground that the use of "contemporary community standards" (as required by the *Miller* test) to determine material harmful to minors made the COPA substantially overbroad. In Ashcroft v. American Civil Liberties Union, 535 U.S. 564 (2002), the Court vacated the Third Circuit's judgment after concluding that the COPA's use of contemporary community standards did not, by itself, render the statute substantially overbroad. Because the scope of the law was narrowed by the requirement that prohibited material be of "prurient interest" to minors and lack any "serious value" to minors, the Court did not think the possibility of widely varying community standards being applied to commercial Internet sites posed a problem of substantial overbreadth. The Court was careful to note that it was not expressing "any view as to whether COPA suffers from substantial overbreadth for other reasons, whether the statute is unconstitutionally vague," or whether the statute will ultimately survive strict scrutiny. The Court left the injunction intact and remanded for further proceedings.

5. Defamation and Other "Civility Torts"

b. Invasion of Privacy

Page 955: Insert the following after subsection (2), "Disclosure of true but private facts," and immediately before subsection (3):

In Bartnicki v. Vopper, 532 U.S. 514 (2001), the Court was presented with the question of whether criminal and civil liability could attach to disclosure of a private communication that was intercepted illegally by someone other than the person making the disclosure but which was obtained lawfully by the publisher of the information. A federal law, 18 U.S.C. §2511(1)(c), imposes criminal penalties on anyone who discloses an illegally intercepted communication if they knew or had reason to know of the illegal nature of the interception. Another statute imposes civil liability for such disclosures. During "contentious" labor negotiations between a teachers' union and a public school board, Bartnicki, the union's chief negotiator, called Kane, the union's president, using a cellular telephone. In the course of the conversation, which focused on the negotiations, Kane suggested that the union might need to "blow off their front porches" to induce the school board to accede to the teachers' demands. An unknown person illegally recorded the conversation and left a tape of it in the mailbox of Yocum, the head of a local taxpayers' organization. Yocum provided the tape to Vopper, a radio commentator, who broadcast the tape as part of his critical commentary on the union.

The Court struck down the two federal statutes, as applied to Vopper, Yocum, and various media defendants who had participated in the disclosure. Even though the laws were "content-neutral law[s] of general applicability" the government failed to justify them under the intermediate level of scrutiny normally applicable to content-neutral speech regulations. See 980-986. The Court acknowledged that "[p]rivacy of communication is an important interest" and that the statutes served that interest by diminishing "the fear of public disclosure of private conversations [that] might well have a chilling effect on private speech." Nevertheless, the Court stressed the fact that the statutes, as applied, implicated "the core purposes of the First Amendment" because they imposed "sanctions on the publication of truthful information of public concern."

6. Commercial Speech

Page 979: Insert the following immediately before section C:

3. Tobacco Advertising. In Lorillard Tobacco Co. v. Reilly, 533 U.S. 525 (2001), the Court applied *Central Hudson* to invalidate Massachusetts's outdoor advertising regulations prohibiting smokeless tobacco or cigar advertising within 1,000 feet of a school or playground. Only the third and fourth prongs of *Central Hudson* were implicated. The regulations directly advanced the governmental interests asserted to justify them because there was ample evidence that (1) there was a problem with underage use of smokeless tobacco and cigars and (2) limiting such tobacco advertising would decrease minors' use of these tobacco products. But the regulations did not satisfy the fourth prong of *Central Hudson*. First, they were exceedingly broad in that they would prohibit tobacco advertising in a substantial portion of Massachusetts's major metropolitan areas and would constitute a near-complete ban on the communication of truthful information. Moreover, the ban applied to indoor advertising if visible from outside and to oral statements. Second, while the governmental interest in preventing minors from using tobacco was substantial, even compelling, the purchase and use of tobacco by adults is legal. A speech regulation cannot unduly impinge on the speaker's ability to propose a commercial transaction and the adult listener's opportunity to obtain information about legal products. Because the broad sweep of these regulations suggested that Massachusetts did not "carefully calculate the costs and benefits associated with the burden on speech imposed," Massachusetts failed its burden of proving that the regulations were not more extensive than necessary.

The Court concluded that the regulations prohibiting indoor, point-of-sale advertising of smokeless tobacco and cigars lower than 5 feet from the floor of a retail establishment located within 1,000 feet of a school or playground failed both the third and fourth prongs of *Central Hudson*. The 5-foot rule failed adequately to advance the goals of preventing minors from using tobacco products and curbing demand for tobacco by limiting youth exposure to advertising. Not all children are less than 5 feet tall, and those who are can look up and take in their surroundings. Moreover the height restriction was an attempt to regulate directly the communicative impact of indoor advertising, and thus not unrelated to expression.

The Court upheld Massachusetts's regulations requiring retailers to place tobacco products behind counters and requiring customers to have contact with a salesperson before handling them. The Court assumed that tobacco vendors have a cognizable speech interest in a particular means of displaying their products, but thought that because unattended displays of tobacco enable access by minors, Massachusetts had demonstrated a substantial interest in preventing access to tobacco products by minors and had adopted an appropriately narrow means of advancing that interest. The regulations left ample alternative means of display to retailers and did not significantly impede adult access to tobacco products.

Page 979: Insert immediately after note 3, Tobacco Advertising, and before section C:

THOMPSON v. WESTERN STATES MEDICAL CENTER
535 U.S. 357 (2002)

JUSTICE O'CONNOR delivered the opinion of the Court.

Section 503A of the Food and Drug Administration Modernization Act of 1997 (FDAMA or Act) exempts "compounded drugs" from the Food and Drug Administration's standard drug approval requirements as long as the providers of those drugs . . . refrain from advertising or promoting particular compounded drugs. [A] group of licensed pharmacies that specialize in compounding drugs sought to enjoin enforcement of [this requirement.] . . . We conclude, as did the courts below, that §503A's provisions regarding advertisement and promotion amount to unconstitutional restrictions on commercial speech, and we therefore affirm.

I. Drug compounding is a process by which a pharmacist or doctor combines, mixes, or alters ingredients to create a medication tailored to the needs of an individual patient. Compounding is typically used to prepare medications that are not commercially available, such as medication for a patient who is allergic to an ingredient in a mass-produced product. It is a traditional component of the practice of pharmacy. . . .

II. The parties agree that the advertising and soliciting prohibited by the FDAMA constitute commercial speech. . . . Neither party has challenged the appropriateness of applying the *Central Hudson* framework . . . here. Although several Members of the Court have expressed doubts about the *Central Hudson* analysis . . . there is no need in this case to break new ground.

III. . . . The Government asserts that three substantial interests underlie the FDAMA[:] an interest in "preserving the effectiveness and integrity of the . . . new drug approval process and the protection of the public health that it provides," . . . an interest in "preserving the availability of compounded drugs for those individual patients who, for particularized medical reasons, cannot use commercially available products that have been approved by the FDA," [and an interest in] "achieving the proper balance between those two independently compelling but competing interests. . . ." Preserving the effectiveness and integrity of the . . . new drug approval process is clearly an important governmental interest, and the Government . . . also has an important interest . . . in permitting the continuation of the practice of compounding so that patients with particular needs may obtain medications suited to those needs. [Because pharmacists] do not make enough money from small-scale compounding to make safety and efficacy testing of their compounded drugs economically feasible, . . . requiring such testing would force pharmacists to stop providing compounded drugs. Given this, the Government needs to be able to draw a line between small-scale compounding and large-scale drug manufacturing. That line must distinguish compounded drugs produced on such a small scale that they could not undergo safety and efficacy testing from drugs produced and sold on a large enough scale that they could undergo such testing and therefore must do so.

The Government argues that the FDAMA's speech-related provisions provide just such a line, i.e., that, in the terms of *Central Hudson*, they "directly advance the governmental interests asserted." . . . The Government argues that advertising particular products is useful in a broad market but is not useful when particular products are designed in response to an individual's "often unique needs" [and] contends that, because of this, advertising is not typically associated with compounding for particular individuals [but] with large-scale production of a drug for a substantial market. The Government argues that advertising, therefore, is "a fair proxy for actual or intended large-scale manufacturing." . . .

[The] Government has failed to demonstrate that the speech restrictions are "not more extensive than is necessary to serve [those] interests." [We] have made clear that if the Government could achieve its interests in a manner that does not restrict speech, or that restricts less speech, the Government must do so. [Rubin v. Coors Brewing Co., 44 Liquormart, Inc. v. Rhode Island.] Several non-speech-related means of drawing a line between compounding and large-scale manufacturing might be possible here. [The] Government could ban the use of "commercial scale manufacturing or testing equipment for compounding drug products," [or] prohibit pharmacists from compounding more drugs in anticipation of receiving prescriptions than in response to prescriptions already received, [or] prohibit pharmacists from "offering compounded drugs at wholesale to other state licensed persons or commercial entities for resale." Alternately, it could limit the amount of compounded drugs, either by volume or by numbers of prescriptions, that a given pharmacist or pharmacy sells out of State. Another possibility . . . would be capping the amount of any particular compounded drug, either by drug volume, number of prescriptions, gross revenue, or profit that a pharmacist or pharmacy may make or sell in a given period of time. . . . The Government has not offered any reason why these possibilities, alone or in combination, would be insufficient to prevent compounding from occurring on such a scale as to undermine the new drug approval process. Indeed, there is no hint that the Government even considered these or any other alternatives. . . . If the First Amendment means anything, it means that regulating speech must be a last — not first — resort. Yet here it seems to have been the first strategy the Government thought to try.

The dissent describes another governmental interest — an interest in prohibiting the sale of compounded drugs to "patients who may not clearly need them" — and argues that "Congress could . . . conclude that the advertising restrictions 'directly advance' " that interest. . . . Although . . . Congress conceivably could have enacted the advertising ban to advance this interest, we have generally only sustained statutes on the basis of hypothesized justifications when reviewing statutes merely to determine whether they are rational. . . . The *Central Hudson* test is significantly stricter than the rational basis test, however. . . .

Even if the Government had argued that the FDAMA's speech-related restrictions were motivated by a fear that advertising compounded drugs would put people who do not need such drugs at risk by causing them to convince their doctors to prescribe the drugs anyway, that fear would fail to justify the restrictions. Aside from the fact that this concern rests on the questionable assumption that doctors would prescribe unnecessary medications (an assumption the dissent is willing to make based on one magazine article and one survey, neither of which was relied upon by the Government), this concern amounts to a fear that people would make bad decisions if given truthful information about compounded drugs. . . . We have previously rejected the notion that the Government has an interest in preventing the dissemination of truthful commercial information in order to prevent members of the public from making bad decisions with the information. [*Virginia Bd. of Pharmacy; 44 Liquormart, Inc.*] . . .

Even if the Government had asserted an interest in preventing people who do not need compounded drugs from obtaining those drugs, the statute does not directly advance that interest [because] the statute does not directly forbid such sales. It instead restricts advertising . . . not just to those who do not need compounded drugs, but also to individuals who do need compounded drugs and their doctors. . . .

JUSTICE THOMAS, concurring.

I concur because I agree with the Court's application of the test set forth in [*Central Hudson,* but] I continue . . . to adhere to my view that [*Central Hudson* should not] "be applied to a restriction of 'commercial' speech" [where] "the asserted interest is one that is to be achieved through keeping would-be recipients of the speech in the dark." [*44 Liquormart, Inc.* (Thomas, J., concurring in part and concurring in judgment).]

JUSTICE BREYER, with whom THE CHIEF JUSTICE, JUSTICE STEVENS, and JUSTICE GINSBURG join, dissenting.

. . . In my view, the advertising restriction "directly advances" the statute's important safety objective [—] to confine the sale of untested, compounded, drugs to where they are medically needed. . . . The restrictions try to assure that demand is generated doctor-to-patient-to-pharmacist, not pharmacist-to-advertisement-to-patient-to-doctor. And they do so in order to diminish the likelihood that those who do not genuinely need untested compounded drugs will not receive them.

[Compounded] drugs carry with them special risks. After all, compounding is not necessarily a matter of changing a drug's flavor, but rather it is a matter of combining different ingredients in new, untested ways [which] can, for some patients, mean infection, serious side effects, or even death. . . . There is considerable evidence that consumer oriented advertising will create strong consumer-driven demand for a particular drug. . . . And there is strong evidence that doctors will often respond affirmatively to a patient's request for a specific drug that the patient has seen advertised. . . .

In these circumstances, Congress could reasonably conclude that doctors will respond affirmatively to a patient's request for a compounded drug even if the doctor would not normally prescribe it. . . . It is consequently not surprising that 71% of the active members of the American Academy of Family Physicians "believe that direct-to-consumer advertising pressures physicians into prescribing drugs that they would not ordinarily prescribe."

Of course, the added risks in any such individual case may be small. But those individual risks added together can significantly affect the public health. At least, the FDA and Congress could reasonably reach that conclusion. And that fact . . . means that the FDA and Congress could also conclude that the advertising restrictions "directly advance" the statute's safety goal. They help to assure that demand for an untested compounded drug originates with the doctor, responding to an individual's special medical needs; they thereby help to restrict the untested drug's distribution to those most likely to need it; and they thereby advance the statute's safety goals. . . .

II. I do not believe that Congress could have achieved its safety objectives in significantly less restrictive ways. [None of] the several alternatives the Court suggests . . . help in any way to assure the kind of individualized doctor-patient need determination that the statute's advertising restriction are designed to help achieve.

III. . . .

I do not deny that the statute restricts the circulation of some truthful information. [But] commercial speech does not warrant application of the Court's strictest speech-protective tests. . . . because restrictions on commercial speech do not often repress individual self-expression; they rarely interfere with the functioning of democratic political processes; and they often reflect a democratically determined governmental decision to regulate a commercial venture in order to protect, for example, the consumer, the public health, individual safety, or the environment. . . . [An] overly rigid "commercial speech" doctrine will transform what ought to be a legislative or regulatory decision about the best way to protect the health and safety of the American public into a constitutional decision prohibiting the legislature from enacting necessary protections. As history in respect to the Due Process Clause shows, any such transformation would involve a tragic constitutional misunderstanding.

C. Content-Neutral Regulations of Speech

1. Time, Place, and Manner of Speech

Page 986: Insert the following immediately before subsection C.2:

Note: Private Communications of Matters of Public Concern

As our lives become ever more technologically complicated, and we communicate vast amounts of information by wireless communications devices and through the porous web of computers that constitutes the Internet, the tension between preserving that privacy and fostering public knowledge of matters of public concern has leaped into the First Amendment arena. Some of this has been fueled by the constant search for partisan advantage in public debate, as was the case with the interception of a cellular phone conference call involving then-Speaker Newt Gingrich by two Democratic partisans and the subsequent release to the media of a tape of that call through Rep. Jim McDermott (D-Washington). See Boehner v. McDermott, 191 F.3d 463 (D.C. Cir. 1999). Prior cases raising aspects of this issue have involved content-based prohibitions on publication, but *Boehner* and Bartnicki v. Vopper, which follows, involved content-neutral prohibitions on disclosure of intercepted communications. For more on the general issue, see Jeffrey Rosen, The Unwanted Gaze: The Destruction of Privacy in America (New York: Random House, 2000).

In Bartnicki v. Vopper, 532 U.S. 514 (2001), the Court invalidated two federal statutes which, as applied, imposed criminal and civil penalties on the disclosure of a private communication that was intercepted illegally by an unknown party but which was obtained lawfully by the person making the disclosure. Under 18 U.S.C. §2511(1)(c), anyone who discloses an illegally intercepted communication if they knew or had reason to know of the illegal nature of the interception is guilty of a crime. Another statute imposes civil liability for such disclosures. An unknown person illegally recorded a cellular telephone between Bartnicki, the chief negotiator for a teachers' union, and Kane, the union's president, that occurred during "contentious" negotiations between the union and a public school board. Kane suggested to Bartnicki that the union might need to "blow off their front porches" to induce the school board to accede to the teachers' demands. A tape of the conversation was left in the mailbox of Yocum, the head of a local taxpayers' organization. Yocum provided the tape to Vopper, a radio commentator, who broadcast the tape as part of his critical commentary on the union.

The Court struck down the two federal statutes, as applied to Vopper, Yocum, and various media defendants who had participated in the disclosure. Even though the laws were "content-neutral law[s] of general applicability" the Court found, with no discussion of the standard of review, that the statutes were unjustified means to the accomplishment of the government's objectives. The Court identified two interests that were served by the statutes: (1) "removing an incentive for parties to intercept private conversations," and (2) "minimizing the harm to persons whose conversations have been illegally intercepted." As to the first interest, the Court observed that the "normal method of deterring unlawful conduct is [to punish] the person who engages in it," and concluded that inasmuch as "it would be quite remarkable to hold that speech by a law-abiding possessor of information can be suppressed in order to deter conduct by a non-law-abiding third party," the government's first justification was "plainly insufficient." (The Court did state that "there are some rare occasions in which a law suppressing one party's speech may be justified by an interest in deterring criminal conduct by another," but noted that such occasions involve speech of "minimal value." The most obvious example is non-obscene child pornography. See Osborne v. Ohio, p. 881; New York v. Ferber, p. 892.)

The Court thought that the second interest, ensuring privacy of private communications, was "considerably stronger." Such privacy encourages "the uninhibited exchange of ideas and information among private parties" and "the fear of public disclosure of private conversations might well have a chilling effect on private speech." Nevertheless, the Court stressed the fact that the statutes, as applied, implicated "the core purposes of the First Amendment" because they imposed "sanctions on the publication of truthful information of public concern." The Court expressly disclaimed any opinion on whether the statutory sanctions might be validly applied to "disclosures of trade secrets or domestic gossip or other information of purely private concern."

Chief Justice Rehnquist, in a dissent joined by Justices Scalia and Thomas, charged that the majority had subjected a content-neutral speech regulation that was conceded to serve "interests of the 'highest order' . . . to the strict scrutiny normally reserved for governmental attempts to censor different viewpoints or ideas." According to the dissent:

> [These] laws are content neutral; they only regulate information that was illegally obtained; they do not restrict republication of what is already in the public domain; they impose no special burdens upon the media; they have a scienter requirement to provide fair warning; and they promote the privacy and free speech of those using cellular telephones. It is hard to imagine a more narrowly tailored prohibition of the disclosure of illegally intercepted communications, and it distorts our precedents to review these

> statutes under the often fatal standard of strict scrutiny. These laws therefore should be upheld if they further a substantial governmental interest unrelated to the suppression of free speech, and they do.

The dissent thought that "sanctioning the knowing disclosure of illegally intercepted communications will deter the initial interception itself, a crime which is extremely difficult to detect," because of the proliferation of illegal "scanners capable of intercepting cellular transmissions." The dissent maintained that the

> "dry up the market" theory, which posits that it is possible to deter an illegal act that is difficult to police by preventing the wrongdoer from enjoying the fruits of the crime, is neither novel nor implausible. It is a time-tested theory that undergirds numerous laws, such as the prohibition of the knowing possession of stolen goods. [The] same logic applies here and demonstrates that the incidental restriction on alleged First Amendment freedoms is no greater than essential to further the interest of protecting the privacy of individual communications. . . . Indeed, demand for illegally obtained private information would only increase if it could be disclosed without repercussion.

3. The "Secondary Effects" Doctrine

Page 1008: Insert at the end of the section, immediately prior to section D:

5. The Evidentiary Standard. In *Erie*, Justice Souter argued that under intermediate scrutiny a government must demonstrate "the harm it claims to flow from expressive activity, and for the alleviation that is expected from the restriction imposed." The problem for Justice Souter was that the City of Erie had purportedly relied on other jurisdictions' experiences in banning nude dancing, but had failed to prove its reliance on those experiences by "demonstrated fact, not speculative supposition."

The problem of the proper evidentiary standard in secondary effects cases came back to the Court in City of Los Angeles v. Alameda Books, 535 U.S. 425 (2002). A four justice plurality ruled that the "substantial government interest" prong of the *Renton* test for secondary effects is satisfied if the evidence "fairly support[s]" the rationale for the law. To overcome such "fairly supportive" evidence, a plaintiff must establish either that the government's evidence does not support the law's rationale or that the government's evidence is factually in dispute, in which case the burden of proving the "substantial government interest" by additional relevant evidence shifts back to the government. Justice Kennedy, concurring in the judgment, argued that the secondary effects doctrine is a narrow exception to the ordinary rule that content-based speech regulations are subject to strict scrutiny. Therefore, to invoke the doctrine successfully it is necessary for a government to establish that its "substantial interest" is to reduce the costs of identified secondary effects of speech *without* suppressing speech. In Kennedy's view, a law that seeks to reduce the secondary effects of, say, pornography by reducing the amount of pornography available would not adequately state a substantial government interest.

Can a government ever have a substantial interest in reducing speech? If so, under what circumstances? What if the government's interest is genuinely something other than suppressing speech, but the only avenue for accomplishment of the non-speech objective is reducing the volume of speech? A tax on pornographic speech alone would be subject to strict scrutiny; was it proper to subject Renton's zoning ordinance (that had the effect of reducing pornographic speech by confining vendors of pornography to a small area with little available land) to intermediate scrutiny? How would Renton's ordinance fare under Justice Kennedy's approach in *Alameda Books*?

D. Regulation of Speech When the Government Is Both Sovereign and Proprietor

1. Public Forum

Page 1015: Insert at the end of note 1.a., Limited public fora:

In Good News Club v. Milford Central School, 533 U.S. 98 (2001), the Court extended its viewpoint discrimination approach to the case of a public school that created a limited public forum by opening its facilities after school hours to a variety of community welfare uses, including education, arts, social, civic, recreational, and entertainment uses, but excluding religious use. The school denied access to the Good News Club, a private Christian organization for children ages 6 to 12 that engaged in Bible lessons, prayer, memorization of Bible passages, and singing of religious songs, on the grounds that the Good News Club was engaged in religious worship. All parties agreed that the school had created a limited public forum. The Court held that the denial of access to the Good News Club was viewpoint discrimination that was not justified on the theory that access must be denied to avoid creation of a forbidden establishment of religion. On the establishment of religion aspects of the case, see the portion of the 2004 Supplement relating to p.1181 of the casebook, below.

Justice Stevens dissented on the ground that it should be permissible for a public entity to create a limited public forum open to speech "from a religious point of view," but closed to religious worship or speech "that is aimed principally at proselytizing or inculcating belief in a particular religious faith." Justice Souter, joined by Justice Ginsburg, also thought that the Good News Club's use of the school "for an evangelical service of worship calling children to commit themselves to an act of Christian conversion" was outside the scope of the limited forum created by the school and that forum limitations that preclude use of the forum for worship should be valid.

Page 1017: Insert at the end of note 1.b., immediately before note 2:

In United States v. American Library Ass'n, 539 U.S. 194 (2003), the Supreme Court upheld portions of the federal Children's Internet Protection Act (CIPA), which denies federal money for Internet access to public libraries unless they install software to block obscene or pornographic images and to prevent minors from accessing material harmful to them. A plurality of the Court rejected the argument that Internet access in public libraries is a public forum. Such access, said the plurality, "is neither a 'traditional' nor a 'designated' public forum. First, this resource — which did not exist until quite recently — has not 'immemorially been held in trust for the use of the public and, time out of mind, . . . been used for purposes of assembly, communication of thoughts between citizens, and discussing public questions.' . . . Nor does Internet access in a public library satisfy our definition of a 'designated public forum.' To create such a forum, the government must make an affirmative choice to open up its property for use as a public forum. . . . A public library does not acquire Internet terminals in order to create a public forum for Web publishers to express themselves, any more than it collects books in order to provide a public forum for the authors of books to speak. . . . As Congress recognized, 'the Internet is simply another method for making information available in a school or library.' It is 'no more than a technological extension of the book stack.' "

4. Public Sponsorship of Speech

Page 1042: Insert the following immediately before section E:

LEGAL SERVICES CORPORATION v. VELASQUEZ
531 U.S. 533 (2001)

JUSTICE KENNEDY delivered the opinion of the Court.

[Congress established the Legal Services Corporation (LSC)] to distribute funds appropriated by Congress to eligible local grantee organizations "for the purpose of providing financial support for legal assistance in noncriminal proceedings or matters to persons financially unable to afford legal assistance.". . . LSC grantees consist of hundreds of local organizations . . . funded by a combination of LSC funds and other public or private sources. The grantee organizations hire and supervise lawyers to provide free legal assistance to indigent clients . . . seeking welfare benefits.

This suit requires us to decide whether one of the conditions imposed by Congress on the use of LSC funds violates the First Amendment rights of LSC grantees and their clients. [Congress barred LSC funded] legal representation . . . if the representation involves an effort to amend or otherwise challenge existing welfare law. As interpreted by the LSC and by the Government, the restriction prevents an attorney from arguing to a court that a state statute conflicts with a federal statute or that either a state or federal statute by its terms or in its application [violates] the United States Constitution.[2]

Lawyers employed by New York City LSC grantees, together with private LSC contributors, LSC indigent clients, and various state and local public officials whose governments contribute to LSC grantees, brought suit in [federal] District Court [to] declare the restriction . . . invalid. The United States Court of Appeals [enjoined] enforcement of the provision as an impermissible viewpoint-based discrimination in violation of the First Amendment. . . . We agree that the restriction violates the First Amendment, and we affirm the judgment of the Court of Appeals. . . .

II. The United States and LSC rely on Rust v. Sullivan [p. 1037] as support for the LSC program restrictions. In *Rust*, Congress established program clinics to provide subsidies for doctors to advise patients on a variety of family planning topics [but specifically] forbade doctors employed by the program from discussing abortion with their patients. . . . We upheld the law, reasoning that Congress had not discriminated against viewpoints on abortion, but had "merely chosen to fund one activity to the exclusion of the other" [and had imposed restrictions necessary] "to ensure that the limits of the federal program [were] observed." . . .

The Court in *Rust* did not place explicit reliance on the rationale that the counseling activities of the doctors . . . amounted to governmental speech; when interpreting the holding in later cases, however, we have explained *Rust* on this understanding. We have said that viewpoint-based funding decisions can be sustained in instances in which the government is itself the speaker, see Board of Regents of Univ. of Wis. System v. Southworth, 529 U.S. 217 (2000), or instances, like *Rust*, in which the government "used private speakers to transmit information pertaining to its own program." Rosenberger v. Rector & Visitors of Univ. of Va., 515 U.S. 819, 833 (1995). As we said in *Rosenberger*, "when the government disburses public funds to private entities to convey a governmental message, it may take legitimate and appropriate steps to ensure that its message is neither garbled nor distorted by the grantee." The latitude which may exist for restrictions on speech where the government's own message is being delivered flows in part from our observation that, "when the government speaks . . . to promote its own policies or to advance a particular idea, it is, in the end, accountable to the electorate and the

2. Congress prohibited funding of any organization "that initiates legal representation or participates in any other way in litigation, lobbying, or rulemaking involving an effort to reform a Federal or State welfare system, except that this paragraph shall not be construed to preclude a recipient from representing an individual eligible client who is seeking specific relief from a welfare agency if such relief does not involve an effort to amend or otherwise challenge existing law in effect on the date of the initiation of the representation." Omnibus Consolidated Rescissions and Appropriations Act of 1996, 110 Stat. 1321-53, §504(a)(16). The prohibition was continued in each subsequent annual appropriations Act. — ED.

political process for its advocacy." [*Southworth.*] [But] "it does not follow . . . that viewpoint-based restrictions are proper when the [government] does not itself speak or subsidize transmittal of a message it favors but instead expends funds to encourage a diversity of views from private speakers." [*Rosenberger.*]

Although the LSC program differs from the program at issue in *Rosenberger* in that its purpose is not to "encourage a diversity of views," the salient point is that, like the program in *Rosenberger*, the LSC program was designed to facilitate private speech, not to promote a governmental message. Congress funded LSC grantees to provide attorneys to represent the interests of indigent clients. In the specific context [at issue], an LSC-funded attorney speaks on the behalf of the client in a claim against the government for welfare benefits. The lawyer is not the government's speaker. The attorney defending the decision to deny benefits will deliver the government's message in the litigation. The LSC lawyer, however, speaks on the behalf of his or her private, indigent client. The Government has designed this program . . . to accomplish its end of assisting welfare claimants in determination or receipt of their benefits. The advice from the attorney to the client and the advocacy by the attorney to the courts cannot be classified as governmental speech even under a generous understanding of the concept. In this vital respect this suit is distinguishable from *Rust.*

[Also,] the Government seeks to use an existing medium of expression and to control it [in] ways which distort its usual functioning. . . . Restricting LSC attorneys in advising their clients and in presenting arguments and analyses to the courts distorts the legal system by altering the traditional role of the attorneys. . . .

An informed, independent judiciary presumes an informed, independent bar. . . . [H]owever, cases would be presented by LSC attorneys who could not advise the courts of serious questions of statutory validity. The disability is inconsistent with the proposition that attorneys should present all the reasonable and well-grounded arguments necessary for proper resolution of the case. By seeking to prohibit the analysis of certain legal issues and to truncate presentation to the courts, the enactment under review prohibits speech and expression upon which courts must depend for the proper exercise of the judicial power. . . . The statute is an attempt to draw lines around the LSC program to exclude from litigation those arguments and theories Congress finds unacceptable but which by their nature are within the province of the courts to consider. . . .

It is fundamental that the First Amendment "was fashioned to assure unfettered interchange of ideas for the bringing about of political and social changes desired by the people." There can be little doubt that the LSC Act funds constitutionally protected expression; and in the context of this statute there is no programmatic message of the kind recognized in *Rust* and which sufficed there to allow the Government to specify the advice deemed necessary for its legitimate objectives. . . . Congress was not required to fund an LSC attorney to represent indigent clients; and when it did so, it was not required to fund the whole range of legal representations or relationships. The LSC and the United States, however, in effect ask us to permit Congress to define the scope of the litigation it funds to exclude certain vital theories and ideas. The attempted restriction is designed to insulate the Government's interpretation of the Constitution from judicial challenge. The Constitution does not permit the Government to confine litigants and their attorneys in this manner. We must be vigilant when Congress imposes rules and conditions which in effect insulate its own laws from legitimate judicial challenge. Where private speech is involved, even Congress's antecedent funding decision cannot be aimed at the suppression of ideas thought inimical to the Government's own interest. . . . Affirmed.

JUSTICE SCALIA, joined by CHIEF JUSTICE REHNQUIST and JUSTICES O'CONNOR and THOMAS, dissenting.

[The statute] defines the scope of a federal spending program. It does not directly regulate speech, and it neither establishes a public forum nor discriminates on the basis of viewpoint. The Court agrees with all this, yet applies a novel and unsupportable interpretation of our public-forum precedents to declare §504(a)(16) facially unconstitutional. This holding not only has no foundation in our jurisprudence; it is flatly contradicted by [*Rust*].

I. [When Congress created the Legal Services Corporation it recognized] that the program could not serve its purpose unless it was "kept free from the influence of or use by it of political pressures." [Thus], from the program's inception [Congress has] tightly regulated the use of its funds. No [LSC] funds may be used, for example, for "encouraging . . . labor or antilabor activities," for "litigation relating to the desegregation of any elementary or secondary school or school system," or for "litigation which seeks to procure a nontherapeutic abortion." Congress discovered through experience, however, that these restrictions did not exhaust the politically controversial uses to which LSC funds could be put, [so] Congress added new restrictions, [including] the one at issue here.

[Under the litigation restriction at issue] the LSC can sponsor neither challenges to *nor* defenses of existing welfare reform law. The litigation ban is symmetrical: Litigants challenging the covered statutes or regulations do not receive LSC funding, and neither do litigants defending those laws against challenge. If a suit for benefits raises a claim outside the scope of the LSC program, the LSC-funded lawyer may not participate in the suit. . . . The lawyers may, however, and indeed *must* explain to the client why they cannot represent him. They are also free to express their views of the legality of the welfare law to the client, and they may refer the client to another attorney who can accept the representation.

II. The LSC Act is a federal subsidy program, not a federal regulatory program, and "there is a basic difference between [the two]." Regulations directly restrict speech; subsidies do not. Subsidies, it is true, may *indirectly* abridge speech, but only if the funding scheme is " 'manipulated' to have a 'coercive effect' " on those who do not hold the subsidized position. National Endowment for Arts v. Finley, 524 U.S. 569, 587 (1998) (quoting Arkansas Writers' Project, Inc. v. Ragland, 481 U.S. 221, 237 (1987) (Scalia, J., dissenting)). Proving unconstitutional coercion is difficult enough when the spending program has universal coverage and excludes only certain speech. [The] Court has found such programs unconstitutional only when the exclusion was "aimed at the suppression of dangerous ideas." Speiser v. Randall, 357 U.S. 513, 519 (1958). Proving the requisite coercion is harder still when a spending program is not universal but limited, providing benefits to a restricted number of recipients. [*Rust.*] The Court has found such selective spending unconstitutionally coercive only once, when the government created a public forum with the spending program but then discriminated in distributing funding within the forum on the basis of viewpoint. [*Rosenberger.*] When the limited spending program does not create a public forum, proving coercion is virtually impossible, because simply denying a subsidy "does not 'coerce' belief," and because the criterion of unconstitutionality is whether denial of the subsidy threatens "to drive certain ideas or viewpoints from the marketplace." Absent such a threat, "the Government may allocate . . . funding according to criteria that would be impermissible were direct regulation of speech or a criminal penalty at stake." [*Finley.*]

[In *Rust* we said there was no] "discrimination on the basis of viewpoint" that triggers strict scrutiny because the "decision not to subsidize the exercise of a fundamental right does not infringe the right." The same is true here. The LSC Act [simply] "placed restrictions on its use of funds." Nor does [the law] discriminate on the basis of viewpoint, since it funds neither challenges to nor defenses of existing welfare law. The provision simply declines to subsidize a certain class of litigation, and under *Rust* that decision "does not infringe the right" to bring such litigation. [The] Court's repeated claims that [the law] "restricts" and "prohibits" speech and "insulates" laws from judicial review are simply baseless. No litigant who, in the absence of LSC funding, would bring a suit challenging existing welfare law is deterred from doing so by [the law]. *Rust* thus controls these cases and compels the conclusion that [the law] is constitutional.

The Court contends that *Rust* is different because the program at issue subsidized government speech, while the LSC funds private speech. This is so unpersuasive it hardly needs response. If the private doctors' confidential advice to their patients at issue in *Rust* constituted "government speech," it is hard to imagine what subsidized speech would *not* be government speech. Moreover, the majority's contention that the subsidized speech in these cases is not government speech because the lawyers have a professional obligation to represent the interests of their clients founders on the reality that the doctors in *Rust* had a professional obligation to serve the interests of their patients. Even respondents agree that "the true speaker in *Rust* was not the government, but a doctor."

The Court further asserts that these cases are different from *Rust* because the welfare funding restriction "seeks to use an existing medium of expression and to control it . . . in ways which distort its usual functioning." This is wrong on both the facts and the law. It is wrong on the law because there is utterly no precedent for the novel and facially implausible proposition that the First Amendment has anything to do with government funding that — though it does not actually abridge anyone's speech — "distorts an existing medium of expression." . . .

The Court's "nondistortion" principle is also wrong on the facts, since there is no basis for believing that [the law], by causing "cases [to] be presented by LSC attorneys who cannot advise the courts of serious questions of statutory validity," will distort the operation of the courts. It may well be that the bar of §504(a)(16) will cause LSC-funded attorneys to decline or to withdraw from cases that involve statutory validity. But that means at most that fewer statutory challenges to welfare laws will be presented to the courts because of the unavailability of free legal services for that purpose. So what? The same result would ensue from excluding LSC-funded lawyers from welfare litigation entirely. . . . Courts must consider only those questions of statutory validity *that are presented by litigants*, and if the Government chooses not to subsidize the presentation of some such questions, that in no way "distorts" the courts' role. . . . Nor will the judicial opinions produced by LSC cases systematically distort the interpretation of welfare laws. [The] statutory validity that courts assume in LSC cases will remain open for full determination in later cases.

Finally, the Court is troubled "because in cases where the attorney withdraws from a representation, the client is unlikely to find other counsel." That is surely irrelevant, since it leaves the welfare recipient in no *worse* condition than he would have been in had the LSC program never been enacted. . . . It is hard to see how providing free legal services to some welfare claimants (those whose claims do not challenge the applicable statutes) while not providing it to others is beyond the range of legitimate legislative choice. *Rust* rejected a similar argument. . . .

This has been a very long discussion to make a point that is embarrassingly simple: The LSC subsidy neither prevents anyone from speaking nor coerces anyone to change speech, and is indistinguishable in all relevant respects from the subsidy upheld in Rust v. Sullivan. There is no legitimate basis for declaring [the law] facially unconstitutional. . . .

I respectfully dissent.

NOTES

1. The Distinction between Government Speech and Private Speech. Why was the physicians' speech at issue in *Rust* the government's speech but the lawyers' speech at issue in *Velasquez* private speech? Both speakers were speaking in the course of delivering a government aid program. Is the difference rooted in the nature of lawyers' speech — that lawyers are employed to speak *for* their clients through advocacy and physicians are employed to speak *to* their patients about medical diagnosis and treatment?

Assess the constitutional validity of a hypothetical federal regulation that bars military chaplains from advocating pacifism, including within their liturgical celebration. Are chaplains private speakers or government speakers?

Suppose Congress subsidizes all teachers of history in public and private nonsectarian schools by providing substantial salary supplements, but provides that any recipient must refrain from criticizing the Framers of the Constitution for their tolerance of slavery. Assess the constitutional validity of the subsidy.

2. The Role of Coercion and Distortion. In *Rust* the Court thought that the abortion counseling restriction was not coercive because indigent women remained free to seek other advice. Was the restriction at issue in *Velasquez* coercive or was coercion simply irrelevant to the Court's analysis in *Velasquez*?

What is the meaning of distortion? Doesn't any speech restriction — even permissible ones that are inextricably connected to legitimate government subsidies — distort speech? Justice Kennedy saw distortion in LSC lawyers' speech and its effect on the judicial process. Justice Scalia saw no distortion there because non-LSC lawyers remained free to say the things that LSC lawyers could not. Is this simply an argument over the level of generality at which the concept of distortion should be determined? If the problem posed by distortion is the effect on the judicial process of the LSC restrictions, should the problem be resolved by assessing whether the LSC restrictions prevent the judiciary from hearing those arguments from anyone? If so, is Justice Scalia correct? If the problem posed by distortion is the effect on LSC lawyers' speech, why did the Court distinguish *Rust* rather than overrule it? Would it be an unconstitutional distortion of speech if Congress simply terminated the LSC?

UNITED STATES v. AMERICAN LIBRARY ASSOCIATION

539 U.S. 194 (2003)

CHIEF JUSTICE REHNQUIST announced the judgment of the Court and delivered an opinion, in which JUSTICE O'CONNOR, JUSTICE SCALIA, and JUSTICE THOMAS joined.

[Congress made federal funds available to public libraries to assist them in providing Internet access to their patrons. To address the problems associated with the availability of Internet pornography in public libraries, Congress enacted the Children's Internet Protection Act (CIPA), under which a public library may not receive federal aid unless it installs software to block images that constitute obscenity or child pornography, and to prevent minors from obtaining access to material that is harmful to them. CIPA permits the library to "disable" the filter "to enable access for bona fide research or other lawful purposes." One federal aid program permitted disabling "during use by an adult"; the other aid program permitted disabling during use by any person.] The District Court held these provisions facially invalid on the ground that they induce public libraries to violate patrons' First Amendment rights. We now reverse.

. . . Congress has wide latitude to attach conditions to the receipt of federal assistance in order to further its policy objectives. South Dakota v. Dole. But Congress may not "induce" the recipient "to engage in activities that would themselves be unconstitutional." [Id.] To determine whether libraries would violate the First Amendment by employing the filtering software that CIPA requires, we must first examine the role of libraries in our society.

Public libraries pursue the worthy missions of facilitating learning and cultural enrichment. . . . To fulfill their traditional missions, public libraries must have broad discretion to decide what material to provide to their patrons. Although they seek to provide a wide array of information, their goal has never been to provide "universal coverage." Instead, public libraries seek to provide materials "that would be of the greatest direct benefit or interest to the community." To this end, libraries collect only those materials deemed to have "requisite and appropriate quality."

We have held in two analogous contexts that the government has broad discretion to make content-based judgments in deciding what private speech to make available to the public. In Arkansas Ed. Television Comm'n v. Forbes, 523 U.S. 666 (1998), we held that public forum principles do not generally apply to a public television station's editorial judgments regarding the private speech it presents to its viewers. [In] National Endowment for Arts v. Finley, 524 U.S. 569 (1998), we upheld an art funding program that required the National Endowment for the Arts (NEA) to use content-based criteria in making funding decisions. We explained that "any content-based considerations that may be taken into account in the grant-making process are a consequence of the nature of arts funding." In particular, "the very assumption of the NEA is that grants will be awarded according to the 'artistic worth of competing applicants,' and absolute neutrality is simply inconceivable." . . . The principles underlying *Forbes* and *Finley* also apply to a public library's exercise of judgment in selecting the material it provides to its patrons. . . . Public library staffs necessarily consider content in making collection decisions and enjoy broad discretion in making them.

. . . A library's need to exercise judgment in making collection decisions depends on its traditional role in identifying suitable and worthwhile material; it is no less entitled to play that role when it collects material from the Internet than when it collects material from any other source. Most libraries already exclude pornography from their print collections because they deem it inappropriate for inclusion. We do not subject these decisions to heightened scrutiny; it would make little sense to treat libraries' judgments to block online pornography any differently, when these judgments are made for just the same reason. Moreover, because of the vast quantity of material on the Internet and the rapid pace at which it changes, libraries cannot possibly segregate, item by item, all the Internet material that is appropriate for inclusion from all that is not. While a library could limit its Internet collection to just those sites it found worthwhile, it could do so only at the cost of excluding an enormous amount of valuable information that it lacks the capacity to review. Given that tradeoff, it is entirely reasonable for public libraries to reject that approach and instead exclude certain categories of content, without making individualized judgments that everything they do make available has requisite and appropriate quality.

[The] dissents fault the tendency of filtering software to "overblock" — that is, to erroneously block access to constitutionally protected speech that falls outside the categories that software users intend to block. . . . Assuming that such erroneous blocking presents constitutional difficulties, any such concerns are dispelled by the ease with which patrons may have the filtering software disabled. When a patron encounters a blocked site, he need only ask a librarian to unblock it or (at least in the case of adults) disable the filter. . . . The District Court viewed unblocking and disabling as inadequate because some patrons may be too embarrassed to request them. But the Constitution does not guarantee the right to acquire information at a public library without any risk of embarrassment.

. . . Appellees argue that CIPA imposes an unconstitutional condition on libraries that receive [federal] subsidies by requiring them, as a condition on their receipt of federal funds, to surrender their First Amendment right to provide the public with access to constitutionally protected speech. The Government counters that this claim fails because Government entities do not have First Amendment rights. We need not decide this question because, even assuming that appellees may assert an "unconstitutional conditions" claim, this claim would fail on the merits. Within broad limits, "when the Government appropriates public funds to establish a program it is entitled to define the limits of that program." Rust v. Sullivan. In *Rust*, [we recognized] that "the Government [was] not denying a benefit to anyone, but [was] instead simply insisting that public funds be spent for the purposes for which they were authorized."

The same is true here. The [federal] programs were intended to help public libraries fulfill their traditional role of obtaining material of requisite and appropriate quality for educational and informational purposes. Congress may certainly insist that these "public funds be spent for the purposes for which they were authorized." Especially because public libraries have traditionally excluded pornographic material from their other collections, Congress could reasonably impose a parallel limitation on its Internet assistance programs. As the use of filtering software helps to carry out these programs, it is a permissible condition under *Rust*.

Appellees mistakenly contend, in reliance on Legal Services Corporation v. Velazquez, that CIPA's filtering conditions "distor[t] the usual functioning of public libraries." In *Velazquez*, the Court concluded that a Government program of furnishing legal aid to the indigent differed from the program in *Rust* "in the vital respect" that the role of lawyers who represent clients in welfare disputes is to advocate *against* the Government, and there was thus an assumption that counsel would be free of state control. . . . Public libraries, by contrast, have no comparable role that pits them against the Government, and there is no comparable assumption that they must be free of any conditions that their benefactors might attach to the use of donated funds or other assistance.

Because public libraries' use of Internet filtering software does not violate their patrons' First Amendment rights, CIPA does not induce libraries to violate the Constitution, and is a valid exercise of Congress' spending power. Nor does CIPA impose an unconstitutional condition on public libraries. Therefore, the judgment of the District Court for the Eastern District of Pennsylvania is

Reversed.

JUSTICE KENNEDY, concurring in the judgment.

If, on the request of an adult user, a librarian will unblock filtered material or disable the Internet software filter without significant delay, there is little to this case. The Government represents this is indeed the fact. . . . If some libraries do not have the capacity to unblock specific Web sites or to disable the filter or if it is shown that an adult user's election to view constitutionally protected Internet material is burdened in some other substantial way, that would be the subject for an as-applied challenge, not the facial challenge made in this case.

JUSTICE BREYER, concurring in the judgment.

. . . I reach the plurality's ultimate conclusion in a different way. . . . I would apply a form of heightened scrutiny . . . . The Act directly restricts the public's receipt of information. And it does so through limitations imposed by outside bodies (here Congress) upon two critically important sources of information — the Internet as accessed via public libraries. For that reason, we should . . . examine the constitutionality of the Act's restrictions here as the Court has examined speech-related restrictions in other contexts where circumstances call for heightened, but not "strict," scrutiny — where, for example, complex, competing constitutional interests are potentially at issue or speech-related harm is potentially justified by unusually strong governmental interests. Typically the key question in such instances is one of proper fit. In such cases the Court has asked whether the harm to speech-related interests is disproportionate in light of both the justifications and the potential alternatives. It has considered the legitimacy of the statute's objective, the extent to which the statute will tend to achieve that objective, whether there are other, less restrictive ways of achieving that objective, and ultimately whether the statute works speech-related harm that, in relation to that objective, is out of proportion. [Cf., e.g., *Central Hudson*; *O'Brien*; *Virginia Bd. of Pharmacy*.]

The Act's restrictions satisfy these constitutional demands. The Act seeks to restrict access to obscenity, child pornography, and, in respect to access by minors, material that is comparably harmful. These objectives are "legitimate," and indeed often "compelling." [Software] filters "provide a relatively cheap and effective" means of furthering these goals. Due to present technological limitations, however, the software filters both "overblock," screening out some perfectly legitimate material, and "underblock," allowing some obscene material to escape detection by the filter. But no one has presented any clearly superior or better fitting alternatives.

At the same time, the Act . . . allows libraries to permit any adult patron access to an "overblocked" Web site; the adult patron need only ask a librarian to unblock the specific Web site or, alternatively, ask the librarian, "Please disable the entire filter." . . . Given the comparatively small burden that the Act imposes upon the library patron seeking legitimate Internet materials, I cannot say that any speech-related harm that the Act may cause is disproportionate when considered in relation to the Act's legitimate objectives. I therefore agree with the plurality that the statute does not violate the First Amendment, and I concur in the judgment.

E. Vagueness, Overbreadth, and Prior Restraints

1. Overbreadth

Page 1049: Insert at the end of the section, immediately before subsection E.2:

4. The Scope and Limits of Overbreadth. Although overbreadth analysis has particular applicability to free speech it is not confined to expression cases. The Court has recognized that overbreadth challenges may be made with respect to laws that inhibit the right to travel, Aptheker v. Secretary of State, 378 U.S. 500 (1964); infringe the right to an abortion, Stenberg v. Carhart, 530 U.S. 914, 938-946 (2000); and exceed Congress's power to enforce the substantive provisions of the Fourteenth Amendment, City of Boerne v. Flores, 521 U.S. 507, 532-535 (1997). Professor Richard Fallon contends that the various substantive tests of constitutional validity in each of these areas plays a significant role in evaluating facial challenges for overbreadth. Richard Fallon, As-Applied and Facial Challenges and Third-Party Standing, 113 Harv. L. Rev. 1321, 1351 (2000). In an earlier work, Professor Henry Monaghan made similar observations about the overbreadth doctrine in the area of free speech. Henry Monaghan, Overbreadth, 1981 S. Ct. Rev. 1, 24.

In Sabri v. United States, 124 S. Ct. 1941 (2004), the Court rejected a challenge to the facial validity of a federal statute that makes bribery of officials of state and local governments that receive at least $10,000 in federal funds a federal crime. In doing so, the Court commented upon the scope and limits of overbreadth. Sabri asserted that the law was void because it failed to predicate criminal liability upon "proof of a connection between the federal funds and the alleged bribe." As applied, it was

> obvious that the acts charged against Sabri himself were well within the limits of legitimate congressional concern. [Sabri's] substantive constitutional claim [was] an overbreadth challenge; the most he could say was that the statute could not be enforced against him, because it could not be enforced against someone else whose behavior would be outside the scope of Congress's Article I authority to legislate. Facial challenges of this sort are especially to be discouraged. Not only do they invite judgments on fact-poor records, but they entail a further departure from the norms of adjudication in federal courts: overbreadth challenges call for relaxing familiar requirements of standing, to allow a determination that the law would be unconstitutionally applied to different parties and different circumstances from those at hand. Accordingly, we have recognized the validity of facial attacks alleging overbreadth (though not necessarily using that term) in relatively few settings, and, generally, on the strength of specific reasons weighty enough to overcome our well-founded reticence. [*Broadrick, Aptheker, Stenberg, City of Boerne.*] Outside these limited settings, and absent a good reason, we do not extend an invitation to bring overbreadth claims.

3. Prior Restraints

a. Licensing

Page 1053: Insert at the end of the section, immediately prior to subsection b:

Content-Neutral Licensing. Any possibility that the *Freedman* standards might be applicable to licensing schemes that are content-neutral was removed by Thomas v. Chicago Park District, 534 U.S. 316 (2002), in which a unanimous Court held that the *Freedman* standards were not applicable to a content-neutral permit ordinance directed "to *all* activity conducted in a public park [in order] to coordinate multiple uses of limited space, to assure preservation of the park facilities, to prevent uses that are dangerous, unlawful, or impermissible under the Park District's rules, and to assure financial accountability for damage caused by the event." The Court viewed licensing to censor the content of speech as totally different from "[r]egulations of the use of a public forum that ensure the safety and convenience of the people. . . . Such a traditional exercise of authority does not raise the censorship concerns that prompted us to impose the extraordinary procedural safeguards on the film licensing process in *Freedman*."

The Court in *Thomas* reemphasized the principle that content-neutral licensing may be done only with clear and definite standards: "Where the licensing official enjoys unduly broad discretion in determining whether to grant or deny a permit, there is a risk that he will favor or disfavor speech based on its content. [*Forsyth County.*] We have thus required that a time, place, and manner regulation contain adequate standards to guide the official's decision and render it subject to effective judicial review. [Here, the 13 grounds for denial of a permit specified by the ordinance] are reasonably specific and objective, and do not leave the decision 'to the whim of the administrator.' They provide 'narrowly drawn, reasonable and definite standards' to guide the licensor's determination [and] they are enforceable on review."

b. Injunctions

Page 1058: Insert at the end of the section, immediately prior to Section F:

Note: Charitable Solicitations

Solicitation of money for charitable purposes is a protected form of expression. See *Schaumburg*, pp. 1047-1048, which identified the speech interests as "communication of information, the dissemination and propagation of views and ideas, and the advocacy of causes." But charitable solicitation is often conducted by for-profit enterprises that retain very large percentages of the donated funds as payment for their solicitation efforts on behalf of the charity. An initial response to this was enactment of flat bans on charitable solicitation if the net contribution to the charity was less than a specified amount. The law at issue in *Schaumberg*, for example, banned in-person solicitation unless at least 75% of the funds raised went to the charity. In *Schaumburg*, *Munson*, p. 1048, and Riley v. National Federation of Blind of N. C., Inc., 487 U.S. 781 (1988), the Court voided laws "that categorically restrained solicitation by charities or professional fundraisers if a high percentage of the funds raised would be used to cover administrative or fundraising costs," on the theory that, as explained in Illinois *ex rel.* Madigan v. Telemarketing Associations, Inc., 538 U.S. 600 (2003), those inflexible restrictions "effectively imposed prior restraints on [charitable] fundraising." In each of *Schaumburg*, *Munson*, and *Riley* the Court acknowledged that the governmental goal of preventing fraud was important but thought that it could be achieved by less draconian means.

In *Telemarketing Associations* the Court was not confronted by a flat ban on high cost charitable solicitations, but by the question of whether a state could sue professional telemarketers soliciting funds for a charity for fraud in connection with the solicitation. The telemarketer defendants had contracted with a charity to raise funds in Illinois for the charity, and the contract stipulated that 85% of the funds raised would be kept by the telemarketers. The Illinois Attorney General contended that the telemarketers had intentionally misled contributors into thinking that most of the money donated would go to the charity when, in fact, it would be kept by the telemarketers. Under Illinois law fraud must be established by clear and convincing evidence that the defendant made a false representation of a material fact knowing that the representation was false, with the intent to mislead, and with the result that the recipient was in fact deceived. The Court permitted Illinois to proceed with its fraud suit, concluding that such "[e]xacting proof requirements . . . provide sufficient breathing room for protected speech," citing New York Times Co. v. Sullivan, p.943.

F. Expression Rights Implicit in the Free Speech Guarantee

1. Freedom of Association

Page 1067: Insert at the end of note 4, immediately prior to note 5:

Forced Contributions for Commercial Speech. In United States v. United Foods, Inc., 533 U.S. 405 (2001), *Keller* and *Abood* were applied to invalidate a provision of federal law that required mushroom producers to pay assessments used primarily to fund advertisements promoting generic mushroom sales. United Foods wanted to convey the message that its brand of mushrooms is superior to those grown by other producers, and so objected to being charged for a contrary message which was apparently desired by most mushroom producers. Regardless of the fact that the compelled speech at issue was "in aid of a commercial purpose" the Court ruled that "First Amendment concerns apply here because of the requirement that producers subsidize speech with which they disagree. [The compelled] message is that mushrooms are worth consuming whether or not they are branded. First Amendment values are at serious risk if the government can compel a particular citizen, or a discrete group of citizens, to pay special subsidies for speech on the side that it favors; and there is no apparent principle which distinguishes out of hand minor debates about whether a branded mushroom is better than just any mushroom. As a consequence, the compelled funding for the advertising must pass First Amendment scrutiny."

In a prior case, Glickman v. Wileman Brothers & Elliott, Inc., 521 U.S. 457 (1997), the Court had upheld a federal requirement that producers of California tree fruits pay assessments for product advertising. The Court distinguished *Glickman* by noting that there "the mandated assessments for speech were ancillary to a more comprehensive program restricting marketing autonomy. Here, for all practical purposes, the advertising itself, far from being ancillary, is the principal object of the regulatory scheme. . . . [*Glickman*] proceeded upon the premise that the producers were bound together and required by the statute to market their products according to cooperative rules. To that extent, their mandated participation in an advertising program with a particular message was the logical concomitant of a valid scheme of economic regulation." *Glickman* was thus roughly analogous to the portion of *Abood* in which the Court upheld mandatory union dues for collective bargaining purposes.

But the "features of the marketing scheme found important in *Glickman*" were not present in *United Foods*. "[A]lmost all of the funds collected under the mandatory assessments are for one purpose: generic advertising. Beyond the collection and disbursement of advertising funds, there are no marketing orders that regulate how mushrooms may be produced and sold [and nothing prevents] individual producers from making their own marketing decisions. . . . The only program the Government contends the compelled contributions serve is the very advertising scheme in question. . . . The cooperative marketing structure relied upon . . . in *Glickman* to sustain an ancillary assessment finds no corollary here; the expression respondent is required to support is not germane to a purpose related to an association independent from the speech itself; and the rationale of *Abood* extends to the party who objects to the compelled support for this speech. [The] assessments are not permitted under the First Amendment."

If the dividing line between valid and invalid forcible contributions is drawn where the forced contribution is ancillary to a valid regulatory program that does not have forced speech as its objective, would the assessment at issue in *United Foods* be valid if it were coupled with a government program requiring that all mushrooms be sold through a single government agency acting as distributor?

Suppose that in an effort to mitigate the secondary effects of non-obscene pornography a city requires all vendors of non-obscene pornography to contribute to a fund that is used for advertisements that seek to discourage demand for pornography. Would such a program be valid after *United Foods*? Would it make any difference if the fund was used to provide additional police protection in neighborhoods with a disproportionately large number of vendors of pornography?

Some states levy taxes on the purchase of cigarettes which are earmarked for advertising campaigns to discourage smoking. If those taxes were levied on the producers of cigarettes instead of the consumer, would *United Foods* cast doubt on their validity?

G. Free Expression and the Political Process

1. Money as Speech: Political Contributions and Expenditures

Page 1096: Insert at the end of note 6:

In Federal Election Commission v. Beaumont, 539 U.S. 146 (2003), the Supreme Court upheld the validity of a federal law that prohibits all corporations from making direct contributions to candidates for federal political office. The law was challenged by North Carolina Right to Life, Inc., a non-profit advocacy corporation dedicated to counseling pregnant women to avoid abortion. In a 7 to 2 decision the Court concluded that the rationales for a blanket ban on all direct corporate contributions to candidates — avoiding the corrupting effect of a candidate financially beholden to a contributor and preventing the use of corporate contributions as a device to avoid limits on individual contributions — were as applicable to non-profit advocacy corporations as to for-profit corporations. The Court distinguished FEC v. Massachusetts Citizens for Life (MCFL) on the ground that *MCFL* had involved expenditures, not contributions. The Court sought to harmonize *MCFL* and *National Right to Work Committee* on this basis, and reiterated its view, expressed in *Buckley* and *Nixon*, that while expenditure limits are subject to strict scrutiny, "a contribution limit involving 'significant interference' with associational rights" is valid "if it satisfies the lesser demand of being 'closely drawn' to match a 'sufficiently important interest.' " Justice Thomas, joined by Justice Scalia, dissented on the ground that all campaign finance limitations, whether on expenditures or contributions, ought to be subject to strict scrutiny.

Page 1096: Insert new note 7 immediately before subsection G.2:

7. *Additional Developments Since* Buckley*: Coordinated Expenditures.* After the Court struck down, in Colorado Republican Federal Campaign Committee v. FEC, 518 U.S. 604 (1996) (*Colorado I*), the spending limits imposed by federal law on a political party's expenditures made independently of a candidate, the case was remanded for consideration of whether all such spending limits imposed on a political party were invalid. In FEC v. Colorado Republican Federal Campaign Committee, 533 U.S. 431 (2001) (*Colorado II*), the Court upheld limits imposed on a political party's expenditures made in coordination with a candidate. The Court rejected as factually inaccurate the contention that limits on coordinated spending posed a special burden to the speech and association interests of political parties. Rather, the Court regarded political parties as "necessarily the instruments of some contributors whose object is not to support the party's message . . . but rather to support a specific candidate . . . who will be obliged to the contributors. [Whether] they like it or not, [parties] act as agents for spending on behalf of those who seek to produce obligated officeholders." Because the Court perceived coordinated party

expenditures as posing a similar, if not identical, risk of corruption as direct contributions to candidates, the Court upheld the Federal Election Campaign Act's spending limits as applied to political party expenditures coordinated with a candidate.

McCONNELL v. FEDERAL ELECTION COMMISSION

540 U.S. 93 (2003)

[Prior to enactment of the Bipartisan Campaign Reform Act of 2002 (the "BCRA"), federal law limiting political contributions did not apply to so-called "soft money": contributions made for some purpose other than the purpose of influencing an election for a federal office. Thus, contributions unlimited in amount could be made to influence state or local elections, to register voters and get them to vote, to promote political parties, and advocate legislation. Soft money could be used to purchase advertising for such purposes, and could mention a candidate's name so long as the advertising did not explicitly urge the election or defeat of a candidate. Accordingly, soft money became the source of funding for so-called "issue ads," which focused on an issue and linked a candidate with that issue, either positively or negatively, but without expressly urging the election or defeat of the mentioned candidate.]

JUSTICE STEVENS and JUSTICE O'CONNOR delivered the opinion of the Court with respect to BCRA Titles I and II.

. . . II. . . . Title I regulates the use of soft money by political parties, officeholders, and candidates. Title II primarily prohibits corporations and labor unions from using general treasury funds for communications that are intended to, or have the effect of, influencing the outcome of federal elections. . . .

III. . . . The cornerstone of Title I is new FECA [Federal Election Campaign Act of 1971, 2 U.S.C. §431 et seq.] §323(a), which prohibits national party committees and their agents from soliciting, receiving, directing, or spending any soft money. In short, §323(a) takes national parties out of the soft-money business. . . . New FECA §323(b) prevents the wholesale shift of soft-money influence from national to state party committees by prohibiting state and local party committees from using such funds for activities that affect federal elections. . . . New FECA §323(d) reinforces these soft-money restrictions by prohibiting political parties from soliciting and donating funds to tax-exempt organizations that engage in electioneering activities. New FECA §323(e) restricts federal candidates and officeholders from receiving, spending, or soliciting soft money in connection with federal elections and limits their ability to do so in connection with state and local elections. Finally, new FECA §323(f) prevents circumvention of the restrictions on national, state, and local party committees by prohibiting state and local candidates from raising and spending soft money to fund advertisements and other public communications that promote or attack federal candidates.

Plaintiffs mount a facial First Amendment challenge to new FECA §323. . . .

In *Buckley* and subsequent cases, we have subjected restrictions on campaign expenditures to closer scrutiny than limits on campaign contributions. [We] have recognized that contribution limits, unlike limits on expenditures, "entail only a marginal restriction upon the contributor's ability to engage in free communication." [*Buckley*, 424 U.S. at 20.] . . . Because the communicative value of large contributions inheres mainly in their ability to facilitate the speech of their recipients, we have said that contribution limits impose serious burdens on free speech only if they are so low as to "prevent candidates and political committees from amassing the resources necessary for effective advocacy." [*Buckley*.] [Although] contribution limits may bear "more heavily on the associational right than on freedom to speak" since contributions serve "to affiliate a person with a candidate" and "enable like-minded persons to pool their resources," . . . contribution limits both "leave the contributor free to become a member of any political association and to assist personally in the association's efforts on behalf of candidates," and allow associations "to aggregate large sums of money to promote effective advocacy." [Because the] "overall effect" of dollar limits on contributions is "merely to require candidates and political committees to raise funds from a greater number of persons," . . . a contribution limit involving even "significant interference" with associational rights is nevertheless valid if it satisfies the "lesser demand" of being "closely drawn" to match a "sufficiently important interest."

Our treatment of contribution restrictions . . . It also reflects the importance of the interests that underlie contribution limits — interests in preventing "both the actual corruption threatened by large financial contributions and the eroding of public confidence in the electoral process through the appearance of corruption." [These] interests directly implicate "the integrity of our electoral process, and, not less, the responsibility of the individual citizen for the successful functioning of that process." Because the electoral process is the very "means through which a free society democratically translates political speech into concrete governmental action," contribution limits, like other measures aimed at protecting the integrity of the process, tangibly benefit public participation in political debate. For that reason, when reviewing . . . contribution limits, "there is no place for a strong presumption against constitutionality, of the sort often thought to accompany the words 'strict scrutiny.' " The less rigorous standard of review we have applied to contribution limits (*Buckley*'s "closely drawn" scrutiny) shows proper deference to Congress' ability to weigh competing constitutional interests in an area in which it enjoys particular expertise. It also provides Congress with sufficient room to anticipate and respond to concerns about circumvention of regulations designed to protect the integrity of the political process. . . .

Like the contribution limits we upheld in *Buckley*, §323's restrictions have only a marginal impact on the ability of contributors, candidates, officeholders, and parties to engage in effective political speech. Complex as its provisions may be, §323, in the main, does little more than regulate the ability of wealthy individuals, corporations, and unions to contribute large sums of money to influence federal elections, federal candidates, and federal officeholders.

Plaintiffs contend that we must apply strict scrutiny to §323 because many of its provisions restrict not only contributions but also the spending and solicitation of funds raised outside of FECA's contribution limits. But [the] relevant inquiry is whether the mechanism adopted to implement the contribution limit, or to prevent circumvention of that limit, burdens speech in a way that a direct restriction on the contribution itself would not. That is not the case here. For example, while §323(a) prohibits national parties from receiving or spending nonfederal money, and §323(b) prohibits state party committees from spending nonfederal money on federal election activities, neither provision in any way limits the total amount of money parties can spend. Rather, they simply limit the source and individual amount of donations. That they do so by prohibiting the spending of soft money does not render them expenditure limitations.

Similarly, the solicitation provisions of §323(a) and §323(e), which restrict the ability of national party committees, federal candidates, and federal officeholders to solicit nonfederal funds, leave open ample opportunities for soliciting federal funds on behalf of entities subject to FECA's source and amount restrictions. Even §323(d), which on its face enacts a blanket ban on party solicitations of funds to certain tax-exempt organizations, nevertheless allows parties to solicit funds to the organizations' federal PACs. As for those organizations that cannot or do not administer PACs, parties remain free to donate federal funds directly to such organizations, and may solicit funds expressly for that purpose. And . . . §323(d) places no limits on other means of endorsing tax-exempt organizations or any restrictions on solicitations by party officers acting in their individual capacities.

Section 323 thus shows "due regard for the reality that solicitation is characteristically intertwined with informative and perhaps persuasive speech seeking support for particular causes or for particular views." Schaumburg v. Citizens for a Better Environment, 444 U.S. 620, 632 (1980). The fact that party committees and federal candidates and officeholders must now ask only for limited dollar amounts or request that a corporation or union contribute money through its PAC in no way alters or impairs the political message "intertwined" with the solicitation. And rather than chill such solicitations, as was the case in *Schaumburg*, the restriction here tends to increase the dissemination of information by forcing parties, candidates, and officeholders to solicit from a wider array of potential donors. As with direct limits on contributions, therefore, §323's spending and solicitation restrictions have only a marginal impact on political speech.

Finally, plaintiffs contend that the type of associational burdens that §323 imposes are fundamentally different from the burdens that accompanied *Buckley*'s contribution limits, and merit the type of strict scrutiny we have applied to attempts to regulate the internal processes of political parties. E.g., California Democratic Party v. Jones, 530 U.S. 567 (2000). [Plaintiffs] greatly exaggerate the effect of §323, contending that it precludes *any* collaboration among national, state, and local committees of the same party in fundraising and electioneering activities. We do not read the provisions in that way. Section 323 merely subjects a greater percentage of contributions to parties and candidates to FECA's source and amount limitations. *Buckley* has already acknowledged that such limitations "leave the contributor free to become a member of any political association and to assist personally in the association's efforts on behalf of candidates." The modest impact that §323 has on the ability of committees within a party to associate with each other does not independently occasion strict scrutiny. None of this is to suggest that the alleged associational burdens imposed on parties by §323 have no place in the First Amendment analysis; it is only that we account for them in the application, rather than the choice, of the appropriate level of scrutiny.

With these principles in mind, we apply the less rigorous scrutiny applicable to contribution limits to evaluate the constitutionality of new FECA §323. Because the five challenged provisions of §323 implicate different First Amendment concerns, we discuss them separately. We are mindful, however, that Congress enacted §323 as an integrated whole to vindicate the Government's important interest in preventing corruption and the appearance of corruption.

New FECA §323(a)'s Restrictions on National Party Committees

. . . The Government defends §323(a)'s ban on national parties' involvement with soft money as necessary to prevent the actual and apparent corruption of federal candidates and officeholders. Our cases have made clear that the prevention of corruption or its appearance constitutes a sufficiently important interest to justify political contribution limits. . . . The question . . . is whether large *soft-money* contributions to national party committees have a corrupting influence or give rise to the appearance of corruption. Both common sense and the ample record in these cases confirm Congress' belief that they do. . . . [C]orporate, union, and wealthy individual donors have been free to contribute substantial sums of soft money to the national parties, which the parties can spend for the specific purpose of influencing a particular candidate's federal election. It is not only plausible, but likely, that candidates would feel grateful for such donations and that donors would seek to exploit that gratitude.

The evidence in the record shows that [parties] kept tallies of the amounts of soft money raised by each officeholder, and "the amount of money a Member of Congress raised for the national political committees often affected the amount the committees gave to assist the Member's campaign." Donors often asked that their contributions be credited to particular candidates, and the parties obliged. . . .

The evidence connects soft money to manipulations of the legislative calendar, leading to Congress' failure to enact, among other things, generic drug legislation, tort reform, and tobacco legislation. . . . To claim that such actions do not change legislative outcomes surely misunderstands the legislative process.

More importantly, plaintiffs conceive of corruption too narrowly. . . . Congress' legitimate interest extends beyond preventing simple cash-for-votes corruption to curbing "undue influence on an officeholder's judgment, and the appearance of such influence." . . . The record . . . is replete with . . . examples of national party committees peddling access to federal candidates and officeholders in exchange for large soft-money donations. . . . In sum, there is substantial evidence to support

Congress' determination that large soft-money contributions to national political parties give rise to corruption and the appearance of corruption. . . .

Accordingly, we reject the plaintiffs' First Amendment challenge to new FECA §323(a).

New FECA §323(b)'s Restrictions on State and Local Party Committees

. . . Congress recognized that, given the close ties between federal candidates and state party committees, BCRA's restrictions on national committee activity would rapidly become ineffective if state and local committees remained available as a conduit for soft-money donations. Section 323(b) is designed to foreclose wholesale evasion of §323(a)'s anticorruption measures by sharply curbing state committees' ability to use large soft-money contributions to influence federal elections. The core of §323(b) is a straightforward contribution regulation: It prevents donors from contributing nonfederal funds to state and local party committees to help finance "Federal election activity." The term "Federal election activity" encompasses four distinct categories of electioneering: (1) voter registration activity during the 120 days preceding a regularly scheduled federal election; (2) voter identification, get-out-the-vote (GOTV), and generic campaign activity that is "conducted in connection with an election in which a candidate for Federal office appears on the ballot"; (3) any "public communication" that "refers to a clearly identified candidate for Federal office" and "promotes," "supports," "attacks," or "opposes" a candidate for that office; and (4) the services provided by a state committee employee who dedicates more than 25% of his or her time to "activities in connection with a Federal election." . . . All activities that fall within the statutory definition must be funded with hard money. . . .

[In] addressing the problem of soft-money contributions to state committees, Congress both drew a conclusion and made a prediction. Its conclusion . . . was that the corrupting influence of soft money does not insinuate itself into the political process solely through national party committees. Rather, state committees function as an alternate avenue for precisely the same corrupting forces. . . . There is at least as much evidence as there was in *Buckley* that such donations have been made with the intent — and in at least some cases the effect — of gaining influence over federal officeholders. Section 323(b) thus promotes an important governmental interest by confronting the corrupting influence that soft-money donations to political parties already have.

Congress also made a prediction. . . . Congress knew that soft-money donors would react to §323(a) by scrambling to find another way to purchase influence. It was "neither novel nor implausible" for Congress to conclude that political parties would react to §323(a) by directing soft-money contributors to the state committees, and that federal candidates would be just as indebted to these contributors as they had been to those who had formerly contributed to the national parties. We "must accord substantial deference to the predictive judgments of Congress," particularly when, as here, those predictions are so firmly rooted in relevant history and common sense. Preventing corrupting activity from shifting wholesale to state committees and thereby eviscerating FECA clearly qualifies as an important governmental interest.

. . . We conclude that §323(b) is a closely-drawn means of countering both corruption and the appearance of corruption. . . . Because voter registration, voter identification, GOTV, and generic campaign activity all confer substantial benefits on federal candidates, the funding of such activities creates a significant risk of actual and apparent corruption. Section 323(b) is a reasonable response to that risk. . . .

New FECA §323(d)'s Restrictions on Parties' Solicitations for, and Donations to, Tax-Exempt Organizations

Section 323(d) prohibits national, state, and local party committees, and their agents or subsidiaries, from "soliciting any funds for, or making or directing any donations" to, any [tax-exempt charitable, educational, or social welfare] organization established under §501(c) of the Internal Revenue Code that makes expenditures in connection with an election for federal office, and any political organizations established under §527 "other than a political committee, a State, district, or local committee of a political party, or the authorized campaign committee of a candidate for State or local office."[3] The District Court struck down the provision on its face. We reverse and uphold §323(d), narrowly construing the section's ban on donations to apply only to the donation of funds not raised in compliance with FECA.

[Section] 323(d)'s ban on solicitations to tax-exempt organizations engaged in political activity [prevents] circumvention of Title I's limits on contributions of soft money to national, state, and local party committees. . . . Absent the solicitation provision, national, state, and local party committees would have significant incentives to mobilize their formidable fundraising apparatuses, including the peddling of access to federal officeholders, into the service of like-minded tax-exempt organizations that conduct activities benefiting their candidates. . . .

Section 323(d)'s solicitation restriction is closely drawn to prevent political parties from using tax-exempt organizations as soft-money surrogates. Though phrased as an absolute prohibition, the restriction does nothing more than subject contributions solicited by parties to FECA's regulatory regime, leaving open substantial opportunities for solicitation and other expressive activity in support of these organizations. . . .

Section 323(d) also prohibits national, state, and local party committees from making or directing "any donation" to qualifying §501(c) or §527 organizations. The Government again defends the restriction as an anticircumvention measure. We agree insofar as it prohibits the donation of soft money. Absent such a restriction,

3. Section 527 "political organizations" are, unlike §501(c) groups, organized for the express purpose of engaging in partisan political activity. They include any "party, committee, association, fund, or other organization (whether or not incorporated) organized and operated primarily for the purpose of directly or indirectly accepting contributions or making expenditures" for the purpose of "influencing or attempting to influence the selection, nomination, or appointment of any individual for Federal, State, or local public office." 26 U.S.C. §527(e).

state and local party committees could accomplish directly what the antisolicitation restrictions prevent them from doing indirectly — namely, raising large sums of soft money to launder through tax-exempt organizations engaging in federal election activities. . . .

New FECA §323(e)'s Restrictions on Federal Candidates and Officeholders

New FECA §323(e) . . . prohibits federal candidates and officeholders from "soliciting, receiving, directing, [transferring], or spending" any soft money in connection with federal elections. It also limits the ability of federal candidates and officeholders to solicit, receive, direct, transfer, or spend soft money in connection with state and local elections. [However, §323(e) permits] federal candidates and officeholders . . . to "attend, speak, or be a featured guest" at a state or local party fundraising event[, solicit] soft money to §501(c) organizations whose primary purpose is not to engage in "Federal election activities" as long as the solicitation does not specify how the funds will be spent[, and solicit soft money] to §501(c) organizations whose primary purpose is to engage in "Federal election activities" as long as the solicitations are limited to individuals and the amount solicited does not exceed $20,000 per year per individual. . . .

Section 323(e)'s restrictions on solicitations are . . . valid anticircumvention measures. Large soft-money donations at a candidate's or officeholder's behest give rise to all of the same corruption concerns posed by contributions made directly to the candidate or officeholder. Though the candidate may not ultimately control how the funds are spent, the value of the donation to the candidate or officeholder is evident from the fact of the solicitation itself. . . .

New FECA §323(f)'s Restrictions on State Candidates and Officeholders

The final provision of Title I is new FECA §323(f), [which] generally prohibits candidates for state or local office, or state or local officeholders, from spending soft money to fund "public communications" . . . — i.e., a communication that "refers to a clearly identified candidate for Federal office . . . and that promotes or supports a candidate for that office, or attacks or opposes a candidate for that office." . . . Section 323(f) places no cap on the amount of money that state or local candidates can spend on any activity[; . . .] it limits only the source and amount of contributions that state and local candidates can draw on to fund expenditures that [have a direct impact upon] federal elections. And, by regulating only contributions used to fund "public communications," §323(f) focuses narrowly on those soft-money donations with the greatest potential to corrupt or give rise to the appearance of corruption of federal candidates and officeholders. . . .

The proliferation of sham issue ads has driven the soft-money explosion. Parties have sought out every possible way to fund and produce these ads with soft money. . . .We will not upset Congress' eminently reasonable prediction that, with . . . other avenues no longer available, state and local candidates and officeholders will become the next conduits for the soft-money funding of sham issue advertising. We therefore uphold §323(f) against plaintiffs' First Amendment challenge. . . .

IV. Title II of BCRA, entitled "Noncandidate Campaign Expenditures," is divided into two subtitles: "Electioneering Communications" and "Independent and Coordinated Expenditures." We consider each challenged section of these subtitles in turn.

BCRA §201's Definition of "Electioneering Communication"

The first section of Title II, §201, comprehensively amends FECA §304, which requires political committees to file detailed periodic financial reports with the FEC. The amendment coins a new term, "electioneering communication," to replace the narrowing construction of FECA's disclosure provisions adopted by this Court in *Buckley*. [That] construction limited the coverage of FECA's disclosure requirement to communications expressly advocating the election or defeat of particular candidates. By contrast, the term "electioneering communication" . . . is defined to encompass any "broadcast, cable, or satellite communication" that . . . "refers to a clearly identified candidate for Federal office; is made within 60 days before a general, special, or runoff election for the office sought by the candidate; or 30 days before a primary or preference election, or a convention or caucus of a political party that has authority to nominate a candidate, for the office sought by the candidate; and in the case of a communication which refers to a candidate other than President or Vice President, is targeted to the relevant electorate." 2 U.S.C. A. §434(f)(3)(A)(i) (Supp. 2003). . . .

BCRA's use of this new term is not, however, limited to the disclosure context: A later section of the Act (BCRA §203, which amends FECA §316(b)(2)) restricts corporations' and labor unions' funding of electioneering communications. Plaintiffs challenge the constitutionality of the new term as it applies in both the disclosure and the expenditure contexts.

The major premise of plaintiffs' challenge . . . is that *Buckley* drew a constitutionally mandated line between express advocacy and so-called issue advocacy, and that speakers possess an inviolable First Amendment right to engage in the latter category of speech. . . . That position misapprehends our prior decisions, for the express advocacy restriction was an endpoint of statutory interpretation, not a first principle of constitutional law. . . . In narrowly reading the FECA provisions in *Buckley* to avoid problems of vagueness and overbreadth, we nowhere suggested that a statute that was neither vague nor overbroad would be required to toe the same express advocacy line.

[The notion] that the First Amendment erects a rigid barrier between express advocacy and so-called issue advocacy . . . cannot be squared with our longstanding recognition that the presence or absence of magic words [e.g., "vote for," "elect," "support," "defeat," or "reject"] cannot meaningfully distinguish electioneering speech from a true issue ad. Indeed, the unmistakable lesson from the record in this litigation . . . is that *Buckley*'s magic-words requirement is functionally meaningless. Not only can advertisers easily evade the line by eschewing the use of magic words, but they would seldom choose to use such words even if permitted. And although the resulting advertisements do not urge the viewer to vote for or against a candidate in so many words, they are no less clearly intended to influence the election. *Buckley*'s express advocacy line, in short, has not aided the legislative effort to combat real or apparent corruption, and Congress enacted BCRA to correct the flaws it found in the existing system.

[We also] observe that new FECA §304(f)(3)'s definition of "electioneering communication" raises none of the vagueness concerns that drove our analysis in *Buckley*. . . . Thus, the constitutional objection that persuaded the Court in *Buckley* to limit FECA's reach to express advocacy is simply inapposite here.

BCRA §203's Prohibition of Corporate and Labor Disbursements for Electioneering Communications

. . . Section 203 of BCRA amends FECA §316(b)(2) to [provide that] corporations and unions may not use their general treasury funds to finance electioneering communications, but they remain free to organize and administer segregated funds, or PACs, for that purpose. . . .

[We] examine the degree to which BCRA burdens First Amendment expression and evaluate whether a compelling governmental interest justifies that burden. The latter question — whether the state interest is compelling — is easily answered by [Austin v. Michigan Chamber of Commerce, 494 U.S. 652 (1990), in which we] sustained legislation aimed at "the corrosive and distorting effects of immense aggregations of wealth that are accumulated with the help of the corporate form and that have little or no correlation to the public's support for the corporation's political ideas."

[Some] plaintiffs contend that it unconstitutionally discriminates in favor of media companies. FECA §304(f)(3)(B)(i) excludes from the definition of electioneering communications any "communication appearing in a news story, commentary, or editorial distributed through the facilities of any broadcasting station, unless such facilities are owned or controlled by any political party, political committee, or candidate." Plaintiffs argue this provision gives free rein to media companies to engage in speech without resort to PAC money, [but the] provision excepts news items and commentary only; it does not afford *carte blanche* to media companies generally to ignore FECA's provisions. The statute's narrow exception is wholly consistent with First Amendment principles. "A valid distinction . . . exists between corporations that are part of the media industry and other corporations that are not involved in the regular business of imparting news to the public." *Austin*.

[We uphold] the constitutionality of FECA §316(b)(2) [as amended by the BCRA.]

BCRA §204's Application to Nonprofit Corporations

Section 204 of BCRA, which adds FECA §316(c)(6), applies the prohibition on the use of general treasury funds to pay for electioneering communications to not-for-profit corporations. Prior to the enactment of BCRA, . . . such corporations, like business corporations, [had] to pay for their express advocacy from segregated funds rather than from their general treasuries. Our recent decision in FEC v.

Beaumont confirmed that the requirement was valid except insofar as it applied to a sub-category of corporations described as "*MCFL* organizations," as defined by our decision in *MCFL*, 479 U.S. 238 (1986).The constitutional objection to applying FECA's segregated-fund requirement to so-called *MCFL* organizations necessarily applies with equal force to FECA §316(c)(6).

Our decision in *MCFL* related to . . . entities "[(1)] formed for the express purpose of promoting political ideas, [not to] engage in business activities; [(2) that have] no shareholders or other persons [that] have a claim on its assets or earnings; [and (3) are] not established by a business corporation or a labor union, and [does not] accept contributions from such entities.". . . Because our decision in the *MCFL* case was on the books for many years before BCRA was enacted, we presume that the legislators who drafted §316(c)(6) were fully aware that the provision could not validly apply to *MCFL*-type entities. . . . As so construed, the provision is plainly valid. . . .

BCRA §214's Changes in FECA's Provisions Covering Coordinated Expenditures

Ever since our decision in *Buckley*, it has been settled that expenditures by a noncandidate that are "controlled by or coordinated with the candidate and his campaign" may be treated as indirect contributions subject to FECA's source and amount limitations. . . . Section 214(a) of BCRA creates a new FECA §315(a)(7)(B)(ii) that applies the same rule to expenditures coordinated with "a national, State, or local committee of a political party.". . .

Plaintiffs [argue] that new FECA §315(a)(7)(B)(ii) and its implementing regulations are overbroad and unconstitutionally vague because they permit a finding of coordination even in the absence of an agreement. . . . We are not persuaded that the presence of an agreement marks the dividing line between expenditures that are coordinated — and therefore may be regulated as indirect contributions — and expenditures that truly are independent. [Expenditures] made after a "wink or nod" often will be "as useful to the candidate as cash" . . . and the resulting expenditure would be "virtually indistinguishable from [a] simple contribution." [*Colorado II*]. . . . The portions of the District Court judgment rejecting plaintiff's challenges to BCRA §214 are affirmed.

V. Many years ago we observed that "to say that Congress is without power to pass appropriate legislation to safeguard . . . an election from the improper use of money is to deny to the nation in a vital particular the power of self protection." Burroughs v. United States, 290 U.S. 534, 545 (1934). We abide by that conviction in considering Congress' most recent effort to confine the ill effects of aggregated wealth on our political system.

CHIEF JUSTICE REHNQUIST delivered the opinion of the Court with respect to BCRA Titles III and IV.

[The Court concluded that the McConnell plaintiffs lacked standing to challenge BCRA §305, which requires broadcasters to sell advertising time in the period immediately before an election at their "lowest unit charge for the same class and amount of time for the same period," but denied the benefits of those low rates to any candidate who refuses to refrain from attacking his rival in such advertising or who fails to identify himself and to state that he approves of the advertisement. Because Senator McConnell's term does not expire until 2009 his] alleged injury in fact is too remote temporally to satisfy Article III standing.

[The Court concluded that neither of two sets of plaintiffs had standing to challenge BCRA §307, which increased the hard money contribution limits and indexed them for inflation. The Adams plaintiffs, a group of voters and candidates who wish to eschew hard money contributions, failed to allege any cognizable injury in fact. The Paul plaintiffs lacked standing because even if the BCRA contribution limits were voided the pre-existing FECA limits, which were not before the Court, would survive; thus a ruling in favor of the Paul plaintiffs] would not redress their alleged injury, and they accordingly lack standing.

[The Court found that the Adams plaintiffs lacked standing, for want of any injury in fact, to challenge the so-called "millionaire provisions" of the BCRA, which operate to increase the] otherwise applicable contribution-to-candidate limits if the candidate's opponent spends a triggering amount of his personal funds.

[The Court upheld BCRA §311, which mandates that all electioneering communications be identified by payor and candidate (if authorized by the candidate), because its disclosure regime bears a sufficient relationship to the important governmental interest of "shedding the light of publicity" on campaign financing.

[The Court struck down BCRA §318, which] prohibits individuals "17 years old or younger" from making contributions to candidates and contributions or donations to political parties. . . . Minors enjoy the protection of the First Amendment. [Tinker v. Des Moines Ind. Community Sch. Dist.] . . . When the Government burdens the right to contribute, we apply heightened scrutiny. . . . We ask whether there is a "sufficiently important interest" and whether the statute is "closely drawn" to avoid unnecessary abridgement of First Amendment freedoms. The Government asserts that the provision protects against corruption by conduit; that is, donations by parents through their minor children to circumvent contribution limits applicable to the parents. But the Government offers scant evidence of this form of evasion [and, in any case,] the provision here sweeps too broadly. . . .

JUSTICE BREYER delivered the opinion of the Court with respect to BCRA Title V, [upholding BCRA §504, which requires broadcasters to keep publicly available records of politically related broadcasting requests.]

CHIEF JUSTICE REHNQUIST, joined by JUSTICES SCALIA and KENNEDY, dissenting with respect to BCRA Titles I and V.

. . . The [linchpin] of Title I, new FECA §323(a), . . . does not regulate only donations given to influence a particular federal election; it regulates *all donations* to national political committees, no matter the use to which the funds are put. The Court attempts to sidestep the unprecedented breadth of this regulation by stating that the "close relationship between federal officeholders and the national parties" makes all donations to the national parties "suspect." But a close association with others, especially in the realm of political speech, is not a surrogate for corruption; it is one of our most treasured First Amendment rights. See California Democratic Party v. Jones, 530 U.S. 567 (2000). . . .

The Court fails to recognize that the national political parties are exemplars of political speech. . . . [Political] parties often foster speech crucial to a healthy democracy and fulfill the need for like-minded individuals to ban together and promote a political philosophy. When political parties engage in pure political speech that has little or no potential to corrupt their federal candidates and officeholders, the government cannot constitutionally burden their speech any more than it could burden the speech of individuals engaging in these same activities. . . .

[T]he Court concludes that because [Congress sought to regulate activities that either] *benefit* federal candidates and officeholders or prevent the circumvention of pre-existing or contemporaneously enacted restrictions it must defer to the "predictive judgments of Congress." Yet the Court cannot truly mean what it says. Newspaper editorials and political talk shows *benefit* federal candidates and officeholders every bit as much as a generic voter registration drive conducted by a state party; there is little doubt that the endorsement of a major newspaper *affects* federal elections, and federal candidates and officeholders are surely "grateful" for positive media coverage. I doubt, however, the Court would seriously contend that we must defer to Congress' judgment if it chose to reduce the influence of political endorsements in federal elections. See Miami Herald Publishing Co. v. Tornillo, 418 U.S. 241 (1974).

It is also true that any circumvention rationale ultimately must rest on the circumvention itself leading to the corruption of federal candidates and officeholders. All political speech that is not sifted through federal regulation circumvents the regulatory scheme to some degree or another, and thus by the Court's standard would be a "loophole" in the current system. Unless the Court would uphold federal regulation of all funding of political speech, a rationale dependent on circumvention alone will not do. By untethering its inquiry from corruption or the appearance of corruption, the Court has removed the touchstone of our campaign finance precedent and has failed to replace it with any logical limiting principle.

But such an untethering is necessary to the Court's analysis. Only by using amorphous language to conclude a federal interest, however vaguely defined, exists can the Court avoid the obvious fact that new FECA §§323(a), (b), (d), and (f) are vastly overinclusive. Any campaign finance law aimed at reducing corruption will almost surely affect federal elections or prohibit the circumvention of federal law, and if broad enough, most laws will generally reduce some appearance of corruption. Indeed, it is precisely because broad laws are likely to nominally further a legitimate interest that we require Congress to tailor its restrictions; requiring all federal candidates to self-finance their campaigns would surely reduce the appearance of donor corruption, but it would hardly be constitutional. In allowing Congress to rely on general principles such as affecting a federal election or prohibiting the circumvention of existing law, the Court all but eliminates the "closely drawn" tailoring requirement and meaningful judicial review.

No doubt Congress was convinced by the many abuses of the current system that something in this area must be done. Its response, however, was too blunt. . . . Today's decision, by not requiring tailored restrictions, has significantly reduced the protection for political speech having little or nothing to do with corruption or the appearance of corruption. . . .

[JUSTICE STEVENS, joined by JUSTICES GINSBURG and BREYER, dissented as to the standing issue raised by BCRA §305, and would have upheld the provision on the merits.]

JUSTICE SCALIA, concurring with respect to BCRA Titles III and IV, dissenting with respect to BCRA Titles I and V, and concurring in the judgment in part and dissenting in part with respect to BCRA Title II.

. . . This is a sad day for freedom of speech. Who could have imagined that the same Court which, within the past four years, has sternly disapproved of restrictions upon such inconsequential forms of expression as virtual child pornography [Ashcroft v. Free Speech Coalition], tobacco advertising [Lorillard Tobacco Co. v. Reilly], dissemination of illegally intercepted communications [Bartnicki v. Vopper], and sexually explicit cable programming [United States v. Playboy Entertainment Group, Inc.], would smile with favor upon a law that cuts to the heart of what the First Amendment is meant to protect: the right to criticize the government. For that is what the most offensive provisions of this legislation are all about. We are governed by Congress, and this legislation prohibits the criticism of Members of Congress by those entities most capable of giving such criticism loud voice: national political parties and corporations, both of the commercial and the not-for-profit sort. . . . To be sure, the legislation is evenhanded: It similarly prohibits criticism of the candidates who oppose Members of Congress in their reelection bids. But as everyone knows, this is an area in which evenhandedness is not fairness. If *all* electioneering were evenhandedly prohibited, incumbents would have an enormous advantage. . . .

Beyond that, however, the present legislation *targets* for prohibition certain categories of campaign speech that are particularly harmful to incumbents. Is it accidental, do you think, that incumbents raise about three times as much "hard money" — the sort of funding generally *not* restricted by this legislation — as do their challengers? Or that lobbyists (who seek the favor of incumbents) give 92 percent of their money in "hard" contributions? Is it an oversight, do you suppose, that the so-called "millionaire provisions" raise the contribution limit for a candidate running against an individual who devotes to the campaign (as challengers often do) great personal wealth, but do not raise the limit for a candidate running against an individual who devotes to the campaign (as incumbents often do) a massive election "war chest"? And is it mere happenstance, do you estimate, that national-party funding, which is severely limited by the Act, is more likely to assist cash-strapped challengers than flush-with-hard-money incumbents? Was it unintended, by any chance, that incumbents are free personally to receive some soft money and even to solicit it for other organizations, while national parties are not?

I wish to address three fallacious propositions that might be thought to justify some or all of the provisions of this legislation — only the last of which is explicitly embraced by the principal opinion for the Court, but all of which underlie, I think, its approach to these cases.

(a) Money is Not Speech

It was said by congressional proponents of this legislation . . . that since this legislation regulates nothing but the expenditure of money for speech, as opposed to speech itself, the burden it imposes is not subject to full First Amendment scrutiny . . . . Until today, however, that view has been categorically rejected by our jurisprudence. As we said in *Buckley*, "this Court has never suggested that the dependence of a communication on the expenditure of money operates itself to introduce a nonspeech element or to reduce the exacting scrutiny required by the First Amendment." Our traditional view was correct, and today's cavalier attitude toward regulating the financing of speech . . . frustrates the fundamental purpose of the First Amendment. In any economy operated on even the most rudimentary principles of division of labor, effective public communication requires the speaker to make use of the services of others. An author may write a novel, but he will seldom publish and distribute it himself. A freelance reporter may write a story, but he will rarely edit, print, and deliver it to subscribers. To a government bent on suppressing speech, this mode of organization presents opportunities: Control any cog in the machine, and you can halt the whole apparatus. License printers, and it matters little whether authors are still free to write. Restrict the sale of books, and it matters little who prints them. Predictably, repressive regimes have exploited these principles by attacking all levels of the production and dissemination of ideas. . . .

Division of labor requires a means of mediating exchange, and in a commercial society, that means is supplied by money. The publisher pays the author for the right to sell his book; it pays its staff who print and assemble the book; it demands payments from booksellers who bring the book to market. This, too, presents opportunities for repression: Instead of regulating the various parties to the enterprise individually, the government can suppress their ability to coordinate by regulating their use of money. What good is the right to print books without a right to buy works from authors? Or the right to publish newspapers without the right to pay deliverymen? The right to speak would be largely ineffective if it did not include the right to engage in financial transactions that are the incidents of its exercise.

This is not to say that *any* regulation of money is a regulation of speech. The government may apply general commercial regulations to those who use money for speech if it applies them evenhandedly to those who use money for other purposes. But where the government singles out money used to fund speech as its legislative object, it is acting against speech as such, no less than if it had targeted the paper on which a book was printed or the trucks that deliver it to the bookstore. . . . It should be obvious, then, that a law limiting the amount a person can spend to broadcast his political views is a direct restriction on speech. . . .

(b) Pooling Money is Not Speech

Another proposition which could explain at least some of the results of today's opinion is that the First Amendment right to spend money for speech does not include the right to combine with others in spending money for speech. Such a proposition fits uncomfortably with the concluding words of our Declaration of Independence: "And for the support of this Declaration, . . . we mutually pledge to each other our Lives, *our Fortunes* and our sacred Honor." (Emphasis added.) The freedom to associate with others for the dissemination of ideas — not just by singing or speaking in unison, but by pooling financial resources for expressive purposes — is part of the freedom of speech. . . . The principle that such financial association does not enjoy full First Amendment protection threatens the existence of all political parties.

(c) Speech by Corporations Can Be Abridged

The last proposition that might explain at least some of today's casual abridgment of free-speech rights is this: that the particular form of association known as a corporation does not enjoy full First Amendment protection. Of course the text of the First Amendment does not limit its application in this fashion, [nor] is there any basis in reason why First Amendment rights should not attach to corporate associations — and we have said so. [First Nat'l Bank of Boston v. Bellotti]. The Court changed course in [*Austin*], upholding a state prohibition of an independent corporate expenditure in support of a candidate for state office. I dissented in that case and remain of the view that it was error. . . . People who associate — who pool their financial resources — for purposes of economic enterprise overwhelmingly do so in the corporate form; and with increasing frequency, incorporation is chosen by those who associate to defend and promote particular ideas — such as the American Civil Liberties Union and the National Rifle Association, parties to these cases. Imagine, then, a government that wished to suppress nuclear power — or oil and gas exploration, or automobile manufacturing, or gun ownership, or civil liberties — and that had the power to prohibit corporate advertising against its proposals. . . . The First Amendment does not in my view permit the restriction of that political speech. And the same holds true for corporate electoral speech: A candidate should not be insulated from the most effective speech that the major participants in the economy and major incorporated interest groups can generate.

But what about the danger to the political system posed by "amassed wealth"? The most direct threat from that source comes in the form of undisclosed favors and payoffs to elected officials — which have already been criminalized, and will be rendered no more discoverable by the legislation at issue here. The use of corporate wealth (like individual wealth) to speak to the electorate is unlikely to "distort" elections — *especially* if disclosure requirements *tell* the people where the speech is coming from. The premise of the First Amendment is that the American people are neither sheep nor fools, and hence fully capable of considering both the substance of the speech presented to them and its proximate and ultimate source. If that premise is wrong, our democracy has a much greater problem to overcome than merely the influence of amassed wealth. Given the premises of democracy, there is no such thing as *too much* speech.

But, it is argued, quite apart from its effect upon the electorate, corporate speech in the form of contributions to the candidate's campaign, or even in the form of independent expenditures supporting the candidate, engenders an obligation which is later paid in the form of greater access to the officeholder, or indeed in the form of votes on particular bills. . . . It cannot be denied . . . that corporate (like noncorporate) allies will have greater access to the officeholder, and that he will tend to favor the same causes as those who support him (which is usually *why* they supported him). That is the nature of politics — if not indeed human nature — and how this can properly be considered "corruption" (or "the appearance of corruption") with regard to corporate allies and not with regard to other allies is beyond me. If the Bill of Rights had intended an exception to the freedom of speech in order to combat this malign proclivity of the officeholder to agree with those who agree with him, and to speak more with his supporters than his opponents, it would surely have said so. . . .

But let us not be deceived. While the Government's briefs and arguments before this Court focused on the horrible "appearance of corruption," the most passionate floor statements during the debates on this legislation pertained to so-called attack ads, which the Constitution surely protects, but which Members of Congress analogized to "crack cocaine," "drive-by shootings," and "air pollution." There is good reason to believe that the ending of negative campaign ads was the principal attraction of the legislation. . . . Another theme prominent in the legislative debates was the notion that there is too much money spent on elections. . . .

Evidently, however, [negative attack] ads *do persuade* voters, or else they would not be so routinely used by sophisticated politicians of all parties. The point, in any event, is that it is not the proper role of those who govern us to judge which campaign speech has "substance" and "depth" (do you think it might be that which is least damaging to incumbents?) and to abridge the rest.

And what exactly are these outrageous sums frittered away in determining who will govern us? A report prepared for Congress concluded that the total amount, in hard and soft money, spent on the 2000 federal elections was between $2.4 and $2.5 billion. *All* campaign spending in the United States, including state elections, ballot initiatives, and judicial elections, has been estimated at $3.9 billion for 2000. Even taking this last, larger figure as the benchmark, it means that Americans spent about half as much electing all their Nation's officials, state and federal, as they spent on movie tickets ($7.8 billion); about a fifth as much as they spent on cosmetics and perfume ($18.8 billion); and about a sixth as much as they spent on pork (the nongovernmental sort) ($22.8 billion). If our democracy is drowning from this much spending, it cannot swim. . . .

Which brings me back to where I began: This litigation is about preventing criticism of the government. . . . I will stipulate that all those who voted for the Act believed they were acting for the good of the country. . . . Those in power, even giving them the benefit of the greatest good will, are inclined to believe that what is good for them is good for the country. . . . The first instinct of power is the retention of power, and, under a Constitution that requires periodic elections, that is best achieved by the suppression of election-time speech. We have witnessed merely the second scene of Act I of what promises to be a lengthy tragedy. In scene 3 the Court, having abandoned most of the First Amendment weaponry that *Buckley* left intact, will be even less equipped to resist the incumbents' writing of the rules of political debate. The federal election campaign laws, which are already (as today's opinions show) so voluminous, so detailed, so complex, that no ordinary citizen dare run for office, or even contribute a significant sum, without hiring an expert advisor in the field, can be expected to grow more voluminous, more detailed, and more complex in the years to come — and always, always, with the objective of reducing the excessive amount of speech.

[JUSTICE THOMAS concurred in part and dissented in part.]

JUSTICE KENNEDY, joined by CHIEF JUSTICE REHNQUIST and, in part, by JUSTICE SCALIA (except to the extent it upholds new FECA §323(e) and JUSTICE THOMAS (with respect to BCRA §213 only).

[The] majority, to make its decision work, must abridge free speech where *Buckley* did not. *Buckley* did not authorize Congress to decide what shapes and forms the national political dialogue is to take. To reach today's decision, the Court . . . replaces discrete and respected First Amendment principles with new, amorphous, and unsound rules, rules which dismantle basic protections for speech. . . . To the majority, [almost all of the BCRA] is not only valid under the First Amendment but also is part of Congress' "steady improvement of the national election laws." We should make no mistake. It is neither. It is the codification of an assumption that the mainstream media alone can protect freedom of speech. It is an effort by Congress to ensure that civic discourse takes place only through the modes of its choosing. And BCRA is only the beginning, as its congressional proponents freely admit. . . . Our precedents teach, above all, that Government cannot be trusted to moderate its own rules for suppression of speech. The dangers posed by speech regulations have led the Court to insist upon principled constitutional lines and a rigorous standard of review. The majority now abandons these distinctions and limitations. . . .

I. . . . In *Buckley,* the Court held that one, and only one, interest justified the significant burden on the right of association involved there: eliminating, or preventing, actual corruption or the appearance of corruption stemming from contributions to candidates. . . . *Buckley* made clear . . . that the corruption interest only justifies regulating candidates' and officeholders' receipt of what we can call the "quids" in the *quid pro quo* formulation. The Court rested its decision on the principle that campaign finance regulation that restricts speech without requiring proof of particular corrupt action withstands constitutional challenge only if it regulates conduct posing a demonstrable *quid pro quo* danger. . . .

The Court ignores these constitutional bounds and in effect interprets the anticorruption rationale to allow regulation not just of "actual or apparent *quid pro quo* arrangements," but of any conduct that wins goodwill from or influences a Member of Congress. . . . This new definition of corruption sweeps away all protections for speech that lie in its path. . . . Access in itself . . . shows only that in a general sense an officeholder favors someone or that someone has influence on the officeholder. There is no basis, in law or in fact, to say favoritism or influence in general is the same as corrupt favoritism or influence in particular. . . .

The generic favoritism or influence theory articulated by the Court is at odds with standard First Amendment analyses because it is unbounded and susceptible to no limiting principle. Any given action might be favored by any given person, so by the Court's reasoning political loyalty of the purest sort can be prohibited. There is no remaining principled method for inquiring whether a campaign finance regulation does in fact regulate corruption in a serious and meaningful way. . . .

Favoritism and influence are not . . . avoidable in representative politics. It is in the nature of an elected representative to favor certain policies, and, by necessary corollary, to favor the voters and contributors who support those policies. It is well understood that a substantial and legitimate reason, if not the only reason, to cast a vote for, or to make a contribution to, one candidate over another is that the candidate will respond by producing those political outcomes the supporter favors. Democracy is premised on responsiveness. . . .

[It] follows that the Court today should not ask, as it does, whether some persons, even Members of Congress, conclusorily assert that the regulated conduct appears corrupt to them. Following *Buckley*, it should instead inquire whether the conduct now prohibited inherently poses a real or substantive *quid pro quo* danger, so that its regulation will stem the appearance of *quid pro quo* corruption.

[Justice Kennedy canvassed the evidence pertinent to new FECA §§323(a), (b), (d), and (f), and concluded that they] cannot stand because they do not . . . further *Buckley*'s corruption interest. [Only new FECA §323 (e)] satisfies *Buckley*'s anti-corruption rationale and the First Amendment's guarantee. . . .

II. . . . The majority permits a new and serious intrusion on speech when it upholds [BCRA] §203, the key provision in Title II that prohibits corporations and labor unions from using money from their general treasury to fund electioneering communications. The majority compounds the error made in [*Austin*] and silences political speech central to the civic discourse that sustains and informs our democratic processes. . . . The majority's holding cannot be reconciled with [*Bellotti*], which invalidated a Massachusetts law prohibiting banks and business corporations from making expenditures "for the purpose of" influencing referendum votes on issues that do not "materially affect" their business interests. . . .

Austin turned its back on this holding, not because the *Bellotti* Court had overlooked the Government's interest in combating *quid pro quo* corruption, but because a new majority decided to recognize "a different type of corruption," the same "corrosive and distorting effects of immense aggregations of wealth" found insufficient to sustain a similar prohibition [in *Bellotti*.]

To be sure, *Bellotti* concerns issue advocacy, whereas *Austin* is about express advocacy. . . . The distinction, however, between independent expenditures for commenting on issues, on the one hand, and supporting or opposing a candidate, on the other, has no First Amendment significance apart from *Austin*'s arbitrary line. *Austin* was based on a faulty assumption. [There] is a general recognition now that discussions of candidates and issues are quite often intertwined in practical terms. . . . To abide by *Austin*'s repudiation of *Bellotti* on the ground that *Bellotti* did not involve express advocacy is to adopt a fiction. . . . .

I surmise that even the majority . . . appreciates these problems with *Austin*. That is why it invents a new justification. We are now told that "the government also has a compelling interest in insulating federal elections from the type of corruption arising from the real or apparent creation of political debts." . . . This rationale has no limiting principle. Were we to accept it, Congress would have the authority to outlaw even pure issue ads, because they, too, could endear their sponsors to candidates who adopt the favored positions. . . . The Government's position would eviscerate the line between expenditures and contributions and subject both to the same "complaisant review under the First Amendment." Complaisant or otherwise, we cannot cede authority to the Legislature to do with the First Amendment as it pleases. . . .

Even under *Austin*, BCRA §203 could not stand. All parties agree strict scrutiny applies; §203, however, is far from narrowly tailored. The Government is unwilling to characterize §203 as a ban, [but this] does not alter the categorical nature of the prohibition on the corporation. "The corporation *as a corporation* is prohibited from speaking." . . .

[BCRA §203's ban on corporate or union issue ads within 30 to 60 days before an election] is a severe and unprecedented ban on protected speech. . . . We are supposed to find comfort in the knowledge that the ad is banned under §203 only if it "is targeted to the relevant electorate. . . ." This Orwellian criterion, however, is analogous to a law, unconstitutional under any known First Amendment theory, that would allow a speaker to say anything he chooses, so long as his intended audience could not hear him. A central purpose of issue ads is to urge the public to pay close attention to the candidate's platform on the featured issues. By banning broadcast in the very district where the candidate is standing for election, §203 shields information at the heart of the First Amendment from precisely those citizens who most value the right to make a responsible judgment at the voting booth. . . .

Neither strict scrutiny nor any other standard the Court has adopted to date permits outlawing speech on the ground that it might influence an election, which might lead to greater access to politicians by the sponsoring organization, which might lead to actual corruption or the appearance of corruption. Settled law requires a real and close connection between end and means. The attenuated causation the majority endorses today is antithetical to the concept of narrow tailoring. . . .

The First Amendment underwrites the freedom to experiment and to create in the realm of thought and speech. Citizens must be free to use new forms, and new forums, for the expression of ideas. The civic discourse belongs to the people and the Government may not prescribe the means used to conduct it. . . . Our pluralistic society is filled with voices expressing new and different viewpoints, speaking through modes and mechanisms that must be allowed to change in response to the demands of an interested public. As communities have grown and technology has evolved, concerted speech not only has become more effective than a single voice but also has become the natural preference and efficacious choice for many Americans. The Court, upholding multiple laws that suppress both spontaneous and concerted speech, leaves us less free than before. Today's decision breaks faith with our tradition of robust and unfettered debate. . . . I dissent.

2. Government Regulation of Elections

Note: Regulating Campaign Speech

Page 1106: Insert at the end of the section, immediately before section H:

In Watchtower Bible & Tract Society of New York, Inc. v. Village of Stratton, 536 U.S. 150 (2002), the Court invalidated a municipal ordinance that prohibited all canvassing upon private property unless a canvasser had first obtained a municipal permit and displayed the permit during the canvassing. Although the ordinance covered all forms of canvassing, not just political canvassing, the Court relied on the fact that the ordinance impinged upon the *McIntyre* right to anonymous distribution of political literature to reach the conclusion that the ordinance was substantially overbroad and invalid on its face.

REPUBLICAN PARTY OF MINNESOTA v. WHITE
536 U.S. 765 (2002)

JUSTICE SCALIA delivered the opinion of the Court.

The question . . . is whether the First Amendment permits the Minnesota Supreme Court to prohibit candidates for judicial election in that State from announcing their views on disputed legal and political issues.

I. Since Minnesota's admission to the Union in 1858, the State's Constitution has provided for the selection of all state judges by popular election. Since 1912, those elections have been nonpartisan. Since 1974, they have been subject to a legal restriction which states that a "candidate for a judicial office, including an incumbent judge," shall not "announce his or her views on disputed legal or political issues." This prohibition, . . . known as the "announce clause," [subjects] judges who violate it . . . to discipline, including removal, censure, civil penalties, and suspension without pay. Lawyers who run for judicial office also must comply with the announce clause [and those] who violate it are subject to . . . disbarment, suspension, and probation.

[A lawyer candidate for election to the Minnesota Supreme Court who] distributed literature criticizing several Minnesota Supreme Court decisions on issues such as crime, welfare, and abortion [became the subject of a complaint that he violated the "announce rule" and filed suit in federal court seeking] a declaration that the announce clause violates the First Amendment and an injunction against its enforcement. [The District Court, on summary judgment, upheld the validity of the "announce rule" and the Eighth Circuit affirmed.]

II. . . . The prohibition [of the announce clause] extends to the candidate's mere statement of his current position, even if he does not bind himself to maintain that position after election. [The announce clause, as interpreted by the Minnesota Supreme Court, permits a judicial candidate to criticize past decisions only if he or she supports *stare decisis*. They] may state their view that prior decisions were erroneous only if they do not assert that they, if elected, have any power to eliminate erroneous decisions. [The announce clause, as interpreted by the Minnesota courts, reaches only "disputed issues that are likely to come before the candidate if he is elected judge." But this] is not much of a limitation at all. One would hardly expect the "disputed legal or political issues" raised in the course of a state judicial election to include such matters as whether the Federal Government should end the embargo of Cuba. Quite obviously, they will be those legal or political disputes that are the proper (or by past decisions have been made the improper) business of the state courts. [It] is clear that the announce clause prohibits a judicial candidate from stating his views on any specific nonfanciful legal question within the province of the court for which he is running. . . .

Respondents contend that this still leaves plenty of topics for discussion on the campaign trail. These include a candidate's "character," "education," "work habits," and "how [he] would handle administrative duties if elected." . . . Whether this list . . . , and other topics not prohibited by the announce clause, adequately fulfill the First Amendment's guarantee of freedom of speech is the question to which we now turn.

III. [The] announce clause both prohibits speech on the basis of its content and burdens a category of speech that is "at the core of our First Amendment freedoms" — speech about the qualifications of candidates for public office. . . . The Court of Appeals concluded that respondents had established two interests as sufficiently compelling to justify the announce clause: preserving the impartiality of the state judiciary and preserving the appearance of the impartiality of the state judiciary. Respondents [argue] that the first is compelling because it protects the due process rights of litigants, and that the second is compelling because it preserves public confidence in the judiciary. Respondents are rather vague, however, about what they mean by "impartiality." . . . Clarity on this point is essential before we can decide whether impartiality is indeed a compelling state interest, and, if so, whether the announce clause is narrowly tailored to achieve it.

A. One meaning of "impartiality" in the judicial context — and of course its root meaning — is the lack of bias for or against either *party* to the proceeding. Impartiality in this sense . . . guarantees a party that the judge who hears his case will apply the law to him in the same way he applies it to any other party. This is the traditional sense in which the term is used. . . . We think it plain that the announce clause is not narrowly tailored to serve impartiality (or the appearance of impartiality) in this sense. Indeed, the clause is barely tailored to serve that interest *at all*, inasmuch as it does not restrict speech for or against particular *parties*, but rather speech for or against particular *issues*. To be sure, when a case arises that turns on a legal issue on which the judge (as a candidate) had taken a particular stand, the party taking the opposite stand is likely to lose. But not because of any bias against that party, or favoritism toward the other party. *Any* party taking that position is just as likely to lose. The judge is applying the law (as he sees it) evenhandedly.

B. It is perhaps possible to use the term "impartiality" in the judicial context (though this is certainly not a common usage) to mean lack of preconception in favor of or against a particular *legal view*. This sort of impartiality would be concerned, not with guaranteeing litigants equal application of the law, but rather with guaranteeing them an equal chance to persuade the court on the legal points in their case. Impartiality in this sense may well be an interest served by the announce clause, but it is not a *compelling* state interest, as strict scrutiny requires. A judge's lack of predisposition regarding the relevant legal issues in a case has never been thought a necessary component of equal justice, and with good reason. For one thing, it is virtually impossible to find a judge who does not have preconceptions about the law. . . . Indeed, even if it were possible to select judges who did not have preconceived views on legal issues, it would hardly be desirable to do so. "Proof that a Justice's mind at the time he joined the Court was a complete *tabula rasa* in the area of constitutional adjudication would be evidence of lack of qualification, not lack of bias." [Laird v. Tatum, 409 U.S. 824, 835 (1972).] The Minnesota Constitution positively forbids the selection to courts of general jurisdiction of judges who are impartial in the sense of having no views on the law. Minn. Const., Art. VI, §5 ("Judges of the supreme court, the court of appeals and the district court shall be learned in the law"). And since avoiding judicial preconceptions on legal issues is neither possible nor desirable, pretending otherwise by attempting to preserve the "appearance" of that type of impartiality can hardly be a compelling state interest either.

C. A third possible meaning of "impartiality" (again not a common one) might be described as openmindedness. This quality in a judge demands, not that he have no preconceptions on legal issues, but that he be willing to consider views that oppose his preconceptions, and remain open to persuasion, when the issues arise in a pending case. This sort of impartiality seeks to guarantee each litigant, not an *equal* chance to win the legal points in the case, but at least *some* chance of doing so. It may well be that impartiality in this sense, and the appearance of it, are desirable in the judiciary, but we need not pursue that inquiry, since we do not believe the Minnesota Supreme Court adopted the announce clause for that purpose. [Minnesota, in fact, encourages encourages judges to] state their views on disputed legal issues outside the context of adjudication — in classes that they conduct, and in books and speeches. . . . That is quite incompatible with the notion that the need for openmindedness (or for the appearance of openmindedness) lies behind the prohibition at issue here. . . .

Moreover, the notion that the special context of electioneering justifies an *abridgment* of the right to speak out on disputed issues sets our First Amendment jurisprudence on its head. "Debate on the qualifications of candidates" is "at the core of our electoral process and of the First Amendment freedoms," not at the edges. "The role that elected officials play in our society makes it all the more imperative that they be allowed freely to express themselves on matters of current public importance." "It is simply not the function of government to select which issues are worth discussing or debating in the course of a political campaign." We have never allowed the government to prohibit candidates from communicating relevant information to voters during an election.

Justice Ginsburg would do so — and much of her dissent confirms rather than refutes our conclusion that the purpose behind the announce clause is not open-mindedness in the judiciary, but the undermining of judicial elections. . . . [We] neither assert nor imply that the First Amendment requires campaigns for judicial office to sound the same as those for legislative office. What we do assert, and what Justice Ginsburg ignores, is that, *even if* the First Amendment allows greater regulation of judicial election campaigns than legislative election campaigns, the announce clause still fails strict scrutiny because it is woefully underinclusive, prohibiting announcements by judges (and would-be judges) only at certain times and in certain forms. . . .

But in any case, Justice Ginsburg greatly exaggerates the difference between judicial and legislative elections. She asserts that "the rationale underlying unconstrained speech in elections for political office — that representative government depends on the public's ability to choose agents who will act at its behest — does not carry over to campaigns for the bench." This complete separation of the judiciary from the enterprise of "representative government" might have some truth in those countries where judges neither make law themselves nor set aside the laws enacted by the legislature. It is not a true picture of the American system. Not only do state-court judges possess the power to "make" common law, but they have the immense power to shape the States' constitutions as well. See, e.g., Baker v. State, 170 Vt. 194 (1999). Which is precisely why the election of state judges became popular.

IV. To sustain the announce clause, the Eighth Circuit relied heavily on the fact that a pervasive practice of prohibiting judicial candidates from discussing disputed legal and political issues developed during the last half of the 20th century. It is true that a "universal and long-established" tradition of prohibiting certain conduct creates "a strong presumption" that the prohibition is constitutional [but the] practice of prohibiting speech by judicial candidates on disputed issues . . . is neither long nor universal. . . .

There is an obvious tension between the article of Minnesota's popularly approved Constitution which provides that judges shall be elected, and the Minnesota Supreme Court's announce clause which places most subjects of interest to the voters off limits. . . . This disparity is perhaps unsurprising, since the ABA, which originated the announce clause, has long been an opponent of judicial elections. . . . That opposition may be well taken (it certainly had the support of the Founders of the Federal Government), but the First Amendment does not permit it to achieve its goal by leaving the principle of elections in place while preventing candidates from discussing what the elections are about. "The greater power to dispense with elections altogether does not include the lesser power to conduct elections under conditions of state-imposed voter ignorance. If the State chooses to tap the energy and the legitimizing power of the democratic process, it must accord the participants in that process . . . the First Amendment rights that attach to their roles."

The Minnesota Supreme Court's canon of judicial conduct prohibiting candidates for judicial election from announcing their views on disputed legal and political issues violates the First Amendment. Accordingly, we reverse the grant of summary judgment to respondents and remand the case for proceedings consistent with this opinion.

JUSTICE O'CONNOR, concurring.

I join the opinion of the Court but write separately to express my concerns about judicial elections generally. Respondents claim that "the Announce Clause is necessary . . . to protect the State's compelling governmental interest in an actual and perceived . . . impartial judiciary." I am concerned that . . . the very practice of electing judges undermines this interest.

We of course want judges to be impartial, in the sense of being free from any personal stake in the outcome of the cases to which they are assigned. But if judges are subject to regular elections they are likely to feel that they have at least some personal stake in the outcome of every publicized case. Elected judges cannot help being aware that if the public is not satisfied with the outcome of a particular case, it could hurt their reelection prospects. See Eule, Crocodiles in the Bathtub: State Courts, Voter Initiatives and the Threat of Electoral Reprisal, 65 U. Colo. L. Rev. 733, 739 (1994) (quoting former California Supreme Court Justice Otto Kaus's statement that ignoring the political consequences of visible decisions is " 'like ignoring a crocodile in your bathtub' "). . . . Even if judges were able to suppress their awareness of the potential electoral consequences of their decisions and refrain from acting on it, the public's confidence in the judiciary could be undermined simply by the possibility that judges would be unable to do so.

Moreover, contested elections generally entail campaigning. And campaigning for a judicial post today can require substantial funds. . . . Unless the pool of judicial candidates is limited to those wealthy enough to independently fund their campaigns, a limitation unrelated to judicial skill, the cost of campaigning requires judicial candidates to engage in fundraising. Yet relying on campaign donations may leave judges feeling indebted to certain parties or interest groups. . . . Even if judges were able to refrain from favoring donors, the mere possibility that judges' decisions may be motivated by the desire to repay campaign contributors is likely to undermine the public's confidence in the judiciary.

Despite these significant problems, . . . Minnesota has chosen to select its judges through contested popular elections; [in] doing so the State has voluntarily taken on the risks to judicial bias described above. As a result, the State's claim that it needs to significantly restrict judges' speech in order to protect judicial impartiality is particularly troubling. If the State has a problem with judicial impartiality, it is largely one the State brought upon itself by continuing the practice of popularly electing judges.

JUSTICE KENNEDY, concurring.

I agree with the Court [and] I join its opinion. I adhere to my view, however, that content-based speech restrictions that do not fall within any traditional exception should be invalidated without inquiry into narrow tailoring or compelling government interests. . . . The political speech of candidates is at the heart of the First Amendment, and direct restrictions on the content of candidate speech are simply beyond the power of government to impose. . . .

Deciding the relevance of candidate speech is the right of the voters, not the State. See Brown v. Hartlage, 456 U.S. 45 (1982). The law in question here contradicts the principle that unabridged speech is the foundation of political freedom. . . . The State may not regulate the content of candidate speech merely because the speakers are candidates. This case does not present the question whether a State may restrict the speech of judges because they are judges — for example, as part of a code of judicial conduct; the law at issue here regulates judges only when and because they are candidates.

[JUSTICE STEVENS, joined by JUSTICE SOUTER, JUSTICE GINSBURG, and JUSTICE BREYER, dissented.]

JUSTICE GINSBURG, with whom JUSTICE STEVENS, JUSTICE SOUTER, and JUSTICE BREYER join, dissenting.

Whether state or federal, elected or appointed, judges perform a function fundamentally different from that of the people's elected representatives. Legislative and executive officials act on behalf of the voters who placed them in office; "judges represent the Law." . . . A judiciary capable of performing this function, owing fidelity to no person or party, is a "longstanding Anglo-American tradition," an essential bulwark of constitutional government, a constant guardian of the rule of law. . . .

[If] Minnesota opts to elect its judges, the Court asserts, the State may not rein in what candidates may say. . . . I would differentiate elections for political offices, in which the First Amendment holds full sway, from elections designed to select those whose office it is to administer justice without respect to persons. Minnesota's choice to elect its judges . . . does not preclude the State from installing an election process geared to the judicial office.

Judges . . . are not political actors. They do not sit as representatives of particular persons, communities, or parties; they serve no faction or constituency. . . . They must strive to do what is legally right, all the more so when the result is not the one "the home crowd" wants. Even when they develop common law or give concrete meaning to constitutional text, judges act only in the context of individual cases, the outcome of which cannot depend on the will of the public. . . . Thus, the rationale underlying unconstrained speech in elections for political office — that representative government depends on the public's ability to choose agents who will act at its behest — does not carry over to campaigns for the bench.

. . . All parties to this case agree that, whatever the validity of the Announce Clause, the State may constitutionally prohibit judicial candidates from pledging or promising certain results. . . . [The] pledges or promises clause advances [the] compelling state interest preserving the public's confidence in the integrity and impartiality of its judiciary. . . . The perception of that unseemly *quid pro quo* — a judicial candidate's promises on issues in return for the electorate's votes at the polls — inevitably diminishes the public's faith in the ability of judges to administer the law without regard to personal or political self-interest. . . .

The constitutionality of the pledges or promises clause is thus amply supported; [the] Announce Clause, however, is equally vital to achieving these compelling ends, for without it, the pledges or promises provision would be feeble, an arid form, a matter of no real importance.

Uncoupled from the Announce Clause, the ban on pledges or promises is easily circumvented. By prefacing a campaign commitment with the caveat, "although I cannot promise anything," or by simply avoiding the language of promises or pledges altogether, a candidate could declare with impunity how she would decide specific issues. . . . By targeting statements that do not technically constitute pledges or promises but nevertheless "publicly make known how [the candidate] would decide" legal issues, the Announce Clause prevents this end run around the letter and spirit of its companion provision. No less than the pledges or promises clause itself, the Announce Clause is an indispensable part of Minnesota's effort to maintain the health of its judiciary, and is therefore constitutional for the same reasons.

NOTES

1. Are All Elections Equal? Consider, in this context, the views of Robert Rantoul, a prominent nineteenth-century lawyer and politician, on the discretion afforded judges by the common law:

> Judge-made law is ex post facto law, and therefore unjust. An act is not forbidden by the statute law, but it becomes void by judicial construction. . . . Judge-made law is special legislation. The judge is human, and feels the bias which the coloring of the particular case gives. If he wishes to decide the next case differently, he has only to distinguish, and thereby make a new law. . . . The Common Law is the perfection of human reason — just as alcohol is the perfection of sugar. The subtle spirit of the Common Law is reason double distilled, till what was wholesome and nutritive becomes rank poison. . . . The judge makes law, by extorting from precedents something which they do not contain [and thus creates] a whole system of law . . . built up without the authority or interference of the legislator.

Robert Rantoul, Oration at Scituate, July 7, 1836, in Kermit L. Hall et al., American Legal History 317-318 (1991).

Rantoul was speaking in favor of the codification movement later associated with the Field Codes promoted by David Dudley Field and his brother, Stephen Field. Suppose that his remarks, however colorful, capture the essence of the freedom of adjudication afforded the common law judge. Does this argue in favor of the majority or the dissent? If elected judges can make the law whatever they want it to be, should they be as accountable as all other elected lawmakers? Or does the freedom of decision possessed by judges require that elected judges be selected in a speech-proscribed process?

Perhaps Rantoul was wrong. Are the opinions in this case premised on a belief that judges do, or do not, exercise the discretionary law-making power of which Rantoul accuses them of possessing?

2. First Amendment Absolutism. Note that Justice Kennedy would strike down, *per se*, all content-based speech restrictions "that do not fall within any traditional exception" to the presumptive invalidity of content-based speech regulation. Such regulations, says Kennedy, "should be invalidated without inquiry into narrow tailoring or compelling government interests." Is Justice Kennedy's view a modern version of Justice Black's free speech views? Does it shift consideration of the justifications for content-based regulation into the categorical balancing that creates the exceptions Kennedy references? If so, is that preferable to evaluating claimed justifications for content-based speech regulations on a case-by-case basis?

Chapter 10

The Religion Clauses

B. The Free Exercise Clause

2. Legislation That Targets Religious Conduct or Belief

Page 1146: Insert at the end of the subsection, immediately before Section C:

LOCKE v. DAVEY
124 S. Ct. 1307 (2004)

CHIEF JUSTICE REHNQUIST delivered the opinion of the Court.

The State of Washington established the Promise Scholarship Program to assist academically gifted students with postsecondary education expenses. In accordance with the State Constitution, students may not use the scholarship at an institution where they are pursuing a degree in devotional theology. We hold that such an exclusion from an otherwise inclusive aid program does not violate the Free Exercise Clause of the First Amendment.

The Washington State Legislature . . . created the Promise Scholarship Program, which provides a scholarship, renewable for one year, to eligible students for postsecondary education expenses. Students may spend their funds on any education-related expense. . . . The scholarships are funded through the State's general fund. . . . The scholarship was worth $1,125 for academic year 1999-2000 and $1,542 for 2000-2001.

To be eligible for the scholarship, a student must meet academic, income, and enrollment requirements. A student must graduate from a Washington public or private high school and either graduate in the top 15% of his graduating class, or attain on the first attempt a cumulative score of 1,200 or better on the Scholastic Assessment Test I or a score of 27 or better on the American College Test. The student's family income must be less than 135% of the State's median. Finally, the student must enroll "at least half time in an eligible postsecondary institution in the state of Washington." . . . Private institutions, including those religiously affiliated, qualify as "eligible postsecondary institutions" if they are accredited. . . . A "degree in theology" is not defined in the statute, but, as both parties concede, the statute simply codifies the State's constitutional prohibition on providing funds to students to pursue degrees that are "devotional in nature or designed to induce religious faith." . . .

Respondent, Joshua Davey, was awarded a Promise Scholarship, and chose to attend Northwest College . . . , a private, Christian college affiliated with the Assemblies of God denomination [that] is an eligible institution under the Promise Scholarship Program. [When] he enrolled in Northwest College, [Davey] decided to pursue a double major in pastoral ministries and business management/administration. There is no dispute that the pastoral ministries degree is devotional and therefore excluded under the Promise Scholarship Program.

At the beginning of the 1999-2000 academic year, Davey . . . learned . . . that he could not use his scholarship to pursue a devotional theology degree. He . . . did not receive any scholarship funds. Davey then brought an action . . . against various state officials (hereinafter State) in [federal] District Court . . . to enjoin the State from refusing to award the scholarship solely because a student is pursuing a devotional theology degree, and for damages. . . . The District Court rejected Davey's constitutional claims and granted summary judgment in favor of the State. A divided panel of the . . . Ninth Circuit reversed, [concluding] that the State had singled out religion for unfavorable treatment and thus under our decision in Church of Lukumi Babalu Aye, Inc. v. Hialeah, [p. 1141], the State's exclusion of theology majors must be narrowly tailored to achieve a compelling state interest. Finding that the State's own antiestablishment concerns were not compelling, the court declared Washington's Promise Scholarship Program unconstitutional. We . . . now reverse.

The Religion Clauses of the First Amendment . . . are frequently in tension. Yet we have long said that "there is room for play in the joints" between them. Walz v. Tax Comm'n of City of New York, 397 U.S. 664, 669 (1970). In other words, there are some state actions permitted by the Establishment Clause but not required by the Free Exercise Clause. This case involves that "play in the joints." [There] is no doubt that the State could, consistent with the [Establishment Clause], permit Promise Scholars to pursue a degree in devotional theology, and the State does not contend otherwise. [*Zelman*, 2004 Supp.; *Zobrest*, p. 1157; *Witters*, p. 1157; *Mueller*, p.1151.] The question before us, however, is whether Washington, pursuant to its own constitution,[1] which has been authoritatively interpreted as prohibiting even indirectly funding religious instruction that will prepare students for the ministry, can deny them such funding without violating the Free Exercise Clause.

---

1. The relevant provision of the Washington Constitution, Art. I, §11, states:

Religious Freedom. Absolute freedom of conscience in all matters of religious sentiment, belief and worship, shall be guaranteed to every individual, and no one shall be molested or disturbed in person or property on account of religion; but the liberty of conscience hereby secured shall not be so construed as to excuse acts of licentiousness or justify practices inconsistent with the peace and safety of the state. No public money or property shall be appropriated for or applied to any religious worship, exercise or instruction, or the support of any religious establishment.

Davey . . . contends that under [*Lukumi*] the program is presumptively unconstitutional because it is not facially neutral with respect to religion. We reject his claim of presumptive unconstitutionality, however; to do otherwise would extend the *Lukumi* line of cases well beyond not only their facts but their reasoning. [Unlike *Lukumi*, here the State] imposes neither criminal nor civil sanctions on any type of religious service or rite. It does not deny to ministers the right to participate in the political affairs of the community. See McDaniel v. Paty, [p. 1141.] And it does not require students to choose between their religious beliefs and receiving a government benefit [because] Promise Scholars may still use their scholarship to pursue a secular degree at a different institution from where they are studying devotional theology. . . . The State has merely chosen not to fund a distinct category of instruction.

[Training] someone to lead a congregation is an essentially religious endeavor. Indeed, majoring in devotional theology is akin to a religious calling as well as an academic pursuit. And the subject of religion is one in which both the United States and state constitutions embody distinct views — in favor of free exercise, but opposed to establishment — that find no counterpart with respect to other callings or professions. That a State would deal differently with religious education for the ministry than with education for other callings is a product of these views, not evidence of hostility toward religion.

Even though the differently worded Washington Constitution draws a more stringent line than that drawn by the United States Constitution, the interest it seeks to further is scarcely novel. . . . Since the founding of our country, there have been popular uprisings against procuring taxpayer funds to support church leaders, which was one of the hallmarks of an "established" religion. . . . Most States that sought to avoid an establishment of religion around the time of the founding placed in their constitutions formal prohibitions against using tax funds to support the ministry. The plain text of these constitutional provisions prohibited any tax dollars from supporting the clergy. . . . That early state constitutions saw no problem in explicitly excluding only the ministry from receiving state dollars reinforces our conclusion that religious instruction is of a different ilk.

Far from evincing the hostility toward religion which was manifest in *Lukumi*, we believe that the entirety of the Promise Scholarship Program goes a long way toward including religion in its benefits. The program permits students to attend pervasively religious schools, so long as they are accredited. . . . And under the Promise Scholarship Program's current guidelines, students are still eligible to take devotional theology courses, [so long as they do not major in the subject.]

In short, we find neither in the history or text of Article I, §11 of the Washington Constitution, nor in the operation of the Promise Scholarship Program, anything that suggests animus towards religion. Given the historic and substantial state interest at issue, we therefore cannot conclude that the denial of funding for vocational religious instruction alone is inherently constitutionally suspect.

Without a presumption of unconstitutionality, Davey's claim must fail. The State's interest in not funding the pursuit of devotional degrees is substantial and the exclusion of such funding places a relatively minor burden on Promise Scholars. If any room exists between the two Religion Clauses, it must be here. We need not venture further into this difficult area in order to uphold the Promise Scholarship Program as currently operated by the State of Washington.

The judgment of the Court of Appeals is therefore

Reversed.

JUSTICE SCALIA, with whom JUSTICE THOMAS joins, dissenting.

In [*Lukumi*] the majority opinion held that "[a] law burdening religious practice that is not neutral . . . must undergo the most rigorous of scrutiny," and that "the minimum requirement of neutrality is that a law not discriminate on its face." . . .

I. . . . When the State makes a public benefit generally available, that benefit becomes part of the baseline against which burdens on religion are measured; and when the State withholds that benefit from some individuals solely on the basis of religion, it violates the Free Exercise Clause no less than if it had imposed a special tax.

That is precisely what the State of Washington has done here. It has created a generally available public benefit, whose receipt is conditioned only on academic performance, income, and attendance at an accredited school. It has then carved out a solitary course of study for exclusion: theology. No field of study but religion is singled out for disfavor in this fashion. Davey is not asking for a special benefit to which others are not entitled. He seeks only equal treatment — the right to direct his scholarship to his chosen course of study, a right every other Promise Scholar enjoys.

The Court's reference to historical "popular uprisings against procuring taxpayer funds to support church leaders" is therefore quite misplaced. That history involved not the inclusion of religious ministers in public benefits programs like the one at issue here, but laws that singled them out for financial aid. . . . One can concede the Framers' hostility to funding the clergy specifically, but that says nothing about whether the clergy had to be excluded from benefits the State made available to all. No one would seriously contend, for example, that the Framers would have barred ministers from using public roads on their way to church.

The Court does not dispute that the Free Exercise Clause places some constraints on public benefits programs, but finds none here, based on a principle of " 'play in the joints.' " . . . Even if "play in the joints" were a valid legal principle, surely it would apply only when it was a close call whether complying with one of the Religion Clauses would violate the other. But that is not the case here. It is not just that "the State could, consistent with the Federal Constitution, permit Promise Scholars to pursue a degree in devotional theology." The establishment question would not even be close, as is evident from the fact that this Court's decision in [Witters] was unanimous. Perhaps some formally neutral public benefits programs are so gerrymandered and devoid of plausible secular purpose that they might raise specters of state aid to religion, but an evenhanded Promise Scholarship Program is not among them.

In any case, the State already has all the play in the joints it needs. There are any number of ways it could respect both its unusually sensitive concern for the conscience of its taxpayers and the Federal Free Exercise Clause. It could make the scholarships redeemable only at public universities (where it sets the curriculum), or only for select courses of study. Either option would replace a program that facially discriminates against religion with one that just happens not to subsidize it. . . .

What is the nature of the State's asserted interest here? It cannot be protecting the pocketbooks of its citizens; given the tiny fraction of Promise Scholars who would pursue theology degrees, the amount of any citizen's tax bill at stake is de minimis. It cannot be preventing mistaken appearance of endorsement; where a State merely declines to penalize students for selecting a religious major, "no reasonable observer is likely to draw . . . an inference that the State itself is endorsing a religious practice or belief." [The] interest to which the Court defers is not fear of a conceivable Establishment Clause violation, budget constraints, avoidance of endorsement, or substantive neutrality. . . . It is a pure philosophical preference: the State's opinion that it would violate taxpayers' freedom of conscience not to discriminate against candidates for the ministry. This sort of protection of "freedom of conscience" has no logical limit and can justify the singling out of religion for exclusion from public programs in virtually any context. The Court never says whether it deems this interest compelling (the opinion is devoid of any mention of standard of review) but, self-evidently, it is not.

II. . . . [The] reason the Court thinks this particular facial discrimination less offensive is that the scholarship program was not motivated by animus toward religion. The Court does not explain why the legislature's motive matters, and I fail to see why it should. If a State deprives a citizen of trial by jury or passes an ex post facto law, we do not pause to investigate whether it was actually trying to accomplish the evil the Constitution prohibits. It is sufficient that the citizen's rights have been infringed. . . . The Court has not approached other forms of discrimination this way. When we declared racial segregation unconstitutional, we did not ask whether the State had originally adopted the regime, not out of "animus" against blacks, but because of a well-meaning but misguided belief that the races would be better off apart. . . .

There is no need to rely on analogies, however, because we have rejected the Court's methodology in this very context. In McDaniel v. Paty, [p. 1141], we considered a Tennessee statute that disqualified clergy from participation in the state constitutional convention. That statute, like the one here, was based upon a state constitutional provision — a clause in the 1796 Tennessee Constitution that disqualified clergy from sitting in the legislature. The State defended the statute as an attempt to be faithful to its constitutional separation of church and state, and we accepted that claimed benevolent purpose as bona fide. Nonetheless, because it did not justify facial discrimination against religion, we invalidated the restriction.

It may be that Washington's original purpose in excluding the clergy from public benefits was benign, and the same might be true of its purpose in maintaining the exclusion today. But those singled out for disfavor can be forgiven for suspecting more invidious forces at work. Let there be no doubt: This case is about discrimination against a religious minority. Most citizens of this country identify themselves as professing some religious belief, but the State's policy poses no obstacle to practitioners of only a tepid, civic version of faith. Those the statutory exclusion actually affects — those whose belief in their religion is so strong that they dedicate their study and their lives to its ministry — are a far narrower set. One need not delve too far into modern popular culture to perceive a trendy disdain for deep religious conviction. In an era when the Court is so quick to come to the aid of other disfavored groups, see, e.g., Romer v. Evans, [p. 672], its indifference in this case, which involves a form of discrimination to which the Constitution actually speaks, is exceptional. . . .

Today's holding is limited to training the clergy, but its logic is readily extendible, and there are plenty of directions to go. What next? [Recall] that France has proposed banning religious attire from schools, invoking interests in secularism no less benign than those the Court embraces today. When the public's freedom of conscience is invoked to justify denial of equal treatment, benevolent motives shade into indifference and ultimately into repression. Having accepted the justification in this case, the Court is less well equipped to fend it off in the future. I respectfully dissent.

NOTES

1. "Play in the Joints:" How Much Room for Government Accommodation of Religion or Refusal to Accommodate Religion? Chief Justice Rehnquist characterized the religion clauses as having "play in the joints" between them, meaning that there is some room for governmental discretion in deciding to accommodate religion or to refuse to accommodate religion. Put another way, the Establishment Clause specifies when governments may not accommodate religion (and must refuse to accommodate religion), while the Free Exercise Clause specifies when governments must accommodate religion. Employment Division v. Smith held in essence that general laws will be applied equally to everybody, including religious believers. Such laws are presumptively valid and will usually be upheld, as they are subject to minimal scrutiny. After *Locke*, Church of Lukumi Babalu Aye v. Hialeah appears to stand for the proposition that laws that are focused on religion and that are purposefully hostile to religion are presumptive violations of the Free Exercise Clause. They may be upheld only if the government can sustain its burden of justification under strict scrutiny. *Locke* establishes that laws that focus on religion or that have an effect on religious practice are presumptively valid and not subject to strict scrutiny unless they manifest hostility to religion. Query: Are such laws subject to minimal scrutiny or to some other level of reduced scrutiny? Justice Scalia charges in dissent that the majority has failed to tell us what level of review applies. How would you answer Justice Scalia? State the components of the scrutiny the Court actually applies in *Locke*.

Does the Court in *Locke* leave too much "play in the joints," as Justice Scalia evidently thinks? What would be the effect on Employment Division v. Smith if Justice Scalia's view had prevailed in *Locke*?

2. Legislative Purpose or Actual Effect: Which Should Matter More? The majority's approach was to ask whether Washington's refusal to fund a Promise Scholarship for the student majoring in devotional theology was motivated by hostility toward religion. Justice Scalia claimed that only the effect of Washington's refusal was relevant to resolution of Davey's Free Exercise claim. Who has the better of this argument? If motivation matters, how do we assess motive if Washington decides to strip churches of the property tax exemption they presently enjoy? If effect matters, how do we assess the effect of a zoning ordinance that treats "charitable organizations, including churches" as commercial enterprises, thus precluding their location in residential neighborhoods? Why should motive matter if the effect is to discriminate against religious practice, and only religious practice? Why should effect matter if the burdens of a general, neutral law unmotivated by religious hostility happen to fall with disproportionate impact on religion? Recall that in cases of race-neutral laws that deliver a disproportionate racial impact the plaintiff is required to prove a racially discriminatory purpose in order to subject the law to strict scrutiny. See Washington v. Davis, p. 701. Does *Locke* simply extend the Washington v. Davis principle to Free Exercise claims? Recall also that if racial discrimination is facially evident the law is automatically subject to strict scrutiny. Cf. Strauder v. West Virginia, p. 700. Does *Locke* ignore that principle in the Free Exercise context?

C. The Establishment Clause

1. Government Financial Aid to Religion

Page 1163: Insert at the end of the subsection, immediately prior to subsection 2:

ZELMAN v. SIMMONS-HARRIS
536 U.S. 639 (2002)

CHIEF JUSTICE REHNQUIST delivered the opinion of the Court.

The State of Ohio has established a pilot program designed to provide educational choices to families with children who reside in the Cleveland City School District. The question presented is whether this program offends the Establishment Clause of the United States Constitution. We hold that it does not.

There are more than 75,000 children enrolled in the Cleveland City School District. The majority of these children are from low-income and minority families. Few of these families enjoy the means to send their children to any school other than an inner-city public school. For more than a generation, however, Cleveland's public schools have been among the worst performing public schools in the Nation. In 1995, a Federal District Court declared a "crisis of magnitude" and placed the entire Cleveland school district under state control. Shortly thereafter, the state auditor found that Cleveland's public schools were in the midst of a "crisis that is perhaps unprecedented in the history of American education." The district had failed to meet any of the 18 state standards for minimal acceptable performance. Only 1 in 10 ninth graders could pass a basic proficiency examination, and students at all levels performed at a dismal rate compared with students in other Ohio public schools. More than two-thirds of high school students either dropped or failed out before graduation. Of those students who managed to reach their senior year, one of every four still failed to graduate. Of those students who did graduate, few could read, write, or compute at levels comparable to their counterparts in other cities.

It is against this backdrop that Ohio enacted, among other initiatives, its Pilot Project Scholarship Program, [which] provides financial assistance to families in any Ohio school district that is or has been "under federal court order requiring supervision and operational management of the district by the state superintendent." Cleveland is the only Ohio school district to fall within that category.

The program provides two basic kinds of assistance to parents of children in a covered district. First, the program provides tuition aid for students in kindergarten through third grade, expanding each year through eighth grade, to attend a participating public or private school of their parent's choosing. Second, the program provides tutorial aid for students who choose to remain enrolled in public school.

The tuition aid portion of the program is designed to provide educational choices to parents who reside in a covered district. Any private school, whether religious or nonreligious, may participate in the program and accept program students so long as the school is located within the boundaries of a covered district and meets statewide educational standards. Participating private schools must agree not to discriminate on the basis of race, religion, or ethnic background, or to "advocate or foster unlawful behavior or teach hatred of any person or group on the basis of race, ethnicity, national origin, or religion." Any public school located in a school district adjacent to the covered district may also participate in the program. Adjacent public schools are eligible to receive a $2,250 tuition grant for each program student accepted in addition to the full amount of per-pupil state funding attributable to each additional student. All participating schools, whether public or private, are required to accept students in accordance with rules and procedures established by the state superintendent.

Tuition aid is distributed to parents according to financial need. Families with incomes below 200% of the poverty line are given priority and are eligible to receive 90% of private school tuition up to $2,250. For these lowest-income families, participating private schools may not charge a parental co-payment greater than $250. For all other families, the program pays 75% of tuition costs, up to $1,875, with no co-payment cap. These families receive tuition aid only if the number of available scholarships exceeds the number of low-income children who choose to participate. Where tuition aid is spent depends solely upon where parents who receive tuition aid choose to enroll their child. If parents choose a private school, checks are made payable to the parents who then endorse the checks over to the chosen school.

The tutorial aid portion of the program provides tutorial assistance through grants to any student in a covered district who chooses to remain in public school. Parents arrange for registered tutors to provide assistance to their children and then submit bills for those services to the State for payment. Students from low-income families receive 90% of the amount charged for such assistance up to $360. All other students receive 75% of that amount. The number of tutorial assistance grants offered to students in a covered district must equal the number of tuition aid scholarships provided to students enrolled at participating private or adjacent public schools.

The program has been in operation within the Cleveland City School District since the 1996-1997 school year. In the 1999-2000 school year, 56 private schools participated in the program, 46 (or 82%) of which had a religious affiliation. None of the public schools in districts adjacent to Cleveland have elected to participate. More than 3,700 students participated in the scholarship program, most of whom (96%) enrolled in religiously affiliated schools. Sixty percent of these students were from families at or below the poverty line. In the 1998-1999 school year, approximately 1,400 Cleveland public school students received tutorial aid. This number was expected to double during the 1999-2000 school year.

The program is part of a broader undertaking by the State to enhance the educational options of Cleveland's schoolchildren in response to the 1995 takeover. That undertaking includes programs governing community and magnet schools. Community schools are funded under state law but are run by their own school boards, not by local school districts. These schools enjoy academic independence to hire their own teachers and to determine their own curriculum. They can have no religious affiliation and are required to accept students by lottery. During the 1999-2000 school year, there were 10 start-up community schools in the Cleveland City School District with more than 1,900 students enrolled. For each child enrolled in a community school, the school receives state funding of $4,518, twice the funding a participating program school may receive.

Magnet schools are public schools operated by a local school board that emphasize a particular subject area, teaching method, or service to students. For each student enrolled in a magnet school, the school district receives $7,746, including state funding of $4,167, the same amount received per student enrolled at a traditional public school. As of 1999, parents in Cleveland were able to choose from among 23 magnet schools, which together enrolled more than 13,000 students in kindergarten through eighth grade. These schools provide specialized teaching methods, such as Montessori, or a particularized curriculum focus, such as foreign language, computers, or the arts.

[Respondents], a group of Ohio taxpayers, . . . filed this action in United States District Court, seeking to enjoin the . . . program on the ground that it violated the Establishment Clause. [The] District Court granted summary judgment for respondents. [A] divided panel of the Court of Appeals affirmed the judgment of the District Court, finding that the program had the "primary effect" of advancing religion in violation of the Establishment Clause. . . . We granted certiorari and now reverse the Court of Appeals.

The Establishment Clause of the First Amendment, applied to the States through the Fourteenth Amendment, prevents a State from enacting laws that have the "purpose" or "effect" of advancing or inhibiting religion. Agostini v. Felton. There is no dispute that the program challenged here was enacted for the valid secular purpose of providing educational assistance to poor children in a demonstrably failing public school system. Thus, the question presented is whether the Ohio program nonetheless has the forbidden "effect" of advancing or inhibiting religion.

To answer that question, our decisions have drawn a consistent distinction between government programs that provide aid directly to religious schools and programs of true private choice, in which government aid reaches religious schools only as a result of the genuine and independent choices of private individuals. [Mueller v. Allen; *Witters; Zobrest.*]

Mueller, *Witters*, and *Zobrest* . . . make clear that where a government aid program is neutral with respect to religion, and provides assistance directly to a broad class of citizens who, in turn, direct government aid to religious schools wholly as a result of their own genuine and independent private choice, the program is not readily subject to challenge under the Establishment Clause. A program that shares these features permits government aid to reach religious institutions only by way of the deliberate choices of numerous individual recipients. The incidental advancement of a religious mission, or the perceived endorsement of a religious message, is reasonably attributable to the individual recipient, not to the government, whose role ends with the disbursement of benefits. "If numerous private choices, rather than the single choice of a government, determine the distribution of aid, pursuant to neutral eligibility criteria, then a government cannot, or at least cannot easily, grant special favors that might lead to a religious establishment.". . . "When government aid supports a school's religious mission only because of independent decisions made by numerous individuals to guide their secular aid to that school, 'no reasonable observer is likely to draw from the facts . . . an inference that the State itself is endorsing a religious practice or belief.' " It is precisely for these reasons that we have never found a program of true private choice to offend the Establishment Clause.

We believe that the program challenged here is a program of true private choice, consistent with *Mueller*, *Witters*, and *Zobrest*, and thus constitutional. As was true in those cases, the Ohio program is neutral in all respects toward religion. It is part of a general and multifaceted undertaking by the State of Ohio to provide educational opportunities to the children of a failed school district. It confers educational assistance directly to a broad class of individuals defined without reference to religion, i.e., any parent of a school-age child who resides in the Cleveland City School District. The program permits the participation of *all* schools within the district, religious or nonreligious. Adjacent public schools also may participate and have a financial incentive to do so. Program benefits are available to participating families on neutral terms, with no reference to religion. The only preference stated anywhere in the program is a preference for low-income families, who receive greater assistance and are given priority for admission at participating schools.

There are no "financial incentives" that "skew" the program toward religious schools. Such incentives "[are] not present . . . where the aid is allocated on the basis of neutral, secular criteria that neither favor nor disfavor religion, and is made available to both religious and secular beneficiaries on a nondiscriminatory basis." [*Agostini.*] The program here in fact creates financial *dis*incentives for religious schools, with private schools receiving only half the government assistance given to community schools and one-third the assistance given to magnet schools. Adjacent public schools, should any choose to accept program students, are also eligible to receive two to three times the state funding of a private religious school. Families too have a financial disincentive to choose a private religious school over other schools. Parents that choose to participate in the scholarship program and then to enroll their children in a private school (religious or nonreligious) must co-pay a portion of the school's tuition. Families that choose a community school, magnet school, or traditional public school pay nothing. Although such features of the program are not necessary to its constitutionality, they clearly dispel the claim that the program "creates . . . financial incentives for parents to choose a sectarian school." [*Zobrest.*]

Respondents suggest that even without a financial incentive for parents to choose a religious school, the program creates a "public perception that the State is endorsing religious practices and beliefs." But we have repeatedly recognized that no reasonable observer would think a neutral program of private choice, where state aid reaches religious schools solely as a result of the numerous independent decisions of private individuals, carries with it the *imprimatur* of government endorsement. [*Mueller; Witters; Zobrest.*] The argument is particularly misplaced here since "the reasonable observer in the endorsement inquiry must be deemed aware" of the "history and context" underlying a challenged program. Any objective observer familiar with the full history and context of the Ohio program would reasonably view it as one aspect of a broader undertaking to assist poor children in failed schools, not as an endorsement of religious schooling in general.

There also is no evidence that the program fails to provide genuine opportunities for Cleveland parents to select secular educational options for their school-age children. Cleveland schoolchildren enjoy a range of educational choices: They may remain in public school as before, remain in public school with publicly funded tutoring aid, obtain a scholarship and choose a religious school, obtain a scholarship and choose a nonreligious private school, enroll in a community school, or enroll in a magnet school. That 46 of the 56 private schools now participating in the program are religious schools does not condemn it as a violation of the Establishment Clause. The Establishment Clause question is whether Ohio is coercing parents into sending their children to religious schools, and that question must be answered by evaluating *all* options Ohio provides Cleveland schoolchildren, only one of which is to obtain a program scholarship and then choose a religious school.

[While it] is true that 82% of Cleveland's participating private schools are religious schools, . . . it is also true that 81% of private schools in Ohio are religious schools. To attribute constitutional significance to this figure, moreover, would lead to the absurd result that a neutral school-choice program might be permissible in some parts of Ohio, such as Columbus, where a lower percentage of private schools are religious schools, but not in inner-city Cleveland, where Ohio has deemed such programs most sorely needed, but where the preponderance of religious schools happens to be greater. Likewise, an identical private choice program might be constitutional in some States, such as Maine or Utah, where less than 45% of private schools are religious schools, but not in other States, such as Nebraska or Kansas, where over 90% of private schools are religious schools.

Respondents and Justice Souter claim that . . . we should attach constitutional significance to the fact that 96% of scholarship recipients have enrolled in religious schools. They claim that this alone proves parents lack genuine choice, even if no parent has ever said so. We need not consider this argument in detail, since it was flatly rejected in *Mueller*, where we found it irrelevant that 96% of parents taking deductions for tuition expenses paid tuition at religious schools. Indeed, we have recently found it irrelevant even to the constitutionality of a direct aid program that a vast majority of program benefits went to religious schools. [*Agostini.*] The constitutionality of a neutral educational aid program simply does not turn on whether and why, in a particular area, at a particular time, most private schools are run by religious organizations, or most recipients choose to use the aid at a religious school. As we said in *Mueller*, "such an approach would scarcely provide the certainty that this field stands in need of, nor can we perceive principled standards by which such statistical evidence might be evaluated." This point is aptly illustrated here. The 96% figure . . . discounts entirely (1) the more than 1,900 Cleveland children enrolled in alternative community schools, (2) the more than 13,000 children enrolled in alternative magnet schools, and (3) the more than 1,400 children enrolled in traditional public schools with tutorial assistance. Including some or all of these children in the denominator of children enrolled in nontraditional schools during the 1999-2000 school year drops the percentage enrolled in religious schools from 96% to under 20%. The 96% figure also represents but a snapshot of one particular school year. In the 1997-1998 school year, by contrast, only 78% of scholarship recipients attended religious schools. The difference was attributable to two private nonreligious schools that had accepted 15% of all scholarship students electing instead to register as community schools, in light of larger per-pupil funding for community schools and the uncertain future of the scholarship program generated by this litigation. . . .

Respondents finally claim that we should look to Committee for Public Ed. & Religious Liberty v. Nyquist, 413 U.S. 756 (1973), to decide these cases. We disagree for two reasons.

First, . . . *Nyquist* involved a New York program that gave a package of benefits exclusively to private schools and the parents of private school enrollees. The program . . . provided direct money grants to religious schools[, and] tax benefits "unrelated to the amount of money actually expended by any parent on tuition," ensuring a windfall to parents of children in religious schools. It similarly provided tuition reimbursements designed explicitly to "offer . . . an incentive to parents to send their children to sectarian schools." Indeed, the program flatly prohibited the participation of any public school, or parent of any public school enrollee. Ohio's program shares none of these features.

Second, were there any doubt that the program challenged in *Nyquist* is far removed from the program challenged here, we expressly reserved judgment with respect to "a case involving some form of public assistance (e.g., scholarships) made available generally without regard to the sectarian-nonsectarian, or public-nonpublic nature of the institution benefited." That, of course, is the very question now before us, and it has since been answered, first in *Mueller*, then in *Witters*, and again in *Zobrest*. To the extent the scope of *Nyquist* has remained an open question in light of these later decisions, we now hold that *Nyquist* does not govern neutral educational assistance programs that, like the program here, offer aid directly to a broad class of individual recipients defined without regard to religion.[1]

In sum, the Ohio program is entirely neutral with respect to religion. It provides benefits directly to a wide spectrum of individuals, defined only by financial need and residence in a particular school district. It permits such individuals to exercise genuine choice among options public and private, secular and religious. The program is therefore a program of true private choice. In keeping with an unbroken line of decisions rejecting challenges to similar programs, we hold that the program does not offend the Establishment Clause.

JUSTICE O'CONNOR, concurring.

. . . I join the Court's opinion. . . . These cases are different from prior indirect aid cases in part because a significant portion of the funds appropriated for the voucher program reach religious schools without restrictions on the use of these funds. The share of public resources that reach religious schools is not, however, as significant as respondents suggest. [At most,] $8.2 million of public funds flowed to religious schools under the voucher program in 1999-2000. Although just over one-half as many students attended community schools as religious private schools on the state fisc, the State spent over $1 million more — $9.4 million — on students in community schools than on students in religious private schools because per-pupil aid to community schools is more than double the per-pupil aid to private schools under the voucher program. Moreover, the amount spent on religious private schools is minor compared to the $114.8 million the State spent on students in the Cleveland magnet schools. Although $8.2 million is no small sum, it pales in comparison to the amount of funds that federal, state, and local governments already provide religious institutions. Religious organizations may qualify for exemptions from the federal corporate income tax, the corporate income tax in many States, and property taxes in all 50 States, and clergy qualify for a federal tax break

---

1. Justice Breyer would raise the invisible specters of "divisiveness" and "religious strife" to find the program unconstitutional. It is unclear exactly what sort of principle Justice Breyer has in mind, considering that the program has ignited no "divisiveness" or "strife" other than this litigation. Nor is it clear where Justice Breyer would locate this presumed authority to deprive Cleveland residents of a program that they have chosen but that we subjectively find "divisive." We quite rightly have rejected the claim that some speculative potential for divisiveness bears on the constitutionality of educational aid programs. [Mitchell v. Helms.]

on income used for housing expenses. In addition, the Federal Government provides individuals, corporations, trusts, and estates a tax deduction for charitable contributions to qualified religious groups. Finally, the Federal Government and certain state governments provide tax credits for educational expenses, many of which are spent on education at religious schools. Most of these tax policies are well established, yet confer a significant relative benefit on religious institutions. . . . Federal dollars also reach religiously affiliated organizations through public health programs such as Medicare and Medicaid, through educational programs such as the Pell Grant program and the G. I. Bill of Rights, and through child care programs such as the Child Care and Development Block Grant Program. . . . These programs are well-established parts of our social welfare system and can be quite substantial. . . . A significant portion of the funds appropriated for these programs reach religiously affiliated institutions, typically without restrictions on its subsequent use.

Against this background, the support that the Cleveland voucher program provides religious institutions is neither substantial nor atypical of existing government programs. While this observation is not intended to justify the Cleveland voucher program under the Establishment Clause, it places in broader perspective alarmist claims about implications of the Cleveland program and the Court's decision in these cases. . . .

JUSTICE THOMAS, concurring.

Frederick Douglass once said that "education . . . means emancipation. It means light and liberty. It means the uplifting of the soul of man into the glorious light of truth, the light by which men can only be made free." Today many of our inner-city public schools deny emancipation to urban minority students. Despite this Court's observation nearly 50 years ago in Brown v. Board of Education, that "it is doubtful that any child may reasonably be expected to succeed in life if he is denied the opportunity of an education," urban children have been forced into a system that continually fails them. These cases present an example of such failures. . . .

I agree with the Court that Ohio's program easily passes muster under our stringent [Establishment Clause] test, but, as a matter of first principles, I question whether this test should be applied to the States. . . . On its face, [the Establishment Clause] places no limit on the States with regard to religion. The Establishment Clause originally protected States, and by extension their citizens, from the imposition of an established religion by the Federal Government. Whether and how this Clause should constrain state action under the Fourteenth Amendment is a more difficult question.

The Fourteenth Amendment fundamentally restructured the relationship between individuals and the States and ensured that States would not deprive citizens of liberty without due process of law. . . . When rights are incorporated against the States through the Fourteenth Amendment they should advance, not constrain, individual liberty. Consequently, in the context of the Establishment Clause, it may well be that state action should be evaluated on different terms than similar action by the Federal Government. "States, while bound to observe strict neutrality, should be freer to experiment with involvement [in religion] — on a neutral basis — than the Federal Government." Walz v. Tax Comm'n of City of New York, 397 U.S. 664, 699 (1970) (Harlan, J., concurring). Thus, while the Federal Government may "make no law respecting an establishment of religion," the States may pass laws that include or touch on religious matters so long as these laws do not impede free exercise rights or any other individual religious liberty interest. . . . Whatever the textual and historical merits of incorporating the Establishment Clause, I can accept that the Fourteenth Amendment protects religious liberty rights. But I cannot accept its use to oppose neutral programs of school choice through the incorporation of the Establishment Clause. There would be a tragic irony in converting the Fourteenth Amendment's guarantee of individual liberty into a prohibition on the exercise of educational choice.

. . . [The] inclusion of religious schools makes sense given Ohio's purpose of increasing educational performance and opportunities. Religious schools, like other private schools, achieve far better educational results than their public counterparts. For example, the students at Cleveland's Catholic schools score significantly higher on Ohio proficiency tests than students at Cleveland public schools. Of Cleveland eighth graders taking the 1999 Ohio proficiency test, 95 percent in Catholic schools passed the reading test, whereas only 57 percent in public schools passed. And 75 percent of Catholic school students passed the math proficiency test, compared to only 22 percent of public school students. But the success of religious and private schools is in the end beside the point, because the State has a constitutional right to experiment with a variety of different programs to promote educational opportunity. . . .

Although one of the purposes of public schools was to promote democracy and a more egalitarian culture, failing urban public schools disproportionately affect minority children most in need of educational opportunity. At the time of Reconstruction, blacks considered public education "a matter of personal liberation and a necessary function of a free society." Today, however, the promise of public school education has failed poor inner-city blacks. [Many] blacks and other minorities now support school choice programs because they provide the greatest educational opportunities for their children in struggling communities. Opponents of the program raise formalistic concerns about the Establishment Clause but ignore the core purposes of the Fourteenth Amendment.

While the romanticized ideal of universal public education resonates with the cognoscenti who oppose vouchers, poor urban families just want the best education for their children, who will certainly need it to function in our high-tech and advanced society. . . . The failure to provide education to poor urban children perpetuates a vicious cycle of poverty, dependence, criminality, and alienation that continues for the remainder of their lives. If society cannot end racial discrimination, at least it can arm minorities with the education to defend themselves from some of discrimination's effects. . . .

Ten States have enacted some form of publicly funded private school choice as one means of raising the quality of education provided to underprivileged urban children. These programs address the root of the problem with failing urban public schools that disproportionately affect minority students. Society's other solution to these educational failures is often to provide racial preferences in higher education. Such preferences, however, run afoul of the Fourteenth Amendment's prohibition against distinctions based on race. By contrast, school choice programs that involve religious schools appear unconstitutional only to those who would twist the Fourteenth Amendment against itself by expansively incorporating the Establishment Clause. Converting the Fourteenth Amendment from a guarantee of opportunity to an obstacle against education reform distorts our constitutional values and disserves those in the greatest need.

As Frederick Douglass poignantly noted "no greater benefit can be bestowed upon a long benighted people, than giving to them, as we are here earnestly this day endeavoring to do, the means of an education."

JUSTICE STEVENS, dissenting.

Is a law that authorizes the use of public funds to pay for the indoctrination of thousands of grammar school children in particular religious faiths a "law respecting an establishment of religion" within the meaning of the First Amendment? In answering that question, I think we should ignore three factual matters that are discussed at length by my colleagues.

First, the severe educational crisis that confronted the Cleveland City School District when Ohio enacted its voucher program is not a matter that should affect our appraisal of its constitutionality. [The] emergency may have given some families a powerful motivation to leave the public school system and accept religious indoctrination that they would otherwise have avoided, but that is not a valid reason for upholding the program. Second, the wide range of choices that have been made available to students *within the public school system* has no bearing on the question whether the State may pay the tuition for students who wish to reject public education entirely and attend private schools that will provide them with a sectarian education. . . . Third, the voluntary character of the private choice to prefer a parochial education over an education in the public school system seems to me quite irrelevant to the question whether the government's choice to pay for religious indoctrination is constitutionally permissible.

For the reasons stated by Justice Souter and Justice Breyer, I am convinced that the Court's decision is profoundly misguided. . . . Whenever we remove a brick from the wall that was designed to separate religion and government, we increase the risk of religious strife and weaken the foundation of our democracy.

JUSTICE SOUTER, with whom JUSTICE STEVENS, JUSTICE GINSBURG, and JUSTICE BREYER join, dissenting.

. . . If there were an excuse for giving short shrift to the Establishment Clause, it would probably apply here. But there is no excuse. . . . Although it has taken half a century since *Everson* to reach the majority's twin standards of neutrality and free choice, the facts show that, in the majority's hands, even these criteria cannot convincingly legitimize the Ohio scheme.

Consider first the criterion of neutrality. . . . Neutrality in this sense refers . . . to evenhandedness in setting eligibility as between potential religious and secular recipients of public money. . . . Here, one would ask whether the voucher provisions . . . were written in a way that skewed the scheme toward benefiting religious schools. This, however, is not what the majority asks. The majority looks not to the provisions for tuition vouchers but to every provision for educational opportunity. . . . The majority then finds confirmation that "participation of *all* schools" satisfies neutrality by noting that the better part of total state educational expenditure goes to public schools, thus showing there is no favor of religion. [The] majority's reasoning would find neutrality in a scheme of vouchers available for private tuition in districts with no secular private schools at all. "Neutrality" as the majority employs the term is, literally, verbal and nothing more. . . .

The majority addresses the issue of choice the same way it addresses neutrality, by asking whether recipients or potential recipients of voucher aid have a choice of public schools among secular alternatives to religious schools. Again, however, the majority asks the wrong question and misapplies the criterion. . . . The question is whether the private hand is genuinely free to send the money in either a secular direction or a religious one. [When] the choice test is transformed from where to spend the money to where to go to school, it is cut loose from its very purpose. . . . If "choice" is present whenever there is any educational alternative to the religious school to which vouchers can be endorsed, then there will always be a choice and the voucher can always be constitutional, even in a system in which there is not a single private secular school as an alternative to the religious school. That is, in fact, just the kind of rhetorical argument that the majority accepts in these cases. . . .

If . . . we ask the right question about genuine choice to use the vouchers, the answer shows that something is influencing choices in a way that aims the money in a religious direction: of 56 private schools in the district participating in the voucher program . . . , 46 of them are religious; 96.6% of all voucher recipients go to religious schools, only 3.4% to nonreligious ones. [There] is no explanation . . . that suggests the religious direction results simply from free choices by parents. One answer . . . which would be consistent with the genuine choice claimed to be operating, might be that 96.6% of families choosing to avail themselves of vouchers choose to educate their children in schools of their own religion. [But] almost two out of three families using vouchers to send their children to religious schools did not embrace the religion of those schools. The families made it clear they had not chosen the schools because they wished their children to be proselytized in a religion not their own, or in any religion, but because of educational opportunity. Even so, the [program] might be consistent with true choice if the students "chose" their religious schools over a wide array of private nonreligious options, or if it could be shown generally that Ohio's program had no effect on educational choices and thus no impermissible effect of advancing religious education. But both possibilities are contrary to fact. First, even if all existing nonreligious private schools in Cleveland were willing to accept large numbers of voucher students, only a few more than the 129 currently enrolled in such schools would be able to attend, as the total enrollment at all nonreligious private schools in Cleveland for kindergarten through eighth grade is only 510 children and there is no indication that these schools have many open seats. Second, the $2,500 cap that the program places on tuition for participating low-income pupils has the effect of curtailing the participation of nonreligious schools: "nonreligious schools with higher tuition (about $4,000) stated that they could afford to accommodate just a few voucher students." By comparison, the average tuition at participating Catholic schools in Cleveland in 1999-2000 was $1,592, almost $1,000 below the cap. . . . There is . . . no way to interpret the 96.6% of current voucher money going to religious schools as reflecting a free and genuine choice by the families that apply for vouchers. The 96.6% reflects, instead, the fact that too few nonreligious school desks are available and few but religious schools can afford to accept more than a handful of voucher students. And . . . public schools in adjacent districts hardly have a financial incentive to participate in the Ohio voucher program, and none has.[2] For the overwhelming number of children in the voucher scheme, the only alternative to the public schools is religious. And it is entirely irrelevant that the State did not deliberately design the network of private schools for the sake of channeling money into religious institutions. The criterion is one of genuinely free choice on the part of the private individuals who choose, and a Hobson's choice is not a choice, whatever the reason for being Hobsonian.

. . . The scale of the aid to religious schools approved today is unprecedented, both in the number of dollars and in the proportion of systemic school expenditure supported. [The] sheer quantity of aid, when delivered to a class of religious primary and secondary schools, [is] suspect on the theory that the greater the aid, the greater its proportion to a religious school's existing expenditures, and the greater the likelihood that public money [is] supporting religious as well as secular instruction. . . . The . . . majority makes no pretense that substantial amounts of tax money are not systematically underwriting religious practice and indoctrination.

It is virtually superfluous to point out that every objective underlying the prohibition of religious establishment is betrayed by this scheme, but something has to be said about the enormity of the violation. . . . [In] the 21st century, the risk is one of "corrosive secularism" to religious schools and the specific threat is to the primacy of the schools' mission to educate the children of the faithful according to the unaltered precepts of their faith. [Religion] "may be compromised . . . as government largesse brings government regulation." The risk is already being realized. In Ohio, for example, a condition of receiving government money under the program is that participating religious schools may not "discriminate on the basis of . . . religion," which means the school may not give admission preferences to children who are members of the patron faith; children of a parish are generally consigned to the same admission lotteries as non-believers. . . . Nor is the State's religious antidiscrimination restriction limited to student admission policies: by its terms, a par-

2. [While] an out-of-district public school that participates will receive a $2,250 voucher for each Cleveland student on top of its normal state funding, [the] basic state funding . . . is a drop in the bucket as compared to the cost of educating that student, as much of the cost (at least in relatively affluent areas with presumptively better academic standards) is paid by local income and property taxes. . . .

ticipating religious school may well be forbidden to choose a member of its own clergy to serve as teacher or principal over a layperson of a different religion claiming equal qualification for the job. Indeed, a separate condition that "the school . . . not . . . teach hatred of any person or group on the basis of . . . religion" could be understood (or subsequently broadened) to prohibit religions from teaching traditionally legitimate articles of faith as to the error, sinfulness, or ignorance of others, if they want government money for their schools.

For perspective on this foot-in-the-door of religious regulation, it is well to remember that the money has barely begun to flow. Prior examples of aid, whether grants through individuals or in-kind assistance, were never significant enough to alter the basic fiscal structure of religious schools; state aid was welcome, but not indispensable. . . . When government aid goes up, so does reliance on it; the only thing likely to go down is independence. . . . A day will come when religious schools will learn what political leverage can do. . . .

As appropriations for religious subsidy rise, competition for the money will tap sectarian religion's capacity for discord. "Public money devoted to payment of religious costs, educational or other, brings the quest for more. It brings too the struggle of sect against sect for the larger share or for any." [It] is enough to say that the intensity of the expectable friction can be gauged by realizing that the scramble for money will energize not only contending sectarians, but taxpayers who take their liberty of conscience seriously. Religious teaching at taxpayer expense simply cannot be cordoned from taxpayer politics, and every major religion currently espouses social positions that provoke intense opposition. Not all taxpaying Protestant citizens, for example, will be content to underwrite the teaching of the Roman Catholic Church condemning the death penalty. Nor will all of America's Muslims acquiesce in paying for the endorsement of the religious Zionism taught in many religious Jewish schools, which combines "a nationalistic sentiment" in support of Israel with a "deeply religious" element. Nor will every secular taxpayer be content to support Muslim views on differential treatment of the sexes, or, for that matter, to fund the espousal of a wife's obligation of obedience to her husband, presumably taught in any schools adopting the articles of faith of the Southern Baptist Convention. Views like these, and innumerable others, have been safe in the sectarian pulpits and classrooms of this Nation not only because the Free Exercise Clause protects them directly, but because the ban on supporting religious establishment has protected free exercise, by keeping it relatively private. With the arrival of vouchers in religious schools, that privacy will go, and along with it will go confidence that religious disagreement will stay moderate. . . .

JUSTICE BREYER, with whom JUSTICE STEVENS and JUSTICE SOUTER join, dissenting.

I write separately . . . to emphasize the risk that publicly financed voucher programs pose in terms of religiously based social conflict. . . . America boasts more than 55 different religious groups and subgroups with a significant number of members [—] among others, Protestants, Catholics, Jews, Muslims, Buddhists,

Hindus, and Sikhs. And several of these major religions contain different subsidiary sects with different religious beliefs.

Under these modern-day circumstances, [and with voucher programs that] may well provide billions of dollars, [why] will different religions not become concerned about, and seek to influence, the criteria used to channel this money to religious schools? . . . If so, just how is the State to resolve the resulting controversies without provoking legitimate fears of the kinds of religious favoritism that, in so religiously diverse a Nation, threaten social dissension? . . . Efforts to respond to these problems not only will seriously entangle church and state, but also will promote division among religious groups, as one group or another fears (often legitimately) that it will receive unfair treatment at the hands of the government. . . .

In a society as religiously diverse as ours, the Court has recognized that we must rely on the Religion Clauses of the First Amendment to protect against religious strife. . . . School voucher programs differ, however, in both *kind* and *degree* from aid programs upheld in the past. They differ in kind because they direct financing to a core function of the church: the teaching of religious truths to young children. . . . History suggests, not that such private school teaching of religion is undesirable, but that *government funding* of this kind of religious endeavor is far more contentious than providing funding for secular textbooks, computers, vocational training, or even funding for adults who wish to obtain a college education at a religious university. . . . Vouchers also differ in *degree.* The aid programs recently upheld by the Court involved limited amounts of aid to religion. But the majority's analysis here appears to permit a considerable shift of taxpayer dollars from public secular schools to private religious schools. That fact, combined with the use to which these dollars will be put, exacerbates the conflict problem. . . .

NOTES

1. The Meaning of Neutral Effect. What is left of the neutral effect prong after *Zelman*? Does it mean that the only effects that count are those that are produced by governments without the intervening choice of private citizens? Assuming a secular purpose for a government program that funnels money to religious institutions through private choice, is neutral effect established by virtue of the existence of meaningful private choice between religious and nonreligious alternatives?

2. The Death of Entanglement? After Agostini v. Felton the "excessive entanglement" prong of *Lemon* was subsumed into the neutral effects prong. Has it now disappeared altogether, as a practical matter? Or is it premature to declare its death? The dissents, particularly Justice Breyer's, sound the warning of religious strife. Was that concern adequately addressed by the Court? The Court regarded Breyer's concerns as speculative; if those concerns become concretely manifested how will (should) the Court respond? Will (should) the response differ if the problem is (i) sectarian conflict over access to government money, or (ii) government regulation of the religious institutions that ultimately receive public funds?

2. Government Endorsement of Religious Beliefs

a. Religion and Public Schools

Page 1181: Insert immediately before subsection b:

GOOD NEWS CLUB v. MILFORD CENTRAL SCHOOL
533 U.S. 98 (2001)

JUSTICE THOMAS delivered the opinion of the Court.

[The Milford Central School opened its facilities to after-hours uses encompassing education, learning, the arts, and social, civic, recreational, and entertainment uses pertaining to community welfare, but not for religious purposes. The school denied access to the Good News Club, a private Christian organization for children ages 6 to 12, because the proposed use — Bible lessons, prayer, memorization of Bible passages, and singing of religious songs — was considered to be religious worship. All parties conceded that Milford Central School had created a limited public forum.] This case presents two questions. The first question is whether Milford Central School violated the free speech rights of the Good News Club when it excluded the Club from meeting after hours at the school. [The Court concluded that the school had violated the free speech guarantee by its viewpoint discrimination in access to the limited public forum.] The second question is whether [that] violation is justified by Milford's concern that permitting the Club's activities would violate the Establishment Clause. We conclude that . . . no Establishment Clause concern justifies that violation. . . .

[While] it is not clear whether a State's interest in avoiding an Establishment Clause violation would justify viewpoint discrimination, [we need not] confront the issue in this case because we conclude that the school has no valid Establishment Clause interest. . . . As in *Lamb's Chapel,* the Club's meetings were held after school hours, not sponsored by the school, and open to any student who obtained parental consent. . . . Milford attempts to distinguish *Lamb's Chapel* . . . by emphasizing that Milford's policy involves elementary school children. According to Milford, children will perceive that the school is endorsing the Club and will feel coercive pressure to participate, because the Club's activities take place on school grounds, even though they occur during non-school hours. This argument is unpersuasive.

First, we have held that "a significant factor in upholding governmental programs in the face of Establishment Clause attack is their *neutrality* towards religion." Mitchell v. Helms, [p. 1161]. Milford's implication that granting access to the Club would do damage to the neutrality principle defies logic. For the "guarantee of neutrality is respected, not offended, when the government, following neutral criteria and evenhanded policies, extends benefits to recipients whose ideologies and viewpoints, including religious ones, are broad and diverse." The Good News Club seeks nothing more than to be treated neutrally and given access to speak about the same topics as are other groups.

Second, to the extent we consider whether the community would feel coercive pressure to engage in the Club's activities, cf. Lee v. Weisman, [p. 1166], the relevant community would be the parents, not the elementary school children. It is the parents who choose whether their children will attend the Good News Club meetings. Because the children cannot attend without their parents' permission, they cannot be coerced into engaging in the Good News Club's religious activities. Milford does not suggest that the parents of elementary school children would be confused about whether the school was endorsing religion. Nor do we believe that such an argument could be reasonably advanced.

Third, whatever significance we may have assigned in the Establishment Clause context to the suggestion that elementary school children are more impressionable than adults, we have never extended our Establishment Clause jurisprudence to foreclose private religious conduct during non-school hours merely because it takes place on school premises where elementary school children may be present. [In] Lee v. Weisman we concluded that attendance at the graduation exercise was obligatory. We did not place independent significance on the fact that the graduation exercise might take place on school premises. Here, where the school facilities are being used for a nonschool function and there is no government sponsorship of the Club's activities, *Lee* is inapposite. . . .

Fourth, [there is no likelihood "that small children would perceive endorsement here" because the meetings were not held] in an elementary school classroom, [the] instructors are not schoolteachers, [and] the children in the group are not all the same age as in the normal classroom setting; their ages range from 6 to 12. . . .

Finally, even if we were to inquire into the minds of schoolchildren in this case, we cannot say the danger that children would misperceive the endorsement of religion is any greater than the danger that they would perceive a hostility toward the religious viewpoint if the Club were excluded from the public forum. . . . We cannot operate [under] the assumption that any risk that small children would perceive endorsement should counsel in favor of excluding the Club's religious activity. We decline to employ Establishment Clause jurisprudence using a modified heckler's veto, in which a group's religious activity can be proscribed on the basis of what the youngest members of the audience might misperceive.

[Separate dissents by JUSTICE STEVENS and JUSTICE SOUTER, joined by JUSTICE GINSBURG, are omitted.]

b. Other Government Adoption of Religious Symbols

Page 1190: Insert at the end of the subsection, immediately before subsection 3:

4. The Pledge of Allegiance: "One Nation, Under God." Under California law and a public school district regulation, each class day begins with a voluntary recitation of the Pledge of Allegiance. In Newdow v. U.S. Congress, 292 F. 3d 597 (9th Cir. 2002), a panel of the Ninth Circuit concluded that the words "under God" in the Pledge of Allegiance constituted a violation of the Establishment Clause. The court thought that the words "under God" conveyed an impermissible endorsement of religion, constituted the same sort of impermissible coercion as was present in Lee v. Weisman, and failed the neutral effects prong of *Lemon* because its primary effect was to endorse religious belief. The dissenting judge viewed the words "under God" as a permissible "ceremonial deism," akin to the legislative prayer upheld in Marsh v. Chambers, the national motto ("In God We Trust"), or the traditional cry opening each session of the U.S. Supreme Court ("God Save the United States and this Honorable Court"). Which is it — forbidden endorsement and coercive as well, or ceremonial deism? What if the pledge said "one nation under Vishnu"? What if the pledge proclaimed "one secular nation"? Is this endorsement or accommodation?

The decision touched a raw political nerve, as politicians of all persuasions rushed to condemn it. In Newdow v. U.S. Congress, 328 F.3d 466 (9th Cir. 2003), a rehearing en banc was denied and the original opinion amended.

In Elk Grove Unified School District v. Newdow, 124 S. Ct. 2301 (2004), the Supreme Court reversed, concluding that Newdow lacked standing because he was not the custodial parent of the public school pupil involved. Chief Justice Rehnquist concurred in the judgment, but on the merits rather than the standing issue. He detailed the history of American public officials recognizing God, including Washington's oath of office, Lincoln's Gettysburg Address and Second Inaugural Address, Wilson's and Franklin Roosevelt's reliance upon God's help in performing their official duties, Eisenhower's invocation of God's blessing upon the D-Day invasion, and the final stanza of The Star-Spangled Banner. In short: "Reciting the Pledge, or listening to others recite it, is a patriotic exercise, not a religious one; participants promise fidelity to our flag and our Nation, not to any particular God, faith, or church."

Justices O'Connor and Thomas also concurred on the merits. Justice O'Connor applied the endorsement test and concluded that the phrase was a "ceremonial deism" that lacked any government endorsement of religion. She based this conclusion on four factors: the history and ubiquity of including reference to God in official actions; the absence of any element of worship or prayer; the absence of any reference to a particular religion (it "acknowledges religion in a general way: a simple reference to a generic 'God' "); and its "minimal reference to religion." Justice Thomas thought that, under Lee v. Weisman, the reference to God in the Pledge was unconstitutional, but he proceeded to reject *Lee*. Justice Thomas thought that "the Establishment Clause is best understood as a federalism provision — it protects state establishments [of religion] from federal interference but does not protect any individual right." Because no Free Exercise rights were at issue, Justice Thomas thought that the case boiled down to whether California's requirement that the Pledge be recited voluntarily involved "actual legal coercion," which Justice Thomas thought was an essential element of a prohibited establishment of religion. Thus, because California's Pledge policy "does not expose anyone to the legal coercion associated with an established religion [it] follows that religious liberty rights are not in question and that the Pledge policy fully comports with the Constitution."

Chapter 11

State Action and the Power to Enforce Constitutional Rights

A. State Action

2. Inextricable Entanglement

Page 1209: Insert the following new section immediately before subsection A.3:

BRENTWOOD ACADEMY v. TENNESSEE SECONDARY SCHOOL ATHLETIC ASSOCIATION
531 U.S. 288 (2001)

JUSTICE SOUTER delivered the opinion of the Court.

The issue is whether a statewide association incorporated to regulate interscholastic athletic competition among public and private secondary schools may be regarded as engaging in state action when it enforces a rule against a member school. The association in question here includes most public schools located within the State, acts through their representatives, draws its officers from them, is largely funded by their dues and income received in their stead, and has historically been seen to regulate in lieu of the State Board of Education's exercise of its own authority. We hold that the association's regulatory activity may and should be treated as state action owing to the pervasive entwinement of state school officials in the structure of the association.

I. Respondent Tennessee Secondary School Athletic Association (Association) is a not-for-profit membership corporation organized to regulate interscholastic sport among the public and private high schools in Tennessee that belong to it. No school is forced to join, but without any other authority actually regulating interscholastic athletics, it enjoys the memberships of almost all the State's public high schools (some 290 of them or 84% of the Association's voting membership), far outnumbering the 55 private schools that belong. A member school's team may play or scrimmage only against the team of another member, absent a dispensation.

The Association's rulemaking arm is its legislative council, [the] voting membership of [which] is limited under the Association's bylaws to high school principals, assistant principals, and superintendents elected by the member schools, and the public school administrators who so serve typically attend meetings during regular school hours. Although the Association's staff members are not paid by the State, they are eligible to join the State's public retirement system for its employees. Member schools pay dues to the Association, though the bulk of its revenue is gate receipts at member teams' football and basketball tournaments, many of them held in public arenas rented by the Association.

The constitution, bylaws, and rules of the Association set standards of school membership and the eligibility of students to play in interscholastic games. . . . Under the bylaws, "in all matters pertaining to the athletic relations of his school," the principal is responsible to the Association, which has the power "to suspend, to fine, or otherwise penalize any member school for the violation of any of the rules of the Association or for other just cause."

Ever since the Association was incorporated in 1925, Tennessee's State Board of Education (State Board) has (to use its own words) acknowledged the corporation's functions "in providing standards, rules and regulations for interscholastic competition in the public schools of Tennessee." More recently, the State Board [in 1972 adopted] a rule expressly "designating" the Association as "the organization to supervise and regulate the athletic activities in which the public junior and senior high schools in Tennessee participate on an interscholastic basis," [providing] that "the authority granted herein shall remain in effect until revoked" and instruct[ing] the State Board's chairman to "designate a person or persons to serve in an ex-officio capacity on the [Association's governing bodies]." [On] several occasions over the next 20 years, the State Board reviewed, approved, or reaffirmed its approval of the recruiting Rule at issue in this case. In 1996, however, the State Board dropped [its rule] expressly designating the Association as regulator; it substituted a statement "recognizing the value of participation in interscholastic athletics and the role of [the Association] in coordinating interscholastic athletic competition," while "authorizing the public schools of the state to voluntarily maintain membership in [the Association]."

The action before us responds to a 1997 regulatory enforcement proceeding brought against petitioner, Brentwood Academy, a private parochial high school member of the Association. The Association [found] that Brentwood violated a rule prohibiting "undue influence" in recruiting athletes, when it wrote to incoming students and their parents about spring football practice. The Association accordingly placed Brentwood's athletic program on probation for four years, declared its football and boys' basketball teams ineligible to compete in playoffs for two years, and imposed a $3,000 fine. When these penalties were imposed, all the [Association's] voting members . . . were public school administrators.

Brentwood sued the Association and its executive director in federal court, . . . claiming that enforcement of the Rule was state action and a violation of the First and Fourteenth Amendments. The District Court entered summary judgment for Brentwood and enjoined the Association from enforcing the Rule. In holding the

Association to be a state actor [the] District Court found that the State had delegated authority over high school athletics to the Association, characterized the relationship between the Association and its public school members as symbiotic, and emphasized the predominantly public character of the Association's membership and leadership. . . . The United States Court of Appeals for the Sixth Circuit reversed. [We] now reverse.

II. A. Our cases try to plot a line between state action subject to Fourteenth Amendment scrutiny and private conduct (however exceptionable) that is not. The judicial obligation is not only to " 'preserve an area of individual freedom by limiting the reach of federal law' and avoid the imposition of responsibility on a State for conduct it could not control," but also to assure that constitutional standards are invoked "when it can be said that the State is *responsible* for the specific conduct of which the plaintiff complains." [Blum v. Yaretsky, pp. 1204, 1208] (emphasis in original). . . . Thus, we say that state action may be found if, though only if, there is such a "close nexus between the State and the challenged action" that seemingly private behavior "may be fairly treated as that of the State itself." [Jackson v. Metropolitan Edison Co., p. 1200.]

What is fairly attributable is a matter of normative judgment, and the criteria lack rigid simplicity. From the range of circumstances that could point toward the State behind an individual face, no one fact can function as a necessary condition across the board for finding state action; nor is any set of circumstances absolutely sufficient, for there may be some countervailing reason against attributing activity to the government. Our cases have identified a host of facts that can bear on the fairness of such an attribution. We have . . . held that a challenged activity may be state action when it results from the State's exercise of "coercive power," when the State provides "significant encouragement, either overt or covert," or when a private actor operates as a "willful participant in joint activity with the State or its agents." [We] have treated a nominally private entity as a state actor when it is controlled by an "agency of the State," when it has been delegated a public function by the State, when it is "entwined with governmental policies" or when government is "entwined in [its] management or control." Evans v. Newton, 382 U.S. 296, 299, 301 (1966) [p. 1200].

[National Collegiate Athletic Ass'n v. Tarkanian, 488 U.S. 179 (1988)] arose when an undoubtedly state actor, the University of Nevada, suspended its basketball coach, Tarkanian, in order to comply with rules and recommendations of the National Collegiate Athletic Association (NCAA). The coach charged the NCAA with state action, arguing that the state university had delegated its own functions to the NCAA, clothing the latter with authority to make and apply the university's rules, the result being joint action making the NCAA a state actor. [We] found no state action on the part of the NCAA [because its] policies were shaped not by the University of Nevada alone, but by several hundred member institutions, most of them having no connection with Nevada, and exhibiting no color of Nevada law. But dictum in *Tarkanian* pointed to a contrary result on facts like ours[:] "The situation would, of course, be different if the [Association's] membership consisted entirely of institutions located within the same State, many of them public institutions created by the same sovereign."

B. Just as we foresaw in *Tarkanian* [there is] state action here. The nominally private character of the Association is overborne by the pervasive entwinement of public institutions and public officials in its composition and workings, and there is no substantial reason to claim unfairness in applying constitutional standards to it. The Association is not an organization of natural persons acting on their own, but [of] public schools to the extent of 84% of the total. Under the Association's bylaws, each member school is represented by its principal or a faculty member, who has a vote in selecting members of the governing legislative council and board of control from eligible principals, assistant principals and superintendents. [Public] school officials act within the scope of their duties when they represent their institutions. [In] Tennessee, nearly every public high school spends money on competitions among schools. Since a pickup system of interscholastic games would not do, these public teams need some mechanism to produce rules and regulate competition. The mechanism is an organization overwhelmingly composed of public school officials who select representatives (all of them public officials at the time in question here), who in turn adopt and enforce the rules that make the system work. . . .

In sum, to the extent of 84% of its membership, the Association is an organization of public schools represented by their officials acting in their official capacity to provide an integral element of secondary public schooling. There would be no recognizable Association, legal or tangible, without the public school officials, who do not merely control but overwhelmingly perform all but the purely ministerial acts by which the Association exists and functions in practical terms. Only the 16% minority of private school memberships prevents this entwinement of the Association and the public school system from being total and their identities totally indistinguishable.

To complement the entwinement of public school officials with the Association from the bottom up, the State of Tennessee has provided for entwinement from top down. State Board members are assigned ex officio to serve as members of the [Association's governing boards], and the Association's ministerial employees are treated as state employees to the extent of being eligible for membership in the state retirement system.

It is, of course, true that [the] State Board's Rule expressly designating the Association as regulator of interscholastic athletics in public schools was deleted in 1996. [But this] affected nothing but words. . . . The most one can say on the evidence is that the State Board once freely acknowledged the Association's official character but now does it by winks and nods. [The] entwinement down from the State Board is therefore unmistakable, just as the entwinement up from the member public schools is overwhelming. Entwinement will support a conclusion that an ostensibly private organization ought to be charged with a public character and judged by constitutional standards; entwinement to the degree shown here requires it. . . .

[Reversed and remanded.]

JUSTICE THOMAS, joined by CHIEF JUSTICE REHNQUIST and JUSTICES SCALIA and KENNEDY, dissenting.

We have never found state action based upon mere "entwinement." Until today, we have found a private organization's acts to constitute state action only when the organization performed a public function; was created, coerced, or encouraged by the government; or acted in a symbiotic relationship with the government. The majority's holding [not] only extends state-action doctrine beyond its permissible limits but also encroaches upon the realm of individual freedom that the doctrine was meant to protect. I respectfully dissent.

I. [The] state-action requirement [excludes] "merely private conduct, however discriminatory or wrongful," [and] thus "preserves an area of individual freedom by limiting the reach of federal law and federal judicial power." Lugar v. Edmondson Oil Co., 457 U.S. 922, 936 (1982). The state-action doctrine also promotes important values of federalism, "avoiding the imposition of responsibility on a State for conduct it could not control." *Tarkanian.*

A. [The] TSSAA's actions cannot fairly be attributed to the State, and thus cannot constitute state action. . . . Although public schools currently compose 84% of the TSSAA's membership, [no] public school need join the TSSAA. The TSSAA's rules are enforced not by a state agency but by its own board of control, which comprises high school principals, assistant principals, and superintendents, none of whom must work at a public school. Of course, at the time the recruiting rule was enforced in this case, all of the board members happened to be public school officials. However, each board member acts in a representative capacity on behalf of all the private and public schools in his region of Tennessee, and not simply his individual school.

The State of Tennessee did not create [or fund] the TSSAA [and] does not pay its employees. [Only] 4% of the TSSAA's revenue comes from the dues paid by member schools; the bulk of its operating budget is derived from gate receipts at tournaments it sponsors. The State does not permit the TSSAA to use state-owned facilities for a discounted fee, and it does not exempt the TSSAA from state taxation. No Tennessee law authorizes the State to coordinate interscholastic athletics or empowers another entity to organize interscholastic athletics on behalf of the State. The only state pronouncement acknowledging the TSSAA's existence is a rule providing that the State Board of Education permits public schools to maintain membership in the TSSAA if they so choose. Moreover, the State of Tennessee has never had any involvement in the particular action taken by the TSSAA in this case [and there] is no indication that the State has ever had any interest in how schools choose to regulate recruiting. . . .

B. . . . The TSSAA has not performed a function that has been "traditionally exclusively reserved to the State." Jackson v. Metropolitan Edison Co. The organization of interscholastic sports is neither a traditional nor an exclusive public function of the States. [The] TSSAA no doubt serves the public, particularly the public schools, but the mere provision of a service to the public does not render such provision a traditional and exclusive public function. [Rendell-Baker v. Kohn.]

It is also obvious that the TSSAA is not an entity created and controlled by the government for the purpose of fulfilling a government objective, as was Amtrak in Lebron v. National Railroad Passenger Corporation. . . . Indeed, no one claims that the State of Tennessee played any role in the creation of the TSSAA as a private corporation in 1925. The TSSAA was designed to fulfill an objective — the organization of interscholastic athletic tournaments — that the government had not contemplated, much less pursued. . . .

[The] State of Tennessee has not "exercised coercive power or . . . provided such significant encouragement [to the TSSAA], either overt or covert," that the TSSAA's regulatory activities must in law be deemed to be those of the State. The State has not promulgated any regulations of interscholastic sports, and nothing in the record suggests that the State has encouraged or coerced the TSSAA in enforcing its recruiting rule. . . . Furthermore, there is no evidence of "joint participation" between the State and the TSSAA in the TSSAA's enforcement of its recruiting rule. [Finally], there is no "symbiotic relationship" between the State and the TSSAA. [The] TSSAA's "fiscal relationship with the State is not different from that of many contractors performing services for the government." The TSSAA provides a service — the organization of athletic tournaments — in exchange for membership dues and gate fees, just as a vendor could contract with public schools to sell refreshments at school events. . . . Also, there is no suggestion in this case that, as was the case in *Burton*, the State profits from the TSSAA's decision to enforce its recruiting rule. . . .

II. Although the TSSAA's enforcement activities cannot be considered state action as a matter of common sense or under any of this Court's existing theories of state action, the majority presents a new theory. Under this theory, the majority holds that the combination of factors it identifies evidences "entwinement" of the State with the TSSAA, and that such entwinement converts private action into state action. The majority does not define "entwinement," and the meaning of the term is not altogether clear. But whatever this new "entwinement" theory may entail, it lacks any support in our state-action jurisprudence. . . .

[Because] the majority never defines "entwinement," the scope of its holding is unclear. If we are fortunate, the majority's fact-specific analysis will have little bearing beyond this case. But if the majority's new entwinement test develops in future years, it could affect many organizations that foster activities, enforce rules, and sponsor extracurricular competition among high schools — not just in athletics, but in such diverse areas as agriculture, mathematics, music, marching bands, forensics, and cheerleading. Indeed, this entwinement test may extend to other organizations that are composed of, or controlled by, public officials or public entities. [I] am not prepared to say that any private organization that permits public entities and public officials to participate acts as the State in anything or everything it does, and our state-action jurisprudence has never reached that far. . . . I respectfully dissent.

NOTES

1. Entwinement as a Distinct Concept. What is the difference between entwinement and the inextricable entanglement of government and private action that was at issue in Burton v. Wilmington Parking Authority, p. 1205? What element(s) are present in *Brentwood Academy* that were absent in *Burton*? What element(s) were present in *Burton* that are absent in *Brentwood Academy*? If there is no difference, why did the Court insist on stating entwinement as a separate, distinct approach to state action?

2. Formalism and Functionalism. Does the difference between the majority and the dissent reflect fundamentally different approaches to state action? Consider the possibility that the majority treats state action as a question of discerning the functional relationship of the challenged action to the state and the dissent regards state action as turning on formal actions of the government. If the defect of formalism is that it allows states to escape constitutional scrutiny by enabling compliant private parties to do their bidding, is the defect of functionalism that it draws no detectable lines between the public and private spheres? Some commentators, especially those aligned with the Critical Legal Studies movement, criticize the entire distinction between public and private as a "false dichotomy." Is the Court in *Brentwood Academy* endorsing that view? If not, what factual elements constitute sufficient "entwinement" to constitute state action? Should it trouble us if it proves to be impossible to give a solid answer to that question?

3. The Value of State Action Doctrine. Justice Souter says that state action should not be found when there is present "some value at odds with finding public accountability in the circumstances." What values might these be? Justice Thomas claims that the state action doctrine "preserves . . . individual freedom by limiting the reach of federal law and federal judicial power," and "promotes important values of federalism [by] 'avoiding the imposition of responsibility on a State for conduct it could not control.' " Presumably, these principles are applicable only at the debatable outer edges of state action, but at what point do they cease to be applicable?

4. Problems. Assess whether the following actions are state action after *Brentwood Academy*:

(a) The Municipal Brotherhood of Police, a voluntary private association whose members are limited to current and retired "peace officers," sponsors a dance for high school graduates each spring and refuses admission to students whom it considers to be gay or lesbian. The term "peace officer" is defined by state law to include law enforcement officers and private security guards. The revenue of the Brotherhood is derived from membership dues and profits from a concession granted the Brotherhood by the municipality at the annual municipal fair. Is the Brotherhood's refusal to admit gay or lesbian students to its dance, otherwise open to all high school seniors, state action?

(b) A public high school's chapter of the Future Farmers of America, an affinity group for high school students interested in agricultural careers, is provided space

in the high school for after-school meetings. The local chapter opens each such meeting with a spoken prayer. Is this practice state action?

(c) A municipality sells its municipal bus service to a private company in return for cash, a share in the profits of the now-private bus service, and two seats on the five person board of directors. Public officials occupy those two director positions. Over the objection of the two public directors, the new owner refuses to permit "punks" (defined by it to describe people with odd or unusual body piercing, hair styles, ragged clothing, or any combination of the above) to ride the buses. Is state action present? Does it matter if the public directors do not object, or vote in favor of the idea?

B. Congressional Power to Enforce Constitutional Rights

2. The Scope of Enforcement Power: Remedial or Substantive?

Page 1226: Erratum: The correct citation for Katzenbach v. Morgan *is 384 U.S. 641 (1966).*

Page 1239: Insert the following at the end:

BOARD OF TRUSTEES OF THE UNIVERSITY OF ALABAMA v. GARRETT
531 U.S. 356 (2001)

CHIEF JUSTICE REHNQUIST delivered the opinion of the Court.

We decide here whether employees of the State of Alabama may recover money damages by reason of the State's failure to comply with the provisions of Title I of the Americans with Disabilities Act of 1990 (ADA or Act). We hold that such suits are barred by the Eleventh Amendment.

The ADA prohibits certain employers, including the States, from "discriminating against a qualified individual with a disability because of the disability of such individual in regard to [the] terms, conditions, and privileges of employment." [The] Act requires employers to "make reasonable accommodations to the known physical or mental limitations of an otherwise qualified individual with a disability who is an applicant or employee, unless [the employer] can demonstrate that the accommodation would impose an undue hardship on the operation of the [employer's] business." . . .

[Garrett and Ash were each employed by units of the state of Alabama. Garrett, a nurse whose cancer treatments necessitated substantial absence from work, was demoted upon her return to work. Ash, a security officer, was denied accommodations for his chronic asthma and sleep apnea.]

Garrett and Ash filed separate lawsuits in [federal] District Court, both seeking money damages under the ADA. Petitioners moved for summary judgment, claiming that the ADA exceeds Congress's authority to abrogate the State's Eleventh Amendment immunity. In a single opinion disposing of both cases, the District Court agreed with petitioners' position and granted their motions for summary judgment. The cases were consolidated on appeal to the Eleventh Circuit, [which court] reversed, [ruling] that the ADA validly abrogates the States' Eleventh Amendment immunity. We granted certiorari. . . .

I. [Although] by its terms the [Eleventh Amendment bars only suits in federal court] against a State by citizens of another State, our cases have extended the Amendment's applicability to suits by citizens against their own States. [Kimel v. Florida Bd. of Regents, 528 U.S. 62, 72-73 (2000); Seminole Tribe of Fla. v. Florida, 517 U.S. 44, 54 (1996); Hans v. Louisiana, 134 U.S. 1, 15 (1890).] The ultimate guarantee of the Eleventh Amendment is that nonconsenting States may not be sued by private individuals in federal court. We have recognized, however, that Congress may abrogate the States' Eleventh Amendment immunity when it both unequivocally intends to do so and "acts pursuant to a valid grant of constitutional authority." The first of these requirements is not in dispute here. The question [is] whether Congress acted within its constitutional authority by subjecting the States to suits in federal court for money damages under the ADA.

Congress may not, of course, base its abrogation of the States' Eleventh Amendment immunity upon the powers enumerated in Article I. See *Kimel*, *Seminole Tribe*. In Fitzpatrick v. Bitzer, 427 U.S. 445 (1976), however, we held that . . . Congress may subject nonconsenting States to suit in federal court when it does so pursuant to a valid exercise of its [power under §5 of the Fourteenth Amendment]. Accordingly, the ADA can apply to the States only to the extent that the statute is appropriate §5 legislation. . . . Section 5 of the Fourteenth Amendment grants Congress the power to enforce the substantive guarantees contained in §1 [e.g., equal protection, due process] by enacting "appropriate legislation." See City of Boerne v. Flores, 521 U.S. 507, 536 (1997). Congress is not limited to mere legislative repetition of this Court's constitutional jurisprudence. "Rather, Congress's power 'to enforce' the Amendment includes the authority both to remedy and to deter violation of rights guaranteed thereunder by prohibiting a somewhat broader swath of conduct, including that which is not itself forbidden by the Amendment's text." *Kimel*; City of Boerne [v. Flores] also confirmed, however, the long-settled principle that it is the responsibility of this Court, not Congress, to define the substance of constitutional guarantees. Accordingly, §5 legislation reaching beyond the scope of §1's actual guarantees must exhibit "congruence and proportionality between the injury to be prevented or remedied and the means adopted to that end."

II. The first step in applying these now familiar principles is to identify with some precision the scope of the constitutional right at issue. Here, that inquiry requires us to examine the limitations §1 of the Fourteenth Amendment places upon States' treatment of the disabled. As we did last Term in *Kimel* we look to our prior decisions under the Equal Protection Clause dealing with this issue. In Cleburne v. Cleburne Living Center, Inc., [p. 684], we [concluded that] the Court of Appeals had erred by holding that mental retardation qualified as a "quasi-suspect" classification under our equal protection jurisprudence. We [held] that such legislation incurs only the minimum "rational-basis" review applicable to general social and economic legislation. . . . Under rational-basis review, where a group possesses "distinguishing characteristics relevant to interests the State has the authority to implement," a State's decision to act on the basis of those differences does not give rise to a constitutional violation. "Such a classification cannot run afoul of the Equal Protection Clause if there is a rational relationship between the disparity of treatment and some legitimate governmental purpose." Moreover, . . . the burden is upon the challenging party to negative "any reasonably conceivable state of facts that could provide a rational basis for the classification." FCC v. Beach Communications, Inc., 508 U.S. 307, 313 (1993).

[The] result of *Cleburne* is that States are not required by the Fourteenth Amendment to make special accommodations for the disabled, so long as their actions towards such individuals are rational. They could quite hard headedly — and perhaps hardheartedly — hold to job-qualification requirements which do not make allowance for the disabled. If special accommodations for the disabled are to be required, they have to come from positive law and not through the Equal Protection Clause.

III. Once we have determined the metes and bounds of the constitutional right in question, we examine whether Congress identified a history and pattern of unconstitutional employment discrimination by the States against the disabled. Just as §1 of the Fourteenth Amendment applies only to actions committed "under color of state law," Congress's §5 authority is appropriately exercised only in response to state transgressions. The legislative record of the ADA, however, simply fails to show that Congress did in fact identify a pattern of irrational state discrimination in employment against the disabled. . . . Congress made a general finding in the ADA that "historically, society has tended to isolate and segregate individuals with disabilities [and] discrimination against individuals with disabilities continues to be a serious and pervasive social problem." The record assembled by Congress includes many instances to support such a finding. But the great majority of these incidents do not deal with the activities of States. . . .

Respondents [do] cite half a dozen examples [that] did involve States. . . . Several of these incidents undoubtedly evidence an unwillingness on the part of state officials to make the sort of accommodations for the disabled required by the ADA. Whether they were irrational under our decision in *Cleburne* is more debatable, [but] even if it were to be determined that each incident [showed] unconstitutional action on the part of the State, these incidents taken together fall far short of even suggesting the pattern of unconstitutional discrimination on which §5 legislation must be based. [Given that Congress] found that "some 43,000,000 Americans have one or more physical or mental disabilities" [and that] the States [employ] more than 4.5 million people [we think it is telling that] Congress assembled only such minimal evidence of unconstitutional state discrimination in employment against the disabled.

Justice Breyer maintains that Congress applied Title I of the ADA to the States in response to a host of incidents representing unconstitutional state discrimination in employment against persons with disabilities. A close review of the relevant materials, however, [discloses only] unexamined, anecdotal accounts of "adverse, disparate treatment by state officials," [which] often does not amount to a constitutional violation where rational-basis scrutiny applies, [and which] were submitted not directly to Congress but to [an advisory task force] which made no findings on the subject of state discrimination in employment. . . .

Even were it possible to squeeze out of these examples a pattern of unconstitutional discrimination by the States, the rights and remedies created by the ADA against the States would raise the same sort of concerns as to congruence and proportionality as were found in City of Boerne [v. Flores]. For example, whereas it would be entirely rational (and therefore constitutional) for a state employer to conserve scarce financial resources by hiring employees who are able to use existing facilities, the ADA requires employers to "make existing facilities used by employees readily accessible to and usable by individuals with disabilities." The ADA does except employers from the "reasonable accommodation" requirement where the employer "can demonstrate that the accommodation would impose an undue hardship on the operation of the business of such covered entity." However, even with this exception, the accommodation duty far exceeds what is constitutionally required in that it makes unlawful a range of alternate responses that would be reasonable but would fall short of imposing an "undue burden" upon the employer. . . .

The ADA's constitutional shortcomings are apparent when the Act is compared to Congress's efforts in the Voting Rights Act of 1965 to respond to a serious pattern of constitutional violations. In South Carolina v. Katzenbach, 383 U.S. 301 (1966), [in which we upheld the Voting Rights Act as a valid exercise of Congress's power under §2 of the Fifteenth Amendment] to enforce the Fifteenth Amendment's protection against racial discrimination in voting, [we] noted that "before enacting the measure, Congress explored with great care the problem of racial discrimination in voting." In that Act, Congress documented a marked pattern of unconstitutional action by the States. . . . Congress's response was to promulgate in the Voting Rights Act a detailed but limited remedial scheme designed to guarantee meaningful enforcement of the Fifteenth Amendment in those areas of the Nation where abundant evidence of States' systematic denial of those rights was identified.

The contrast between this kind of evidence, and the evidence that Congress considered in the present case, is stark. . . . Congress is the final authority as to desirable public policy, but in order to authorize private individuals to recover money damages against the States, there must be a pattern of discrimination by the States which violates the Fourteenth Amendment, and the remedy imposed by Congress must be congruent and proportional to the targeted violation. Those requirements are not met here, and to uphold the Act's application to the States would allow

Congress to rewrite the Fourteenth Amendment law laid down by this Court in *Cleburne.*[1] Section 5 does not so broadly enlarge congressional authority. . . .

Reversed.

JUSTICE KENNEDY, joined by JUSTICE O'CONNOR, concurring.

. . . If the States had been transgressing the Fourteenth Amendment by their mistreatment or lack of concern for those with impairments, one would have expected to find in decisions of the courts of the States and also the courts of the United States extensive litigation and discussion of the constitutional violations. This confirming judicial documentation does not exist. . . .

JUSTICE BREYER, joined by JUSTICES STEVENS, SOUTER and GINSBURG, dissenting.

Reviewing the congressional record as if it were an administrative agency record, the Court holds the statutory provision before us unconstitutional. . . . Section 5 [grants] Congress the "power to enforce, by appropriate legislation" the Fourteenth Amendment's equal protection guarantee. As the Court recognizes, state discrimination in employment against persons with disabilities might "run afoul of the Equal Protection Clause" where there is no "rational relationship between the disparity of treatment and some legitimate governmental purpose." In my view, Congress reasonably could have concluded that the remedy before us constitutes an "appropriate" way to enforce this basic equal protection requirement. And that is all the Constitution requires.

I. . . . Congress compiled a vast legislative record documenting "massive, society-wide discrimination" against persons with disabilities. [The] powerful evidence of discriminatory treatment throughout society in general . . . implicates state governments as well. [There] is no particular reason to believe that they are immune from the "stereotypic assumptions" and pattern of "purposeful unequal treatment" that Congress found prevalent. . . .

[In] any event, there is no need to rest solely upon evidence [of] general societal discrimination. There are roughly 300 examples of discrimination by state governments themselves in the legislative record. . . . Congress, unlike courts, must, and does, routinely draw general conclusions [from] anecdotal and opinion-based evidence of this kind. . . .

II. [The] Court fails to find in the legislative record sufficient indication that Congress has "negatived" the presumption that state action is rationally related to a le-

---

1. Our holding here that Congress did not validly abrogate the States' sovereign immunity from suit by private individuals for money damages under Title I does not mean that persons with disabilities have no federal recourse against discrimination. Title I of the ADA still prescribes standards applicable to the States. Those standards can be enforced by the United States in actions for money damages, as well as by private individuals in actions for injunctive relief under Ex parte Young, 209 U.S. 123 (1908). In addition, state laws protecting the rights of persons with disabilities in employment and other aspects of life provide independent avenues of redress.

gitimate objective. The problem with the Court's approach is that neither the "burden of proof" that favors States nor any other rule of restraint applicable to *judges* applies to *Congress* when it exercises its §5 power. Rational-basis review — with its presumptions favoring constitutionality — is "a paradigm of *judicial* restraint." And the Congress of the United States is not a lower court. . . .

There is simply no reason to require Congress, seeking to determine facts relevant to the exercise of its §5 authority, to adopt rules or presumptions that reflect a court's institutional limitations. Unlike courts, Congress can readily gather facts from across the Nation, assess the magnitude of a problem, and more easily find an appropriate remedy. Unlike courts, Congress directly reflects public attitudes and beliefs, enabling Congress better to understand where, and to what extent, refusals to accommodate a disability amount to behavior that is callous or unreasonable to the point of lacking constitutional justification. Unlike judges, Members of Congress can directly obtain information from constituents who have first-hand experience with discrimination and related issues. . . . To apply a rule designed to restrict courts as if it restricted Congress's legislative power is to stand the underlying principle [of] judicial restraint on its head.

III. The Court argues . . . that the statute's damage remedy is not "congruent" with and "proportional" to the equal protection problem that Congress found. The Court suggests that the Act's "reasonable accommodation" requirement and disparate impact standard "far exceed what is constitutionally required." [In] other words, the requirement may exceed what is necessary to avoid a constitutional violation. But it is just that power — the power to require more than the minimum — that §5 grants to Congress. [In Katzenbach v. Morgan, p. 1226, the Court stated] that §5's "draftsmen sought to grant to Congress . . . the same broad powers expressed in the Necessary and Proper Clause," [and] that "it is not for us to review the congressional resolution of . . . the various conflicting considerations — the risk or pervasiveness of the discrimination in governmental services . . ., the adequacy or availability of alternative remedies, and the nature and significance of the state interests that would be affected. . . . It is enough that we be able to perceive a basis upon which the Congress might resolve the conflict as it did." . . .

IV. . . . The Court, through its evidentiary demands, its non-deferential review, and its failure to distinguish between judicial and legislative constitutional competencies, improperly invades a power that the Constitution assigns to Congress. Its decision saps §5 of independent force, effectively "confining the legislative power . . . to the insignificant role of abrogating only those state laws that the judicial branch [is] prepared to adjudge unconstitutional." . . . I respectfully dissent.

NOTES

1. Determining the Scope of the Enforcement Power. The Court tied the substance of the rights protected by the Fourteenth Amendment (in this case, equal protection) to the judicial standards for ascertaining equal protection violations. Because Congress sought to outlaw discrimination against the disabled, the Court applied the judicial standards for determination of when such discrimination is unconstitutional. That standard, of course, is minimal scrutiny. As with judicial applications of minimal scrutiny the Court placed the burden of proof on Congress to demonstrate that state employment discrimination against the disabled was irrational or illegitimate. Thus, the Court required Congress to make a convincing demonstration that (1) such discrimination actually exists and (2) it is an irrational means to accomplish legitimate government ends or an illegitimate end in itself.

a. Congressional determination of the existence of constitutional violations. How much should the Court defer to congressional judgment about the existence of constitutional violations? The dissent contended that "sponsors and supporters of the [Fourteenth] Amendment were primarily interested in augmenting the power of Congress." Should that dictate greater judicial deference to Congress on the question of identifying constitutional violations, or would such deference eviscerate the principle established in City of Boerne v. Flores that Congress's enforcement power is limited to a remedial power? Is it true, as Justice Breyer argued, that Congress has more institutional competence to determine when constitutional violations are occurring? Isn't that inquiry the special province of courts? Perhaps Congress is better situated than courts to assess when states are engaging in actions that, while not constitutional violations, are so close to the line that their continued tolerance will likely produce constitutional violations. If so, Congress would simply be acting to *prevent* constitutional violations before they occur. Justice Kennedy's apparent response to this argument was to suggest that if there was any realistic likelihood of constitutional violations, one would observe at least a few surfacing in the courts. Is it fair to say that without such evidence there is no reason to believe that there are any constitutional violations to be prevented?

b. Congruence and proportionality. What is the difference between congruence and proportionality? Was Congress's remedy not congruent with the constitutional violation because the remedy — subjecting states to private suit for damages for their failure to provide "reasonable accommodations" — prohibited much more conduct than is constitutionally forbidden, or was it because Congress had not identified constitutional violations that were as extensive as the remedy it provided? Did Congress's remedy lack proportionality for the same reasons? Note that the Court contrasted the ADA with the 1965 Voting Rights Act, legislation that prohibited conduct (e.g., literacy prerequisites for voting) that was closely associated with unlawful racial discrimination in voting access and which did so only in jurisdictions that displayed substantial circumstantial evidence of such violations. Are congruence and proportionality simply terms to describe a requirement of narrow tailoring, such that Congress may not validly invoke its enforcement power unless it limits that which it forbids to what the Fourteenth Amendment forbids or, if broader, to conduct that Congress has established is a pretext for accomplishing constitutionally forbidden ends, and then only to the extent that the geographic scope of its application is dovetailed to the extent of the violations?

2. *The Role of the Eleventh Amendment and the Scope of* Garrett. The majority was careful to point out that the case raised only the narrow issue of whether Congress could use its enforcement power to abrogate the states' Eleventh Amendment immunity. Does the scope of the enforcement power vary with the purpose for which Congress is invoking that power? Put another way, does Congress have greater latitude to use its enforcement power when it prohibits state activities that it thinks violate the Constitution but does not subject the states to private suits for damages for those actions? Why should this be so, if it is the case? Does the principle of state sovereign immunity occupy an unstated but actual preferred position? If there is nothing special about the Eleventh Amendment, does *Garrett* augur a diminished ability of Congress to prohibit state action that is not itself constitutionally improper but that implicates widely held societal notions of justice?

Consider the following possibilities:

(1) In Alexander v. Sandoval, 532 U.S. 275 (2001), the Court held that Title VI of the 1964 Civil Rights Act does not furnish a private cause of action to enforce "disparate impact" regulations issued under its authority. Title VI bars national origin discrimination in any covered "program or activity" and authorizes federal agencies to make implementing regulations. The federal Justice and Transportation Departments issued regulations barring recipients of federal funds (who are thus subject to Title VI) from "utilizing criteria or methods of administration which have the effect of subjecting individuals to discrimination because of their race, color, or national origin." Alabama made English the state's official language and refused to administer driver's license examinations in any language other than English. Sandoval brought a class action, contending that the English-only examination practice violated the federal regulations "because it had the effect of subjecting non-English speakers to discrimination based on their national origin." The Court ruled that there was no private right of action to enforce the regulation and thus never addressed the merits of the claim, or even whether the regulations were authorized by the statute.

Suppose that after *Sandoval* Congress were to invoke its §5 enforcement power to amend Title VI to create an express private cause of action to enforce by injunctive relief Title VI and all regulations issued under its authority. Would Congress's action be valid, either on its face or as applied to the disparate impact regulations at issue in *Sandoval*? On what might resolution of this issue depend?

(2) In United States v. Virginia, p. 781, the Court ruled that Virginia's exclusion of women from its publicly funded Virginia Military Institute was a violation of equal protection, but left open the question of when, if ever, single-sex public schooling might be constitutionally valid. Suppose that Congress used its §5 enforcement power to prohibit all single-sex public schools, and a girl who alleges that the presence of boys in her classroom hinders her ability to learn challenges the validity of Congress's action, introducing voluminous evidence that supports her contention, evidence that Congress ignored in enacting the bar. What result?

(3) Suppose that Congress invokes its §5 enforcement power to bar consideration of race by public universities in its admissions decisions. What result?

NEVADA DEPARTMENT OF HUMAN RESOURCES v. HIBBS
538 U.S. 721 (2003)

[The "family leave" provision of the Family and Medical Leave Act of 1993 (FMLA or the Act), 29 U.S.C. §2612(a)(1)(C), requires employers, including state governments, to grant up to 12 weeks of unpaid leave annually in order to permit an employee to care for a "serious health condition" in an employee's spouse, child, or parent. The Act creates a private right of action to seek both equitable relief and money damages. Hibbs, an employee of the Nevada Department of Human Resources, sued the state agency for money damages after his termination, allegedly in violation of the family leave provision of FMLA. A federal District Court granted summary judgment to the state agency on the grounds that the FMLA claim was barred by the Eleventh Amendment and that Hibbs's Fourteenth Amendment rights had not been violated. The Ninth Circuit reversed and the Supreme Court affirmed.]

CHIEF JUSTICE REHNQUIST delivered the opinion of the Court.

. . . This case turns . . . on whether Congress acted within its constitutional authority when it sought to abrogate the States' immunity for purposes of the FMLA's family-leave provision.

. . . Congress may, in the exercise of its §5 power, do more than simply proscribe conduct that we have held unconstitutional. . . . Congress may enact so-called prophylactic legislation that proscribes facially constitutional conduct, in order to prevent and deter unconstitutional conduct.

. . . *City of Boerne* [confirmed] that it falls to this Court, not Congress, to define the substance of constitutional guarantees. Section 5 legislation reaching beyond the scope of §1's actual guarantees must be an appropriate remedy for identified constitutional violations, not "an attempt to substantively redefine the States' legal obligations."[*Kimel.*] We distinguish appropriate prophylactic legislation from "substantive redefinition of the Fourteenth Amendment right at issue," by applying the test set forth in *City of Boerne:* Valid §5 legislation must exhibit "congruence and proportionality between the injury to be prevented or remedied and the means adopted to that end."

. . . The FMLA aims to protect the right to be free from gender-based discrimination in the workplace. [Statutory] classifications that distinguish between males and females are [presumed to violate equal protection, and may be sustained only if "the discriminatory means employed" are "substantially related" to the achievement of actual "important governmental objectives" that do "not rely on overbroad generalizations about the different talents, capacities, or preferences of males and females."] We now inquire whether Congress had evidence of a pattern of constitutional violations on the part of the States in this area.

. . . According to evidence that was before Congress when it enacted the FMLA, States continue to rely on invalid gender stereotypes in the employment context, specifically in the administration of leave benefits. Reliance on such stereotypes cannot justify the States' gender discrimination in this area. [The] persistence of such unconstitutional discrimination by the States justifies Congress'[s] passage of prophylactic §5 legislation.

[The] FMLA's legislative [revealed] differential leave policies [that] were not attributable to any differential physical needs of men and women, but rather to the pervasive sex-role stereotype that caring for family members is women's work. . . . Congress had evidence that, even where state laws and policies were not facially discriminatory, they were applied in discriminatory ways. . . . In sum, the States' record of unconstitutional participation in, and fostering of, gender-based discrimination in the administration of leave benefits is weighty enough to justify the enactment of prophylactic §5 legislation.

We reached the opposite conclusion in *Garrett* and *Kimel*. In those cases, the §5 legislation under review responded to a purported tendency of state officials to make age- or disability-based distinctions. [Such discrimination is presumptively constitutional and is void only if it is proven to lack a rational connection to any legitimate government objective.] Thus, in order to impugn the constitutionality of state discrimination against the disabled or the elderly, Congress must identify, not just the existence of age- or disability-based state decisions, but a "widespread pattern"of irrational reliance on such criteria. We found no such showing [in *Kimel* and *Garrett*.] Here, however, Congress directed its attention to state gender discrimination, which triggers a heightened level of scrutiny. Because the standard for demonstrating the constitutionality of a gender-based classification is more difficult to meet than our rational-basis test . . . it was easier for Congress to show a pattern of state constitutional violations. . . .

The impact of the discrimination targeted by the FMLA is significant. . . . Stereotypes about women's domestic roles are reinforced by parallel stereotypes presuming a lack of domestic responsibilities for men. Because employers continued to regard the family as the woman's domain, they often denied men similar accommodations or discouraged them from taking leave. These mutually reinforcing stereotypes created a self-fulfilling cycle of discrimination that forced women to continue to assume the role of primary family caregiver, and fostered employers' stereotypical views about women's commitment to work and their value as employees. Those perceptions, in turn, Congress reasoned, lead to subtle discrimination that may be difficult to detect on a case-by-case basis.

[Congress's] chosen remedy, the family-care leave provision of the FMLA, is "congruent and proportional to the targeted violation." Congress had already tried unsuccessfully to address this problem through Title VII and the amendment of Title VII by the Pregnancy Discrimination Act. Here, as in [South Carolina v. Katzenbach, p. 1225] Congress again confronted a "difficult and intractable problem," where previous legislative attempts had failed. Such problems may justify added prophylactic measures in response.

By creating an across-the-board, routine employment benefit for all eligible employees, Congress sought to ensure that family-care leave would no longer be stigmatized as an inordinate drain on the workplace caused by female employees, and that employers could not evade leave obligations simply by hiring men. By setting a minimum standard of family leave for *all* eligible employees, irrespective of gender, the FMLA attacks the formerly state-sanctioned stereotype that only women are responsible for family caregiving, thereby reducing employers' incentives to engage in discrimination by basing hiring and promotion decisions on stereotypes. . . . Unlike the statutes at issue in *City of Boerne*, *Kimel*, and *Garrett*, which applied broadly to every aspect of state employers' operations, the FMLA is narrowly targeted at the fault line between work and family — precisely where sex-based overgeneralization has been and remains strongest — and affects only one aspect of the employment relationship.

. . . Affirmed.

[Concurring opinions by Justice Souter, joined by Justices Ginsburg and Breyer, and Justice Stevens are omitted.]

JUSTICE SCALIA, dissenting.

. . . The constitutional violation that is a prerequisite to "prophylactic" congressional action to "enforce" the Fourteenth Amendment is a violation *by the State against which the enforcement action is taken*. There is no guilt by association, enabling the sovereignty of one State to be abridged under §5 of the Fourteenth Amendment because of violations by another State, or by most other States, or even by 49 other States. . . . Today's opinion for the Court . . . treats "the States" as some sort of collective entity which is guilty or innocent as a body. . . . This will not do. Prophylaxis in the sense of extending the remedy beyond the violation is one thing; prophylaxis in the sense of extending the remedy beyond the violator is something else. . . .

JUSTICE KENNEDY, joined by JUSTICE SCALIA and JUSTICE THOMAS, dissenting.

. . . The Court is unable to show that States have engaged in a pattern of unlawful conduct which warrants the remedy of opening state treasuries to private suits. The inability to adduce evidence of alleged discrimination, coupled with the inescapable fact that the federal scheme is not a remedy but a benefit program, demonstrate the lack of the requisite link between any problem Congress has identified and the program it mandated.

In examining whether Congress was addressing a demonstrated "pattern of unconstitutional employment discrimination by the States," the Court gives superficial treatment to the requirement that we "identify with some precision the scope of the constitutional right at issue." *Garrett*. . . . The relevant question . . . is whether . . . the States . . . engage in widespread discrimination on the basis of gender in the provision of family leave benefits. . . . The evidence to substantiate this charge must be far more specific . . . than a simple recitation of a general history of employment discrimination against women. . . .

Respondents fail to make the requisite showing. [The] evidence considered by Congress concerned discriminatory practices of the private sector, not those of state employers. . . . While the evidence of discrimination by private entities may be relevant, it does not, by itself, justify the abrogation of States' sovereign immunity. *Garrett*. . . . The question is not whether the family leave provision is a congruent and proportional response to general gender-based stereotypes in employment which "have historically produced discrimination in the hiring and promotion of women;" the question is whether it is a proper remedy to an alleged pattern of unconstitutional discrimination by States in the grant of family leave. The evidence of gender-based stereotypes is too remote to support the required showing. [Nor] does the Constitution require States to provide their employees with any family leave at all. A State's failure to devise a family leave program is not, then, evidence of unconstitutional behavior. Considered in its entirety, the evidence fails to document a pattern of unconstitutional conduct sufficient to justify the abrogation of States' sovereign immunity. . . .

Our concern with gender discrimination, which is subjected to heightened scrutiny, . . . does not alter this conclusion. The application of heightened scrutiny is designed to ensure gender-based classifications are not based on the entrenched and pervasive stereotypes which inhibit women's progress in the workplace. This consideration does not divest respondents of their burden to show that "Congress identified a history and pattern of unconstitutional employment discrimination by the States." . . . Congress was not responding with a congruent and proportional remedy to a perceived course of unconstitutional conduct. Instead, it enacted a substantive entitlement program of its own. If Congress had been concerned about different treatment of men and women with respect to family leave, a congruent remedy would have sought to ensure the benefits of any leave program enacted by a State are available to men and women on an equal basis. Instead, the Act imposes, across the board, a requirement that States grant a minimum of 12 weeks of leave per year. This requirement may represent Congress'[s] considered judgment as to the optimal balance between the family obligations of workers and the interests of employers. . . . It does not follow, however, that if the States choose to enact a different benefit scheme, they should be deemed to engage in unconstitutional conduct and forced to open their treasuries to private suits for damages. . . .

The scheme enacted by the Act does not respect the States' autonomous power to design their own social benefits regime.

Were more proof needed to show that this is an entitlement program, not a remedial statute, it should suffice to note that the Act does not even purport to bar discrimination in some leave programs the States do enact and administer. Under the Act, a State is allowed to provide women with, say, 24 weeks of family leave per year but provide only 12 weeks of leave to men. [A] law of this kind might run afoul of the Equal Protection Clause or Title VII, but it would not constitute a violation of the Act. The Act on its face is not drawn as a remedy to gender-based discrimination in family leave.

[The principle that Congress's prophylactic power under §5 is limited to instances where there has been a "widespread and persisting deprivation of constitutional rights" that constitutes a "difficult and intractable problem" is illustrated by the] Court's precedents upholding the Voting Rights Act of 1965 as a proper exercise of Congress'[s] remedial power. . . . In South Carolina v. Katzenbach, [p. 1225] the Court concluded that the Voting Rights Act's prohibition on state literacy tests was an appropriate method of enforcing the constitutional protection against racial discrimination in voting . . . because "Congress documented a marked pattern of unconstitutional action by the States." Congress'[s] response [was] congruent, because it "aimed at areas where voting discrimination has been most flagrant," and proportional, because it was necessary to "banish the blight of racial discrimination in voting, which has infected the electoral process in parts of our country for nearly a century." . . .

For the same reasons, the abrogation of state sovereign immunity pursuant to Title VII was a legitimate congressional response to a pattern of gender-based discrimination in employment. Fitzpatrick v. Bitzer, 427 U.S. 445 (1976). The family leave benefit conferred by the Act is, by contrast, a substantive benefit Congress chose to confer upon state employees. . . . What is at issue is only whether the States can be subjected, without consent, to suits brought by private persons seeking to collect moneys from the state treasury. Their immunity cannot be abrogated without documentation of a pattern of unconstitutional acts by the States, and only then by a congruent and proportional remedy. There has been a complete failure by respondents to carry their burden to establish each of these necessary propositions. I would hold that the Act is not a valid abrogation of state sovereign immunity and dissent with respect from the Court's conclusion to the contrary.

NOTES AND QUESTIONS

1. *What (if Anything) Changed from* Garrett? Apart from the result, did anything change from *Garrett* to *Hibbs*? Did the Court in *Hibbs* alter the standard — congruence and proportionality? Did the Court in *Hibbs* apply the same standard in a different way? Or did the Court in *Hibbs* review the family leave provision of the FMLA in a fashion completely consistent with *Garrett* and its predecessors? Does *Hibbs* suggest that the evidentiary burden that Congress must carry to invoke its section five power lessens as the presumptive invalidity of the problem attacked increases, or does *Hibbs* suggest only that it will be easier for Congress to meet the same evidentiary burden when it addresses state behavior that is presumptively invalid? Is this a distinction without a difference?

2. *New Developments: Access to Courts.* In Tennessee v. Lane, 124 S. Ct. 1978 (2004), the Court was confronted with the question of whether Title II of the Americans with Disabilities Act of 1990 ("ADA") was a valid use of §5 of the Fourteenth Amendment to abrogate state sovereign immunity. Title II provides that "no qualified individual with a disability shall, by reason of such disability, be excluded from participation in or be denied the benefits of the services, programs or activities of a public entity, or be subjected to discrimination by any such entity." 42 U.S.C. §12132. George Lane, a paraplegic confined to a wheelchair, was required to appear twice at a county courthouse to answer criminal charges against him. The first time he appeared he crawled up two flights of stairs because the courthouse lacked an elevator and the hearing room was on the second floor. The second time he refused the court's offer to carry him up the stairs or to move the hearing room to a wheelchair accessible courtroom in a nearby town and, as a result, was arrested for his failure to appear. In federal court, Lane invoked Title II of the ADA to seek damages from and equitable relief against Tennessee.

In a 5-4 decision the Court, in an opinion by Justice Stevens, applied the *City of Boerne* congruence and proportionality test to uphold the validity of Title II as applied to the narrow issue raised by Lane: "[W]e conclude that Title II, as it applies to the class of cases implicating the fundamental right of access to the courts, constitutes a valid exercise of Congress' §5 authority to enforce the guarantees of the Fourteenth Amendment." The majority reasoned that this right of access is "subject to more searching judicial review," a factor that, according to *Hibbs*, makes it easier for Congress to show a pattern of state constitutional violations sufficient to support exercise of its enforcement power in a fashion congruent with the constitutional right at issue. The *Lane* majority thought that Congress had adequately documented "pervasive unequal treatment in the administration of state services and programs, including systematic deprivations of [such] fundamental rights" as voting, jury service, and marriage.[1] The majority relied on a study submitted to Congress that "some 76% of public services and programs housed in state-owned buildings were inaccessible to and unusable by persons with disabilities" to bolster the case for the congruence of Congress's "exercise of its prophylactic power" in Title II and the constitutionally fundamental right of access to such state services as courts.

The majority found Title II to be proportional to the asserted constitutional violation by declining to rule on the entire scope of Title II. Taken as a whole, Title II subjects states to monetary liability for denying disabled persons access to such things as "state-owned hockey rinks" as well as "voting-booth access." Tennessee argued that "the broad range of Title II's applications," mandating access to constitutionally fundamental state services and programs as well as constitutionally trivial services and programs, fatally impeached its claim to appropriate proportionality. However, the majority declined to consider Title II "as an undifferentiated whole." Instead, it thought that "the question presented in this case is not whether Congress can validly subject the States to private suits for money damages for failing to provide reasonable access to hockey rinks, or even to voting booths, but whether Congress had the power under §5 to enforce the constitutional right of access to the courts. Because we find that Title II unquestionably is valid §5 legislation as it applies to the class of cases implicating the accessibility of judicial services, we need go no further."

In a dissent, Chief Justice Rehnquist, joined by Justices Kennedy and Thomas, chided the majority for relying "on a wide-ranging account of societal discrimination against the disabled" to prove the much narrower claim that states have systematically deprived disabled people of access to courts. "Some of this evidence would be relevant if the Court were considering the constitutionality of the statute as a whole; but the Court rejects that approach in favor of a narrower 'as-applied' inquiry." Accordingly, the dissenters thought that this "outdated, generalized evidence" was "irrelevant to Title II's purported enforcement of Due Process access-to-the-courts rights." The dissenters charged that "there is *nothing* in the legislative

---

1. The laws cited by the majority generally impose a categorical disqualification upon "idiots," "lunatics," or the mentally disabled, without any individualized assessment of mental competence to vote, serve on a jury, or marry.

record or statutory findings to indicate that disabled persons were systematically denied the right to be present at criminal trials, denied the meaningful opportunity to be heard in civil cases, unconstitutionally excluded from jury service, or denied the right to attend criminal trials." Finally, the dissent contended that it was incorrect to determine the validity of Title II on an as-applied basis because "the congruence-and-proportionality test" is designed to determine

> whether Congress has attempted to statutorily redefine the constitutional rights protected by the Fourteenth Amendment. This question can only be answered by measuring the breadth of a statute's coverage against the scope of the constitutional rights it purports to enforce and the record of violations it purports to remedy. In conducting its as-applied analysis, however, the majority posits a hypothetical statute, never enacted by Congress, that applies only to courthouses. The effect is to rig the congruence-and-proportionality test by artificially constricting the scope of the statute to closely mirror a recognized constitutional right. But Title II is not susceptible of being carved up in this manner; it applies indiscriminately to all "services," "programs," or "activities" of any "public entity." Thus, the majority's approach is not really an assessment of whether Title II is "appropriate *legislation*" at all, but a test of whether the Court can conceive of a hypothetical statute narrowly tailored enough to constitute valid prophylactic legislation. . . .
>
> [The] Court's adoption of an as-applied approach eliminates any incentive for Congress to craft §5 legislation for the purpose of remedying or deterring actual constitutional violations. Congress can now simply rely on the courts to sort out which hypothetical applications of an undifferentiated statute . . . may be enforced against the States. All the while, States will be subjected to substantial litigation in a piecemeal attempt to vindicate their Eleventh Amendment rights.

Justice Scalia, dissenting separately, rejected the congruence-and-proportionality test entirely because it, "like all such flabby tests, is a standing invitation to judicial arbitrariness and policy-driven decisionmaking. Worse still, it casts this Court in the role of Congress's taskmaster. Under it, the courts (and ultimately this Court) must regularly check Congress's homework to make sure that it has identified sufficient constitutional violations to make its remedy congruent and proportional." Justice Scalia would replace this test with one focusing on Congress's power, textually limited in §5, to *enforce* the Fourteenth Amendment: "Nothing in §5 allows Congress to go *beyond* the provisions of the Fourteenth Amendment to proscribe, prevent, or 'remedy' conduct that does not *itself* violate any provision of the Fourteenth Amendment. So-called 'prophylactic legislation' is reinforcement rather than enforcement." The only exception to this rule that Justice Scalia would permit would be, "principally for reasons of *stare decisis*," applicable

> to congressional measures designed to remedy racial discrimination by the States. I would not, however, abandon the requirement that Congress may impose prophylactic §5 legislation only upon those particular States in which there has been an identified history of relevant constitutional violations. I would also adhere to the requirement that the prophylactic remedy predicated upon such state violations must be directed against the States or state actors rather than the public at large. And I would not, of course,

permit any congressional measures that violate other provisions of the Constitution. When those requirements have been met, however, I shall leave it to Congress, under constraints no tighter than those of the Necessary and Proper Clause, to decide what measures are appropriate under §5 to prevent or remedy racial discrimination by the States.